CAMBRIDGE STUDIES IN CRIMINOLOGY, VOLUME XXIV

*Editor:* Leon Radzinowicz

# THE POLICE: A STUDY IN MANPOWER

THE HEINEMANN LIBRARY OF CRIMINOLOGY

AND PENAL REFORM

# THE POLICE: A STUDY IN MANPOWER

*The Evolution of the Service in England and Wales 1829-1965*

*by*

## J. P. Martin

*and*

## Gail Wilson

HEINEMANN

LONDON

Heinemann Educational Books Ltd
LONDON   MELBOURNE   TORONTO
SINGAPORE   JOHANNESBURG
HONG KONG   AUCKLAND
IBADAN   NAIROBI

SBN 435 82576 3

*Publisher's note:* This series is continuous with the
Cambridge Studies in Criminology, Volumes I to
XIX, published by Macmillan & Co, London

Published by
Heinemann Educational Books Ltd
48 Charles Street, London W1X 8AH

Printed in Great Britain by
Morrison and Gibb Ltd, London and Edinburgh

# Table of Contents

*Page*

**Foreword** by L. Radzinowicz            vii

**Acknowledgements**          x

*Chapter*

   I.   Introduction        1

  II.   Laying the Foundations—1829–1919      6

 III.   The Inter-War Years      36

 IV.   The Post-War Period—1950–65      68

  V.   The Design of a Manpower Survey      119

 VI.   The Pattern of Police Work      138

 VII.   Criminal Investigation and Traffic Work      166

VIII.   Court Work and the Policing of Holiday Areas      196

 IX.   Policewomen, Traffic Wardens and Civilians      210

  X.   Aspects of Operational Organization      228

 XI.   General Conclusions      248

**Appendices**

A.   Recording Booklet and Instructions      263

B.   Statistical Methods: 1. *Method of Calculation of Police Service Man Hours 1861–1965*      270

                2. *Test of Significance of correlation co-efficient*      273

                3. *Method of Calculating Overtime*      274

                4. *Test for Representativeness of Number of Crimes Committed During Survey Period*      275

**C.** Selection and Characteristics of Sample of Forces     276

**D.** Tables used as basis for data included in text     278

**E.** The employment of Traffic Wardens in some survey areas     286

*Index*     288

# Foreword

*by*

*Leon Radzinowicz*

Iᴛ is often said that the police should be catching criminals, not directing traffic, waiting about in the courts or engaged on 'extraneous' duties. It is also often lamented that they are chronically short of manpower. But what share of police time has been devoted to each of their various functions? And is the remedy for inadequacy to be sought in larger numbers, or in linking the men more effectively, through better training, administration and equipment, to modern techniques and modern knowledge? An examination of past facts cannot, in itself, decide what duties, what methods, should be given priority in future planning. But it does provide an essential basis for such decisions.

This report by Professor Martin and Miss Wilson is one of the first attempts in this country to apply social accounting techniques to the study of police manpower. It has made an important contribution in showing how much work of various kinds there is and how it has been distributed between different sections of the service. The increase in numbers has been such that, in spite of considerable improvements in their conditions, the total of hours worked by the police in proportion to population is higher than at any time in their history.

The fact that the police are shown in historical as well as economic perspective gives the work an interest beyond the relatively narrow circle of specialists, and should make it of value to social scientists and public administrators.

At the present time bold and systematic steps are being taken to re-shape the traditional police forces: to increase their striking power in the prevention and detection of crime; to enable them to come to grips with its most threatening forms, especially with organized criminals; to combine efficiency with economy of effort. These emphasize the need to adapt the service to technical change, to face such problems as specialization. All this adds to the special topicality of the monograph.

The enquiry was launched, and the empirical material accumulated, whilst Professor Martin was an Assistant Director of Research at the Institute of Criminology. In his Preface he has acknowledged the help of the many who have co-operated in its preparation. On behalf of the Institute, I should like to thank the Consultative and Reviewing Committee, whose names appear on page ix, a committee of experience and distinction, and particularly its Chairman, Mr C. W. Guillebaud.

It is good to have this report by Professor Martin and Miss Gail Wilson as one of the volumes of the Cambridge Series. I hope that the work they have initiated in this still largely unexplored field will be taken up by others.

CAMBRIDGE, *November* 1968.

# Reviewing and Consultative Committee

Mr C. W. Guillebaud, C.B.E. (Chairman), *Emeritus Reader in Economics and Politics, University of Cambridge.*

Mr R. E. Beard, F.I.A., M.B.E., *Actuary, General Manager, Pearl Assurance Company.*

Professor R. M. Jackson, LL.D., F.B.A., *Downing Professor of Laws of England, University of Cambridge.*

Mr T. S. Lodge, C.B.E., *Statistical Adviser and Director, Home Office Research Unit.*

Mr R. L. Morrison, *Director, National Association for the Care and Resettlement of Offenders.*

Mr K. A. L. Parker, C.B., *Receiver, Metropolitan Police.*

Mr H. R. Pratt, *Chief Constable, Bedfordshire and Luton Constabulary.*

Professor L. Radzinowicz, LL.D., *Wolfson Professor of Criminology, Director, Institute of Criminology, University of Cambridge.*

Mr H. W. Stotesbury, *Assistant Under-Secretary of State, Home Office, Police Division.*

Mr H. B. Wilson, *Assistant Under-Secretary of State, Home Office, Criminal Division.*

# Acknowledgements

In addition to the members of the Consultative and Reviewing Committee, whose help has been acknowledged in Professor Radzinowicz's Foreword, we are indebted to many colleagues and friends who worked on the project or assisted or advised us at various stages.

On sampling and statistical matters we had valuable advice from Professors C. A. Moser and Alan Stuart, Miss Hilary Gibbs and Mr G. N. G. Rose. The design and execution of the surveys owed much to Mr Joseph Bradley, whose sudden death robbed the project of an experienced research worker whose energy and executive skill had contributed considerable impetus to the early stages. Mr R. Gwilliam gave invaluable help in completing the field-work.

Many people helped with data processing, but the bulk of the work was undertaken by Miss G. Wisbey, Mrs P. Ardrey and Mrs P. Bruce. For secretarial work we are indebted to Mrs P. Bruce, Mrs J. Bartlett, Mrs I. Bason, Mrs P. Fortescue, Mrs S. Harvey, Mrs L. Leadbitter, Mrs C. Mills and Miss K. M. Pratt.

We are most grateful to Miss Diana Marshallsay of the Ford Library of Parliamentary Papers, University of Southampton, who compiled the index and gave valuable bibliographical assistance.

All or parts of the manuscript were read by Mr B. N. Bebbington, Mrs G. Sutherland, Mr H. Glennerster, Dr C. H. Feinstein, Professor Alan Williams and Professor J. H. Smith. Mr T. Critchley generously allowed us to see *A History of the Police in England and Wales 900–1966* before publication, and his wide knowledge and experience saved us from many errors. Any errors that remain, however, are our responsibility.

Finally, we must thank those members of the police service, of all ranks, who not only took part in the surveys, but took so much trouble to assist us and to increase our knowledge of their work.

J.P.M.
G.W.

# Bibliographical Note

Frequent reference is made throughout this book to a number of official reports. In order to save cumbersome repetition in the footnotes short forms of the titles have been used as follows:

Commissioner of Police of the = Report of the Commissioner of
Metropolis                         Police of the Metropolis for the
year . . . . .

Desborough Report              = Police Service of England, Wales and Scotland. Committee. Report, Parts I & II, Minutes of Evidence; 1919 Cmd. 253, XXVII. 1920 Cmd. 574, Cmd. 874, XXII.

Inspector(s) of Constabulary  = Report of H.M. Inspectors (or Chief Inspector) of Constabulary for the year . . . . .

Taverne Report               = Home Office: Police Manpower, Equipment and Efficiency. Working Parties. Reports. London, H.M.S.O., 1967.

# I

# Introduction

OUR first conception of this book was that it should simply be an analysis of the financial aspects of law enforcement. As the work developed we found that the police service was sufficient as a subject in itself, but a purely financial study seemed an inadequate basis for discussing its work and problems. Many of these, we concluded, centred around the use of manpower, and this has become our main theme.

With all British institutions it is necessary to know about their past in order to understand the present; of few is this more true than the police. The foundations of the modern service were well and truly laid in the nineteenth century, and our account, therefore, begins historically. It goes on, however, to consider the modern period in detail, ending with the results of surveys into the use of manpower made in 1965 and 1966.

Chapter II sets the scene by describing the structure of the service as established under the Police Acts of the nineteenth century, and draws attention to the early problems of manpower —recruitment, wastage, pay, leave and standards of living. It is a salutary reminder of how far the service has come since the days when drunkenness among policemen was a major problem, when leave was virtually non-existent and when the level of pay, and thereby status, of the constable was deliberately related to that of the agricultural labourer.

Our next chapter starts with the report of the Desborough Committee of 1919–20 which, when implemented, gave the policeman a new status, and effectively began the process of standardizing conditions of service. Despite the cuts in pay which resulted from the economic crises of the nineteen twenties and thirties it seems clear that for nearly two decades the service enjoyed a degree of stability that it had not achieved before, and which did not survive the second world war. Considering how recent this period was it is surprising to be able to show how many features of today's service had their origin as experiments in a few years before the war—traffic patrols, forensic laboratories, wireless communication and, above all, the introduction of training courses.

Recent history (1950–65) is the subject of Chapter IV. At this point it becomes possible to relate expenditure on the police to that on other public services and to Gross National Expenditure. This analysis demonstrates how the police share of public resources grew more rapidly than that of other public services and, indeed, Gross National Expenditure. Shortage of manpower, however, came to be seen as an almost insoluble problem. Nevertheless we show that the strength of the service reached the highest point ever recorded and more hours were worked per head of population than in any previous period.

After the second world war investment became a matter of major importance, and we describe its scope and form. It is notable that whereas housing and buildings came first, expenditure on equipment only increased substantially towards the end of the period. Possibly of equal importance was a new form of investment —training. The future historian of the service may well conclude that, in the long run, the systematic development of training at all levels, and particularly of the Police College, had a more lasting effect on its morale, quality (and thereby status) than any other single development during the twenty years that followed the war.

In the second half of our study we look more closely at what this money has been used for. In order to obtain evidence we conducted a survey into the use of manpower based on records kept by 8,225 police officers and civilians employed in some twelve provincial forces, in two land divisions and in the central traffic division of the Metropolitan police.

In analysing the results of the surveys we consider such questions as the effective strength of the police, the amount of overtime worked and the variation in work load between departments. We show, for example, that the legitimate requirements of leave, sickness, refreshments and training meant that, in effect, the proportion of police strength available for duty was only 57·7 per cent. Marked differences were also found between the Metropolitan police and other forces and, within forces, between the C.I.D. and other departments.

The most significant facts concerning the nature of the work load were the amount of time spent on patrolling (which accounted for about a third of active duty), the claims of the administration of Justice (which on average occupied just over 10 per cent of all police time),[1] and of traffic. Traffic work took up very nearly a quarter of all working time in the provincial forces, and almost a fifth in the Metropolitan. These figures were well above those already condemned by the Select Committee on Estimates in 1966.

Chapters VII to X discuss various aspects of police work in more detail. Our examination of criminal investigation work showed that in most forces the case load per detective was still below 150 a year, but there were some where the load was substantially greater. Such forces appeared to have reached the limit of expanding the C.I.D. to keep pace with the increase in crime; this raises the important question of the relationship between the C.I.D. and uniformed branches and, indeed, of the role of specialist units in the service. The introduction of Unit Beat Policing represents a new attempt to solve this problem, and its significance is discussed in Chapter VII.

The volume of traffic work undertaken in a force seemed, to some extent, to be a matter of policy related to the structure of the force. In spite of the existence of specialized traffic departments the bulk of supervision and handling of accidents and incidents was done by beat patrol officers and, where employed, by traffic wardens. Considerable differences were found to exist in the relationship between traffic court work and the time spent on dealing with traffic accidents and incidents. Generally speaking provincial forces spent more time on traffic court work than on the incidents which generated it, while the reverse was true of the Metropolitan police.

Possibly the most significant result concerning court work, apart from its volume which we have already mentioned, is that traffic cases in total involved as much time as crime, in spite of the expeditious way in which they were handled.

We made seasonal comparisons of work in holiday areas and found that, contrary to expectation, the actual amount of extra

---

[1] This information has been used by Williams to show that the police contribution to the total cost of the administration of justice is at least equal to the entire costs of the courts and judiciary. See Alan Williams: *Output Budgeting and the Contribution of Micro-Economics to Efficiency in Government.* C.A.S. Occasional Paper No. 4, London, H.M.S.O., 1967.

work in terms of hours was small; its inconvenience, however, may have been considerable. The only branch of work which increased in all areas was traffic, and the extra work very largely fell upon non-specialists rather than on the traffic departments.

Chapter IX deals with policewomen, traffic wardens and civilians. Our results suggest that policewomen have a more varied and interesting job than policemen, and they work virtually the same hours. Traffic wardens are shown to do as much traffic supervision as about seven beat officers in the course of their ordinary patrol, but their employment may only save manpower if they relieve officers on fixed points. The institution of wardens has largely allowed the police to do traffic work that previously they had been forced to neglect. They are not so much an economy as the instruments of a policy of traffic supervision.

Civilians are shown to make a substantial contribution, mainly because they do not have to spend time on training. Hence although their working hours are shorter than those of police officers they are close to the police figures for active duty. Great discrepancies existed between forces in the use they made of civilians, but these are likely to be reduced as the result of amalgamations.

Chapter X deals with aspects of mobility. It shows that slightly more than 40 per cent of all police service time is spent in police stations. With beat patrol officers the proportion was about 25 per cent due mainly to the claims of refreshment breaks, report writing and occasional periods as station reserve. When out and about the majority of beat patrol officers worked on foot or with pedal cycles. It seemed to us, however, that with the development of personal radios, the principles upon which men are deployed and mechanical transport is used need to be re-examined.

In our last chapter we discuss two underlying themes; first, the amount of national resources devoted to the police and the amount of cover obtained in return; second, the place of specialization in the service, particularly in relation to technical change. We end by emphasizing the fact that the country now enjoys more police protection in terms of man hours than ever before, and suggest that what may now be most urgent is a reappraisal of the use of that time, rather than a continuation of attempts to make the service larger and larger.

Finally it should be said that we have made no attempt to

extend our study beyond 1965. We are well aware of the rapid developments in administration, particularly in the form of amalgamations, and in operational methods (such as the introduction of Unit Beat Policing, described in Chapter VII, p. 180). These changes are still taking place, and it would have been impossible to chronicle them with the same thoroughness as we applied to the years up to 1965. In a sense, therefore, our study is already an historical one, marking as it did the end of an era. Such recent history, however, not only conveys the lessons to be learned from the evolution of the service, but portrays the milieu in which most members of the present service were trained and developed their beliefs about the nature of police work. Only if the nature of this formative experience is adequately taken into account can the service hope to achieve the full benefits of the changes it is now undergoing.

# II

# Laying the Foundations—1829–1919

THE traditions of the British police service were laid down in the nineteenth century. Although, on the surface, police work has changed tremendously over the last hundred years, the old order survived with remarkable strength and there were few radical changes between 1856 and 1964. Since then there have been many far-reaching developments. Even so, apart from such obvious evidence of the past as police buildings dating from the last century, many aspects of organization were relatively little changed. The number of individual police forces has certainly declined, but even in 1966 there were still many that had existed as self-contained units in the same areas for over a hundred years. The power of local police authorities over their forces has weakened, but only gradually and it is still strong. Above all, the beat system which was first developed as an efficient means of policing by the Metropolitan police[1] was slowly being modified, but was still the basis of police work throughout the country up to 1964. Since then the Unit Beat system of policing has been introduced and become relatively widespread.[2]

The purpose of this chapter is to trace the main threads in the development of the police from a barely literate and drunken body of ex-labourers with a rapidly changing membership, to a force enjoying, in the twentieth century, a respected quasi-professional status. In the process many of the virtues which have made the British police famous were developed. At the same time, however, the very durability of the structure established in the early years led to delays and difficulties when the time for modernization had clearly arrived.

Throughout the nineteenth century the police forces of England and Wales were characterized more by their diversity than their similarity. Individual forces slowly replaced the old systems of

---

[1] Founded in 1829.
[2] See pp. 164 f. and 180 f.

night-watchmen in the towns and parish constables in the counties as, at different times and for different reasons, these were rejected as inefficient.

The first modern force was the Metropolitan police founded in 1829. Its establishment was preceded by a long series of disorders and criminal outrages which had caused passing concern, but had no lasting effect. The Metropolitan Police Act of 1829 replaced a number of more or less inefficient bodies by one organization under two commissioners. An amendment of 1839 enlarged the area to form the Metropolitan Police District which has hardly changed since then.[1] It appears to have proved its usefulness in the first few years of operation. The beat system, which was to some extent a rationalization of the old night watches, was brought to a high degree of efficiency and was the main source of success. A policeman patrolled a given area in a given time, inspecting property and keeping a look out for suspicious characters. Attention to duty was assured by a system of checks and meeting points with constables on neighbouring beats, and written reports were required. Men on 'point' duty were available at fixed points to assist members of the public or to act in emergency. Higher ranks supervised the constables and manned the stations. The system was adopted by all efficient forces as they were set up.[2]

The impetus that led to the establishment of the Metropolitan police was to some extent a result of criminal outrages, but the great emphasis in police work throughout the nineteenth century was on the preservation of public order. Prevention and detection of crime were secondary and did not assume prominence until much later in police history. The French revolution had shown the danger of uncontrolled mobs in fearsome and conclusive fashion. The long series of riots which occurred in the first half of the century made the fear of mobs an ever present reality. Growing urbanization made for larger crowds and the mobs were noticeably more destructive and dangerous than they had been in the eighteenth century. There were agricultural risings in 1816 and 1830, and the Plug Plot riots in the industrial north in 1842,

---

[1] The major change was the incorporation of the Romford district of Essex in 1965 when the London Government Act 1963 came into force.

[2] See T. A. Critchley, *A History of the Police in England and Wales 1900–1966*, London, Constable, 1967, pp. 64 and 145 n for examples of Metropolitan Officers organizing provincial forces.

to mention but a few of the disorders. The threat from the Chartists was also very real right up till 1848.[1] The riots and Chartist demonstrations were at first controlled by the army, but the military were too few to cover the country effectively, despite the advent of rail transport. They also became less popular as liberal public opinion turned against the spectacle of soldiers firing on defenceless crowds. By the middle of the century there was a further cause of unease as transportation went out of use and, as a result, it was feared that the number of able-bodied criminals roaming the country would increase.

All these factors had their effect on local and national opinion at different times and in different parts of the country. The efficiency of provincial police forces, and even in the case of the counties, the date of their establishment, varied from place to place. The 'new police' on the Metropolitan model were expensive and the cost had to be locally justified.

The first move to provide a legislative framework for the police was the Borough and Municipal Corporations Act 1835. The Act established the legal and financial limits within which local government bodies could provide the common services which urban life was showing to be vitally necessary. It obliged all boroughs to set up watch committees and appoint a force of full-time paid constables. However, boroughs varied greatly in size and efficiency. Many merely established nominal forces and as late as 1857 there were thirteen boroughs which had ignored the police clauses in the Act entirely. Even the smallest of the existing boroughs came under the Act but often they were too small to afford, or even to need, an efficient force on the Metropolitan police model. In places the police consisted of a Superintendent or Head Constable and two or three constables, often working part-time. The senior officers frequently drew part of their salaries for service as inspectors of weights and measures or as head firemen and appear to have done little police work. In such circumstances there was no possibility of maintaining a police force which differed much from the discredited system of night-watchmen. The watchmen were in fact often taken into the new borough forces. They were characterized as old, short, drunken, illiterate

---

[1] See for example J. L. and B. Hammond, *The Village Labourer, 1760–1832*, London, Longmans Green, 1911, and F. C. Mather, *Public Order in the Age of the Chartists*, Manchester University Press, 1959.

and lazy. Clearly they were not ideal recruits and their short-comings had frequently been responsible for the agitation which led to demands for a proper police force, first in London and then in various parts of the provinces. They were later to become an early drain on the borough pension funds.

The Act of 1835 applied only to the boroughs. In the counties the problem was somewhat different. The old parish constables were not intended to deal with rioting mobs and were in any case quite inadequate to do so. Although the military were used to control riots, and had the advantage of being cheaper than police, the Chartist threat resulted in a demand for the 'new style' police in some counties. An enabling act was quickly passed in 1839 and further legislation followed in 1840. The Acts allowed the justices of the peace to set up a force for a county or any division of a county. These acts did not compel the establishment of a police force as the 1835 Act had done and there were other differences. In the counties there was no existing local administrative frame-work which could organize a police force, as there had been in the boroughs. As a result the central government had greater freedom of action. The regulations which accompanied the Acts of 1839 and 1840 laid down common conditions for any force which was established. Recruits were to be at least five foot seven inches tall, under 40 years old, able to read and write, in good health and of irreproachable character and connections. Most watchmen of the old order and the part-time parish constables were thus disqualified from joining the new forces. The number of constables was not to exceed one per thousand inhabitants and wages scales were laid down. Chief Constables were to be appointed by the justices of the peace but only with the Home Secretary's approval. Once in office the county chief constable was virtually irremoveable and was allowed full disciplinary powers over his force.

The differences between county and borough forces were thus established at an early date. County forces were theoretically more closely controlled by the Home Office but were in actual fact more or less free to operate as the chief constable wished. Borough forces, however, were closely supervised by the watch committee, and in general only the largest cities delegated disciplinary powers to their head constables. Divisions between the two types of force were often accentuated by political and social differences between town and county. The amalgamation of a borough with a county force was thus a rarity and the difference persisted. Even in 1919 Sir Leonard Dunning, Inspector of Constabulary, prefaced his evidence to the Desborough Committee by saying that there were 'two sorts of police'—county and borough.[1]

The next major development was the Police Act of 1856. It was designed to bring a certain unity to the policing of England and Wales. It did impose a few common conditions but was unable to alter much that already existed. The metropolis, the boroughs and the counties all operated their police forces under different legislation, and some counties still had no force at all. Centralization and standardization were prevented by political and administrative realities. There was strong opposition to the establishment of any form of national police force. Such a development was characterized as 'French' and 'spying'.[2] Even the Act of 1856 was widely attacked as dictatorial and un-English.[3]

The other major force which prevented standardization was the generally low level of central government activity. In particular, the Home Office police branch appears to have been unable or unwilling to do more than the minimum.[4] Even after 1856 reports from Chief Constables, though statutorily obligatory, were not called for, county forces ignored Home Office regulations on wages[5] and borough forces, though required to submit rules made by watch committees to the Home Secretary, were 'almost entirely independent of Home Office control'.[6] The Home Office did, of course, exercise some powers, particularly after 1856 through the

---

[1] *Report of the Committee on the Police Service of England, Wales and Scotland* (Desborough Report), Part II, Minutes of evidence, p. 79, q. 1431 (1920 Cmd. 874, xxii).—'one must remember that outside the metropolis there are in England and Wales two sorts of police forces, the County Constabularies and the Borough Police Forces, which differ from each other in disciplinary conditions, hours of duty and closeness of supervision, and remuneration.'

[2] J. Hart, 'The County and Borough Police Act, 1856', *Public Administration*, Vol. XXXIV (1956), p. 405.

[3] T. A. Critchley, *op. cit.*, p. 117.

[4] See H. Parris, 'The Home Office and the Provincial Police in England and Wales, 1856–1870', *Public Law* (1961), pp. 230–55.

[5] *Inspectors of Constabulary, 1872*, 1873 (16), xxxi, and *Report of the Select Committee on the Police Weekly Rest Day*, Minutes of Evidence, p. 104, evidence of the Chief Constable of Lancashire; 1908 (353,354), ix.

[6] Desborough Report, Part II, Minutes of Evidence, p. 1, evidence from the Home Office; 1920 Cmd. 874, xxii.

Inspectors of Constabulary, but the emphasis was on the police as a local service dealing with local disorders and local criminals. In the circumstances of the 1850's this was not unreasonable, but improved communications and a shift in the balance of police work away from the preservation of public order towards the prevention and detection of individual crimes, showed up the weaknesses of the County and Borough system as the years passed.

The Police Act 1856 consolidated the existing situation. At that date nearly all the boroughs had set up police forces and many, such as Birmingham or Liverpool, were efficient and modern by the standards of the time. There were forces in twenty-five counties and in parts of seven others. The new Act compelled all counties to establish forces. The provinces were divided into three Districts, and an Inspector of Constabulary was assigned to each District. Their duties were to visit each force annually and certify that it was efficient. Efficiency was, however, measured in terms of numbers and discipline and the state of police buildings.[1] There was no reference to crime rates or the state of public order. On the other hand it is clear that shortage of men, in particular of active men, and poor discipline which resulted in drunkenness and absence from duty, were the main obstacles in the way of efficient policing in 1856. A solution to the problems of the 1850's was, therefore, built into the administrative framework and came to dominate police thinking in a way that has only recently begun to break down. The number of men needed was measured in terms of population. The county forces were limited by statute to less than one man per thousand inhabitants, but the boroughs were expected to have more. Discipline was also closely connected with numbers since it was judged mainly by the ratio of sergeants and other supervisory ranks to constables. It was reckoned that a force of less than six men (sixty-nine forces in 1857) could not be adequate in point of discipline, even if fewer men could in theory police the area. Three constables were needed to maintain twenty-four hour beat coverage and three officers of higher rank were necessary for supervision, since with only two there was no allowance for absence on leave or sickness.

All forces in the counties and those in boroughs with more than

[1] See H. Parris, 'The Home Office and the Provincial Police in England and Wales, 1856–1870', *Public Law* (1961), p. 231.

5,000 people were eligible for a grant of one quarter (increased to a half in 1874) of the cost of the pay and clothing of the force if they were certified as efficient. The small boroughs were given the choice of being policed by the surrounding county or of continuing without a grant. This was the first attempt to deal with the problem of small forces and was, like many that followed, not very successful, since most chose independence. The grant was also too low to make it worthwhile for some of the smallest and most inefficient forces to qualify.

The result of the Act was that in 1857 there were 239 police forces in England and Wales and though the total fell slightly, particularly after the Local Government Act in 1888, it remained in the region of 200 for the rest of the century. These forces were unlike each other in size, type of recruit, pay, pensions, hours of duty, chain of command and style of uniform. They had in common adherence to the beat system, the annual inspection and, after the first few years, the Home Office grant. By 1890, although standards varied, there were no chronically inefficient forces.

In the years after 1856 the police service developed many of the characteristics which were to remain until the 1960's. The professional competence and status of the ordinary policeman slowly improved, the foundations of the pension system were laid and the individual and local character of the separate forces was strengthened.

*Recruitment*

Recruitment appears never to have been a serious problem in the nineteenth century, though there were occasional regional difficulties. Complaints of the increasing competition from other branches of local government were voiced from the early years of the twentieth century onwards. The type of men recruited obviously varied from force to force. The most important requirements were literacy, tallness and a strong constitution. Although agricultural labourers were the largest single group of recruits, they were by no means the only source and were often not even in the majority. A survey of 300 entrants to the Metropolitan police in 1872 to 1873 showed that 31 per cent came from the land, 13 per cent from the services, another 13 per cent from general labouring and 6 per cent from other police forces. The rest were from a very wide variety of occupations but, significantly, only three could be classed as non-manual.[1]

Vacancies were, on average, consistently low. In the 1860's the average for England and Wales was about 3 per cent, but by the 1880's it was down to less than 1 per cent. The number of vacancies did not reflect recruiting difficulties but was an inevitable result of the high rates of turnover experienced in the nineteenth century. The problem was not to attract recruits, but to keep them in the service.

TABLE II.1

**Rates of separation from police forces in England, Wales and the Metropolis (1860-95)**
**Percentage of establishment leaving annually**

|      | Metropolis | England and Wales |
|------|------------|-------------------|
| 1860 | 13·3       | —                 |
| 1865 | 13·5       | —                 |
| 1870 | 9·9        | —                 |
| 1875 | 10·2       | 13·8              |
| 1880 | 6·8        | 11·9              |
| 1885 | 5·0        | 8·9               |
| 1890 | 5·4        | 7·9               |
| 1895 | 4·8        | 6·3               |

SOURCE: *Annual Reports of the Inspectors of Constabulary and of the Commissioner of Police of the Metropolis.*

Table II.1 shows that by modern standards (when a rate of 3 per cent causes great concern), the rate of separation was almost intolerably high, though it fell by more than half as the century passed. There is some evidence to suggest that the fall was partly a function of the age and growing traditions of the forces as well as a response to improved conditions of pay and service. For example, the rate of separation in the Metropolitan police, founded several years earlier than the majority of borough forces, and acknowledged as the most experienced and efficient, fell earlier than the provincial rate. It was in the region of 14 per cent from 1860 to 1866, fell to a rate of 10 or 11 per cent until 1873 and after that fell again to remain around 5 per cent from 1884 till the outbreak of the first world war. The provincial forces repeated the pattern, but with a time lag. Separations were averaging 15 per cent in the seventies but fell steadily to about 6 per cent in

[1] *Commissioner of Police of the Metropolis, 1873,* 1874 C. 1059, xxvii.

1885. Rates remained steady, and slightly above those for London, until 1899 when the statistics ceased to be published.

A different pattern emerges from an analysis of the causes of separation. In the Metropolitan police, voluntary resignations and the occasional desertion accounted for about half the separations, or 7 per cent of the force, until 1867. After that the position improved and voluntary separation settled at about a quarter of the total. Dismissals and compulsory resignations, on the other hand, remained high, fluctuating between a half and a third of all removals. In the provinces, however, voluntary resignations stayed at a higher level. Although after 1879 they were rarely more than half of those leaving, in most years the proportion was at least a third. In contrast, dismissals in the provinces fell steadily from 1876 onwards and by the end of the century were reduced to a fifth of those leaving or under 1 per cent of the established forces.

## Wages

During the years from 1860 to 1913 there was a general improvement in the standard of living in Britain.[1] The rate at which average wages rose or the cost of living fell did, of course, vary from time to time, and different occupations were affected in different ways, but the general trend was for the better. Money wages rose and there were long periods when the cost of living was either stationary or declining. Early studies of wages and earnings estimated that wages rose on average by 40 per cent from 1860 to 1891 and that when the fall in the cost of living was taken into account the real value of the increase was nearer 90 per cent.[2]

The changes affected the police in a number of different ways. Their wages varied very greatly between different parts of the country (see below), and also tended to remain fixed for several years at a time. It was therefore possible for police wages to fall behind the national average, and this was especially true in the years between 1894 and 1913. During this time the cost of living

[1] See the works of A. L. Bowley for much of what follows. Detailed aspects of Bowley's work have been challenged, but further research is needed before the general outline can be refuted.

[2] A. L. Bowley, 'Changes in Average Wages (Nominal and Real) in the United Kingdom between 1860 and 1891', *Journal of the Royal Statistical Society* (June 1895), Vol. LVIII, Pt. II, p. 224.

rose slowly and average national wages followed. Those on fixed wages, such as the police, therefore found themselves becoming worse off.

Police pay scales were decided by the watch committee in the borough forces. In the counties one of a number of scales laid down by the Home Office was theoretically obligatory, and a rise in pay could not be given without Home Office approval. In fact, the pay scales were not revised often enough by the Home Office and came to be disregarded by counties which found themselves losing men to more highly paid borough forces. The rise in the average level of wages was by no means steady and was interrupted by a fall from 1875 to 1880 and another slight drop from 1891 to 1896. The period of most rapid upward movement occurred between 1870 and 1874.

TABLE II.2

**Changes in the weekly maximum and minimum wages for police constables in England and Wales (1860–90)**

|  | Maximum wage | | Minimum wage | |
|---|---|---|---|---|
|  | *Median* | *Range* | *Median* | *Range* |
|  | *shillings* | *shillings* | *shillings* | *shillings* |
| 1860 | 20 | 19 | 18 | 19 |
| 1870 | 22 | 22 | 19 | 19 |
| 1880 | 27 | 20 | 23 | 11 |
| 1890 | 29 | 19 | 23 | 8 |

SOURCE: *Reports of H.M. Inspectors of Constabulary.*

The improvement in police wages shown in Table II.2 therefore has to be seen against the background of better conditions for wage-earners as a whole. However, by 1890 the police had more than kept up with the national average and had substantially improved their status. The Table is constructed from records showing the highest and lowest pay of constables in each force in the country. The majority of policemen could of course expect to earn a weekly wage which was somewhere between the limits shown.

In the years following 1856 police wages appear to have been low in relation to other occupations. They were then, as throughout the period, generally several shillings a week above those of agricultural labourers, but this difference was in part illusory. Agricultural earnings often included payments in kind.[1] The

[1] A. L. Bowley, *Wages in the United Kingdom in the Nineteenth Century*, Cambridge, 1900, p. 7.

practice declined over the century,[1] but even when no actual payment in goods was made there were hidden advantages in the country, such as produce obtained at farm prices, free pasture or subsidized housing. The difference in real earnings between the police and the agricultural labourer was therefore less than at first appears.

Before the 1870's, although police wages were high enough to attract men from many different callings at a rate of 10 to 15 per cent of the total force each year, once in the force the absence of fringe benefits (rent allowances or free houses do not appear to have become at all general until the 1890's), the contrast with national average wage rates and the often uncongenial work, had their effect. Even in 1874 an investigation showed that over half of all recruits left after less than two years' service.[2]

Soon after 1870 an improvement set in. The disturbances in economic activity generated by the Franco-Prussian war resulted in a rapid, though uneven, rise in national wages in the years 1870 to 1874. Police wages lagged behind at first but caught up over the next decade. In 1870 the national average for a constable on his maximum was 22s. a week (Table II.2). Only four years later it was estimated that the average wage for all constables was 24s.[3] and by 1879 this was the minimum wage in the Northern District and the overall national minimum was only a shilling lower. During these years wages were therefore undergoing a slow though irregular improvement. An example of the piecemeal method adopted appears in a report for 1872. In that year recruiting was difficult and the Inspector of the Midlands District noted that the boroughs were raising their rates of pay and attracting men from the counties. The counties, though officially bound by Home Office scales, had no alternative but to raise their rates and were widely doing so. In the same year the Metropolitan police successfully negotiated an increase in pay and a slight decrease in working hours.

After 1880 the overall rise in police wages appears to have been small, but the disparity in the wages paid by different forces lessened. This development towards greater equality appears to

---

[1] The series of Truck Acts passed from 1831 to 1896 finally eliminated it.
[2] *Report from the Select Committee on Police Superannuation Funds*, p. 7; 1877 (158), xv.
[3] *Ibid.*, p. 70.

have been a response to national economic trends rather than the result of a consistent policy on the part of the Home Office or local forces.[1] Between 1880 and 1890 the range between the highest and lowest wages fell from 11s. to 8s. There were more forces paying less than the national average in 1890 but those with the lowest rates had been obliged to raise them.

In the 1890's, the police were comparatively well off financially and their conditions of service were improving. Charles Booth found in 1894 that 'as a rule the men are now satisfied with their lot; the policeman's position, if not indeed "a happy one", is equal to that of most skilled workmen'.[2] Booth was looking on the bright side since, from his own observations, the average wages of a constable were 31s. a week, while those of a skilled workman were 40s. He estimated that rent allowance, boot and other allowances, pension and a week's holiday made up the difference. However that may be there is no doubt that during the 1890's the policeman and his family were able to live as respectable members of the working classes, a position which was a considerable advance on the early image of him as akin to the agricultural labourer. After 1900, however, police earnings fell in relation to the national average and discontent grew.

Table II.2 also shows the average maximum wage for constables. The lowest figures for maximum wages were recorded in the years 1860 and 1870 when some forces were still paying a single rate for all constables and this rate was recorded both as a maximum and a minimum. In 1880 and 1890 the total range was much the same but the number of forces paying the lowest rates declined. In general rates of pay differed less between counties than between boroughs, as might be expected, but there was no coherent pattern of regional variation.

Although the national trend was for police wages to rise and the difference between forces to be reduced, the persistence of wide disparities between Districts and between forces influenced later events. The inequalities of police pay encouraged, and were

[1] 'The general policy of the Home Office till last year (1918) was to treat the several forces as independent of each other.' Desborough Report, Part 1, p. 5; 1919 Cmd. 253, xxvii.

[2] C. Booth, *Life and Labour of the People in London. Second Series. Industry 4. Public, Professional and Domestic Service, Unoccupied Classes, Inmates of Institutions*, London, Macmillan, 1903, p. 51.

encouraged by, the lack of communication between forces, so intensifying the local character of police work. Another legacy has been the persistence with which the police fought any reintroduction of differentials when once the principle of a single national scale had been accepted in 1919. Forces which found themselves seriously short of men after 1945 were thus unable to pay higher rates to attract recruits, and even in 1966 differentials were meant to be only temporary expedients and were not considered as part of normal pay.[1]

TABLE II.3

**Regional differences in the average police minimum weekly wage in England and Wales (1860–90)**

|  | Northern | | Southern | | Midland | |
|  | Median shillings | Range shillings | Median shillings | Range shillings | Median shillings | Range shillings |
|---|---|---|---|---|---|---|
| 1860 | 18 | 12 | 18 | 18 | 17 | 15 |
| 1870 | 20 | 7 | 19 | 8 | 19 | 15 |
| 1880 | 24 | 6 | 21 | 9 | 22 | 5 |
| 1890 | 24 | 8 | 23 | 6 | 22 | 5 |

SOURCE: *Reports of H.M. Inspectors of Constabulary.*

Table II.3 shows the range of variation among minimum wages at different dates. In 1860 variations between forces were wide but were more or less evenly spread over the three Police Districts of England and Wales. Even where variations were least, i.e. among the counties, wages for constables at the bottom of the scale varied from 18s. to 22s., a range of over 20 per cent. The counties, being tied to Home Office pay scales, naturally had less freedom in fixing wages than the boroughs. They were also, except in the North, less directly in competition with urban industrial wages. Boroughs, on the other hand, were at liberty to pay whatever wages they wished and the range was very wide. There were small boroughs all over the country which paid very low wages that appear to have been based on the rate for part-time parish constables. Even some large boroughs also paid badly, for example Bristol where the starting pay was 14s. in 1860. At the other end of the scale there were boroughs, also generally with small forces, paying the highest wages. An example was Bideford which paid 25s. a week.

[1] See the discussion by the Select Committee on Estimates. *First Report from the Estimates Committee, Police,* p. xxii and related evidence; 1966–67 (145).

Differentials between the three Police Districts began to develop after 1860. The Northern District which comprised the north of England as far south as Cheshire, Derbyshire, Nottinghamshire (after 1868) and Yorkshire, was the most homogeneous. With the exception of police forces in country districts such as the county force of East Riding and the joint force of Cumberland and Westmorland and a few isolated boroughs like Richmond, employment was dominated by the great industrial centres of the late nineteenth century. The Midland, Eastern Counties and North Wales District extended as far south as Merionethshire, Shropshire, Worcestershire, Oxfordshire, Bedfordshire, Huntingdonshire and Essex. The rest of the country (with the exception, of course, of the Metropolitan Police District and the City of London), was in District No. 3, Southern Counties and South Wales. The Midland and Southern Districts exhibited more variety than did the North. The Midland District ranged from the Birmingham and Black Country industrial areas to the sparsely inhabited counties of North Wales and the farm lands of East Anglia. There was naturally a wide variation between forces. The same was true of the South which included industrial Wales, South East England and the farming areas of the South West. The South West was to some extent a unique area— agricultural wages were among the lowest in the country throughout the period[1] and the number of small borough forces was only surpassed in Kent. In the counties of Devon and Cornwall there were nineteen borough forces in 1860 and still seventeen in 1870. Low wages and inefficient forces were the dominant characteristics of the South West, and the poor pay lowered the average for the whole Southern District.

From 1860 to 1870 the average starting wage rose by one shilling overall (Table II.3), but regional differences became more marked. The range within the Districts fell except for Northern county forces. Starting wages in the Southern and Midland counties remained below average but the boroughs in the North went ahead. The levelling up (if that is not too strong a term) of wages was most marked in the boroughs. The difference between the highest and lowest wages had been over three times as great as

[1] A. L. Bowley, 'The Statistics of Wages in the United Kingdom during the last Hundred Years (Part 1) Agricultural Wages', *Journal of the Royal Statistical Society*, Vol. LXI (1898), pp. 704-5.

in the counties, and the change was brought about mainly by a reduction in the number of boroughs paying the lowest rates. There was no increase in the top rate paid by boroughs, and even a decrease in the South. (For example, Bideford which had paid 25s. in 1860 reduced the starting wage to 18s. in 1870.)

Bowley's figures showed that by 1880 a general national wage rise had occurred and the rise in police wages must be viewed in this context. The average starting rate for police constables was 4s., or 21 per cent higher than it had been in 1870. The counties and boroughs in the North were, at 24s., paying above the national average, though wages in the counties covered a wider range below the average than in the boroughs. It is clear that police in the South benefited least from the general wage rise. Southern counties had the lowest average starting wages (3s. below the national average), and the range in the boroughs was wider than in the rest of the country. At the bottom it extended 7s. below the national average and at the top only went 2s. above it.

Wages were fairly stable over the following decade. The average did not change except in Northern counties and Southern boroughs, but there was a gradual reduction in the range of wages and a drift upwards in the worst forces. The Southern District was the most affected.

Table II.4 gives the wages of sergeants and is designed to show how promotion might affect the ordinary recruit. A sergeant on the maximum scale could expect to earn at least a third more than the starting pay of a recruit (33s. in 1890) and the differential increased slightly over the period. The range between the highest and lowest paying forces was in general less for sergeants' pay than for constables'. At the maximum the range increased over the period. This was mainly a result of very high rates being paid in the Northern boroughs (for example 49s. in Manchester in 1890).

It is clear that wages were bound to vary from force to force. In the first place the work was different and called for different skills. For example, the rural constable in Central Wales led a different life from his counterpart in Kent. The same went for the borough constables in Peterborough and Birmingham. In the absence of national negotiating machinery these differences were naturally reflected in the wages paid. However, the wide variations recorded cannot be explained solely in terms of differences in the nature of police duties, or even as a reflection of the regional variations in wage levels, though wages in the North were in part a response to competition from industry. One important reason was the lack of communication. The men in the separate police forces were, in general, subject to very strict discipline and had little opportunity for meeting their colleagues and forming comparisons. Attempts to form a police union were increasingly successful after 1900 and there is no doubt that as opportunities for communication between forces grew, discontent over unequal pay and conditions flourished as well.

TABLE II.4

**Maximum and minimum average weekly wages for police sergeants in England and Wales (1860–90)**

|  | Maximum wage | | Minimum wage | |
|---|---|---|---|---|
|  | Median shillings | Range shillings | Median shillings | Range shillings |
| 1860 | 23 | 4 | 23 | 10 |
| 1870 | 26 | 11 | 25 | 11 |
| 1880 | 32 | 20 | 29 | 15 |
| 1890 | 33 | 22 | 31 | 11 |

SOURCE: *Reports of H.M. Inspectors of Constabulary.*

As wages rose the opportunities open to the police for making money in other ways diminished. Their forerunners, such as the parish constables and Bow Street runners, had performed services directly for members of the public and were privately paid. The practice was replaced by a ban on nearly all forms of off-duty work, which was more and more strictly enforced as discipline improved. A few forms of approved public and private duty were open to policemen, e.g. as attendants in municipal galleries or doormen at weddings, but these had to be performed in off-duty hours and were not available to all forces. The regulations were a hardship to men with unusually large families but helped to raise the police in the public esteem—though the practice of tipping constables was common until well into this century.

## Conditions of work

The working conditions of the police, like the wages, have to be compared with those of other occupations. At first it seems that ten-hour tours of duty were not uncommon, but these soon fell to eight or nine hours for constables in most forces. The higher ranks continued to work longer hours, for example, inspectors and sergeants in central London stations worked twelve-hour shifts until 1887.[1]

The policeman who worked an eight- or nine-hour day was at first sight better off than the majority of working men. A Ten Hour Day Act limiting the length of the working day was first passed in 1847, but throughout the country there were many occupations where ten or more hours were normally worked. In 1894 a survey of 206 occupations showed that in 142, or nearly 70 per cent, a ten-hour day (with Sundays and one afternoon off) was being worked.[2] However, the length of a shift was not the most important consideration in calculating police hours. Night shifts were generally done in a single block of eight hours, but day duty was divided into split shifts in nearly all forces. The constable divided his time into a spell of four hours before noon and four or five hours in the early or late evening. As a result his working day could easily extend to twelve hours. Men were also expected to parade for up to fifteen minutes before joining their beats, and again when coming off. On a single shift, therefore, an extra half-hour might have to be worked, but with split shifts the extra might easily be an hour. (This system was considered essential if constables were to be briefed and information received, but it amounted to hidden overtime.) In addition reports had to be written in the constable's free time and for the many barely literate recruits in the early years the labour was no doubt very tedious.

Before 1900 meal breaks were uncommon and constables were expected to eat on duty. Some carried small stoves for warming tea on night duty and others were sent hot drinks from the nearest station. After 1900 forces began to introduce a short meal break, generally of fifteen minutes, but this was by no means universal even by 1919. For example, in 1908 it was still possible to see a constable on point duty (where he remained for eight hours), in Oxford Street 'munching something' in the middle of the traffic.[3]

---

[1] *Inspectors of Constabulary, 1887*, p. 4; 1888 (19), lvii.

[2] C. Booth, *Life and Labour of the People in London. Second Series: Industry 5. Comparisons, Survey and Conclusions*, London, Macmillan, 1904, p. 182.

[3] *Report of the Select Committee on the Police Weekly Rest Day*, Minutes of Evidence, p. 44; 1908 (353, 354), ix.

Even where the meal break was given it was sometimes made up by lengthening the shift from eight to eight and a half hours.

A policeman was expected to walk an average of twenty miles a day in all weathers at a steady pace. The work was for the most part boring, but was occasionally enlivened by violent encounters with gangs of poachers, wandering navvies or able-bodied vagrants.[1] There were some 13,000 assaults a year on the police in the 1870's, 11,000 in the 1890's but only about 6,000 since the first world war. (This represents a drop of 50 per cent, and it would be even greater if allowance were made for the increase in police and population.)

The work continued day in and day out. In the more advanced forces constables received a week's paid annual leave and one, or even two, days off per month. But in others, especially the counties, the only respite was one week of unpaid leave. After 1890 there was a gradual improvement. By 1900 most counties gave one day off a month and most boroughs two. However, by this time the average workman had 52 Sundays off a year, 52 half-days and six Bank Holidays—a total of 84. A policeman had, if he were lucky, 26 days off and ten days' annual holiday—less than half as much. The police working week was therefore very much longer than at first appeared and by the end of the period it was increasingly above the national average.

Much was written by the early reformers about the disadvantages of piece work, seasonal work and uncertain employment. A policeman in contrast to others, had a steady job and the faint chance of a pension. The advantages were undeniable, but it is clear that many preferred insecurity and time off—even if it was enforced idleness—to the unending routine of police work.

An added disadvantage was the increasingly pervasive discipline of the police service. As the police became more professional, they became more disciplined. For example, in the early days many men were dismissed for drunkenness. In times when agricultural wages included free beer or cider, as they often did even in 1890,[2] drinking by rural recruits was perhaps only to be expected. With

[1] Critchley gives a vivid account of these aspects of the life of the Victorian policeman. *Op. cit.*, pp. 157–9.
[2] A. L. Bowley, *Wages in the United Kingdom in the Nineteenth Century*, Cambridge, 1900, p. 26.

a high turnover it was hard to eliminate, but the practice appears to have virtually died out by the end of the period.[1]

Discipline was most restrictive in the counties where the doctrine that the whole of a policeman's time was at the disposal of the force was furthest developed. A man was commonly not allowed to leave his house during off-duty hours without permission. The rules preventing a policeman or his family from having anything to do with business appear to have been strictly enforced everywhere and opportunities for finding approved employment outside duty hours diminished.

*Training*

In the early days when police duties virtually comprised pounding the beat and acting as a riot squad when needed, there was very little training. No special skills were needed over and above the basic qualifications for recruits, turnover was high and many men left after a few months. As the complexity of police work developed, the larger forces at least, did more training. In the 1860's instruction for recruits was limited to drill, but thirty years later a month's course in basic law and police responsibilities followed by one or two months on the beat with an experienced officer was normal in large forces. However as late as 1918 many forces had no formal training schemes.[2] Specialized departments with their different training needs also developed slowly. An embryonic Criminal Investigation Department was first formed in the Metropolitan police in 1842, but in the early years detective work tended to be equated with spying. The Department was reorganized under Sir Howard Vincent in 1878 and a few years later a Special Irish Branch of the C.I.D. was set up to protect Ministers of the Crown from terrorist activities. Its activities gradually broadened and it became known by its present title of the Special Branch.[3] The larger provincial forces also had detective departments. In these more advanced forces detection slowly became more

---

[1] In Liverpool in 1882 it was unusual to find a man who did not drink on duty while by 1908, the exception was the man who did. *Report of the Select Committee on the Police Weekly Rest Day*, Minutes of Evidence, p. 136; 1908 (353, 354), ix.

[2] Desborough Report, Part II, Minutes of Evidence, p. 88; 1920 Cmd. 874, xxii.

[3] T. A. Critchley, *op. cit.*, p. 161.

scientific. Fingerprints were collected by the Metropolitan police from 1901 and the system was general by 1907. Two years later Major Atcherley, later to be one of Her Majesty's Inspectors, began the system of classifying and identifying criminals by their methods and idiosyncrasies (modus operandi), in the West Riding. Detective training courses (mainly in criminal law) were instituted in the larger forces and in 1918 the Metropolitan courses were opened to provincial officers. The other main field of specialization appears to have been in clerical work. The various licensing activities of the police (cabs, pedlars, etc.) early called for full-scale clerical departments. This specialization, however, had only a limited impact as beat work was by far the most important aspect of police work throughout the nineteenth and early twentieth centuries.

*Equipment*

During the whole of this period the police operated with very little equipment. The early police were, in fact, almost devoid of equipment other than their uniforms and their truncheons. Bicycles first became general in the 1890's and were used by borough criminal investigation departments as an aid to mobility. Higher ranks usually moved on horseback or by carriage. Communications were slow. The Metropolitan police installed a telegraph system early in the period but a committee enquiring into the riot of 1886 found that the system was inadequate and out of date.[1]

*Extra duties*

One important factor which helped to establish the police as a civilian quasi-professional body, despite their duties as a riot squad, was the wide range of non-police functions they came to perform. The practice was deplored by the police but there is little doubt that these activities, often socially useful, and always calling for integrity, helped to establish a favourable picture of the police in the public mind (particularly of the middle classes). The most time-consuming appears to have been the fire service,

[1] *Report of the Committee appointed to enquire into the Administration and Organization of the Metropolitan Police Force*, p. 5; 1886 C. 4892, xxxiv.

which in many boroughs was entirely manned by the police. More important politically were the inspection of weights and measures and, after 1872, the enforcement of the various Licensing and Hours acts. One result was that small boroughs sometimes refused to amalgamate their forces with the neighbouring county because the trading and brewing interests on the council did not wish to see an independent county man as Inspector.[1]

Other duties came and went. In the 1880's the issue of tickets to vagrants took up much time, but soon ceased. Enforcement of the Chimney Sweeps Act likewise declined. However, the general trend was for extraneous duties to increase. To quote Sir Leonard Dunning, Inspector of Constabulary in 1909, 'Before concluding I would like to draw attention to the multifarious duties which the police are called upon to perform in the present day, and the increasing tendency to throw new work on to them. Originally established for the special purpose of preventing and detecting crime, they are now engaged at all times on such work as Weights and Measures, Contagious Diseases (Animals), Food and Drugs, Explosives Acts, Swine and Cattle Licences and sheep dipping and during the past year local taxation duties have been thrown in. It is a serious question whether any more miscellaneous work can be put upon the police, without destroying their efficiency in the performance of their more primary duties.'[2]

*Pensions*

The most frequently quoted advantage of police work was the pension, but few men received one until after 1890. There were many reasons why this was so. Pension funds were not obligatory at first. Boroughs were allowed to set up funds by the act of 1835. The sources of income for the fund and the pension rates payable were laid down, but very few boroughs took advantage of the provisions. In county forces funds were obligatory after 1840. They were to be financed by deductions from pay not exceeding $2\frac{1}{2}$ per cent, stoppages of pay during sickness (generally a flat rate of 1s. per day throughout the period), disciplinary fines, money from the sale of old uniforms and such proportions of various

---

[1] T. A. Critchley, *op. cit.*, 1967, pp. 102 and 157 n, and also W. L. Burn, *The Age of Equipoise*, London, Allen and Unwin, 1964, p. 175.

[2] *Inspectors of Constabulary, 1909*, p. 3; 1910 (106), lxxv.

fines imposed in the magistrates' courts as the courts should decide. Under the regulations a man who had reached the age of 60 could retire on half pay if he had served between fifteen and twenty years and on two-thirds pay after twenty or more years' service. Men could retire earlier provided they were medically certified as unfit for duty, but it seems that few actually did so.

Table II.5 shows the number and percentage of establishment leaving with a pension in various years. The numbers ran at a very low level until 1891 and, since all witnesses agreed that most men were not fit for beat duty by the age of 55,[1] it is clear that

### TABLE II.5

#### Superannuation (1861–1911)

| | Metropolitan | | England and Wales | |
|---|---|---|---|---|
| | *No.* Pensioned | *Pensioned per 1,000\* establishment* | *No.* Pensioned | *Pensioned per 1,000 establishment* |
| 1861 | 114 | 16 | n.a. | n.a. |
| 1866 | 206 | 27 | 79 | 5 |
| 1871 | 177 | 18 | n.a. | n.a. |
| 1876 | 234 | 23 | 196 | 11 |
| 1881 | 187 | 16 | 270 | 14 |
| 1886 | 209 | 15 | 309 | 14 |
| 1891 | 468 | 31 | 845 | 36 |
| 1896 | 470 | 31 | 501 | 20 |
| 1901 | 403 | 25 | n.a. | n.a. |
| 1906 | 454 | 26 | n.a. | n.a. |
| 1911 | 527 | 26 | n.a. | n.a. |

\* Metropolitan authorized strength.

SOURCE: *Annual Reports of Inspectors of Constabulary: England and Wales, and of the Commissioner of Police of the Metropolis.*

the majority struggled on in the hope that they would be awarded a pension at 60. In 1859 the county rules were extended to the boroughs.[2] The rules, however, only laid down what a man might get if the justices or the watch committee decided to award him

[1] *Report from the Select Committee on Police Superannuation Funds*, 1877 (158), xv and *Report of the Select Committee on the Police Weekly Rest Day, passin*; 1908 (353, 354), ix.

[2] The rules were virtually the same except that fees for summonses and warrants went to the borough pension funds while in the counties they were used to offset general police expenses.

a pension. No constable was entitled to a pension by right. It could be refused, or he could be dismissed and so forfeit his pension. Until 1906 dismissal could occur at any time even when a man had completed twenty-five years' service. There was a right of appeal to the watch committee in the boroughs, but in the counties dismissal was final. This continued until the 1906 Police Act ruled that a pension could not be cancelled after twenty-six years' service unless a man were convicted of a crime or similar misdemeanour.

Since virtually all pension funds were chronically insolvent throughout the period, there was every incentive to dismiss men before they reached retiring age. The major reason for insolvency was that actuarial calculations were either not made or were not sufficiently thorough. As a result contributions were too small and the income of the funds was never high enough for them to meet their obligations after the first wave of retirements.

Inefficiencies in administration contributed. For example, men who left in their first year of service rarely paid contributions, and they amounted to 5 per cent of the force in the early years— even if they were the lowest-paid 5 per cent. Funds were not infrequently misappropriated. There were other unforeseen and unavoidable problems. The borough funds generally had a higher income but the former watchmen who had been recruited in 1835 reached retiring age early and had not contributed to the pension fund for most of their service. The boroughs were thus in as bad a position as the counties. Rising wages over the country also had their effect since pensions were calculated on final pay while contributions had been made on the basis of the lower wages of the past.

In 1872 concern over the funds led to part of the revenue from the new beer and spirit licenses being allocated to the funds. Five years later a committee was set up to investigate the position, but little was done until 1890. A Police Act of that year made pensions obligatory unless a man was dismissed. It laid down maximum and minimum scales for pensions. The Act also brought the administration of police funds under Home Office control for the first time. From 1893 the accounts of all funds had to be published. Additional central revenue from the licensing acts was also allocated to the funds.

The response to the Act was mixed. Some police authorities

were naturally concerned about the prospect of many more men being pensioned and becoming a burden on funds which were already unsound. Others quickly adopted the maximum pension scales and lowered the age limit or substituted length of service as the qualification for retirement. The immediate result of the Act was that the numbers pensioned rose from 505 in 1890 to 1,313 in 1891. Promotion opportunities improved in all but the forces where the age limit had not been changed or was even raised.

*Promotion*

The question of promotions was an important one. From the earliest days it was possible for all members of the force to rise to the rank of superintendent. The first rules for promotion in county forces laid down the qualifications which were desirable for sergeants, inspectors and superintendents and advocated promotion from the ranks. Examinations were instituted in the larger forces in the 1860's.

TABLE II.6

**Percentage of different ranks in the police force (1861–1911)**

|      | Chief Officers | Supt. & Clerks | Inspectors | Sergeants | Constables† | Total estab. |
|------|------|------|------|------|------|------|
| 1861 | 1·0 | 2·3 | 3·5 | 10·1 | 83·1 | 20,488 |
| 1872* | 0·8 | 1·9 | 3·4 | 10·3 | 83·6 | 27,247 |
| 1881 | 0·7 | 1·6 | 4·5 | 10·2 | 83·0 | 31,596 |
| 1891 | 0·5 | 1·5 | 4·1 | 11·6 | 82·3 | 39,198 |
| 1901 | 0·4 | 1·4 | 3·4 | 12·2 | 82·6 | 44,705 |
| 1911 | 0·5 | 1·2 | 3·2 | 11·9 | 83·2 | 54,314 |

    * Figures for 1871 are not available.
    † Additional constables who were not officially part of the establishment but performed normal police duties have been included with constables.

SOURCE: *Annual Reports of the Inspectors of Constabulary* and *Annual Reports of the Commissioner of Police of the Metropolis.*

Table II.6 shows the changing proportions of the various ranks. Chief officers and superintendents both declined in number as the smaller forces were amalgamated. The proportion of inspectors, as shown by the figures for 1881 and 1891, rose considerably, partly as a result of an expansion in the Metropolitan police after a riot in 1886 had shown that the command structure was completely inadequate. Sergeants increased steadily in numbers until

1901. Improved schemes of command and growing standards of efficiency clearly demanded more sergeants. They performed the main supervisory and disciplinary functions, while administration and policy were carried out at a higher level. It is perhaps significant that in the nineteenth and early twentieth centuries sergeants increased while the proportion of higher ranks actually declined. The converse has been true in recent years.

Chances of promotion were, of course, very uneven from force to force. In the small boroughs promotion tended to be either very rapid or very slow. Borough chief constables who had risen from the ranks were often appointed in their early thirties. Some remained in post until long after the normal retiring age (chief constables in their seventies were not unknown), while others moved on to larger boroughs. Indeed, one of the arguments advanced in favour of maintaining the small borough forces was that young men of talent could rise to a chief constableship early in their careers, and from there progress to the higher ranks of large forces. On the other hand all promotion might be completely blocked for decades. In some small borough forces the higher positions were taken in 1856 by members of the old watch, and in others men designated as superintendents were appointed relatively young and remained at the top for many years, blocking advancement for the rest of the force. These superintendents were not comparable in importance with those of a large force but there was no effort to standardize ranks and duties until 1919 and the designation remained. Favouritism was not unknown even at the highest level. In 1918 His Majesty's Inspector told the Desborough Committee that men did get appointed as chief constables, especially of small boroughs, 'not on their merits as policemen'.[1] In the counties the situation was somewhat different because appointments as chief constable from the ranks were rare. County chiefs were frequently young military men and also tended to remain long in office. The practice of appointing such candidates direct to the rank of superintendent also declined gradually. By 1918 only Devon still did so, and the Desborough Committee was not in favour of appointments from outside the service.[2] In the larger forces there were more opportunities, and men who

[1] Desborough Report, Part II, Minutes of Evidence, p. 87; 1920 Cmd. 874, xxii.

[2] Desborough Report, Part II, p. 11; 1920 Cmd. 874, xxii.

stayed in the force and had ability could reasonably expect to rise to the rank of sergeant. This brought them a wage approximately equal to that of a skilled workman and made the police an attractive career for a man who had not been apprenticed in his youth.[1] In 1878 it took, on average, four to five years to be promoted to sergeant and a further eight to ten years to become an inspector.[2]

It appears that the rate of promotion was becoming increasingly unfavourable by the late 1880's. There was some relief after the Police Pensions Act of 1890, but the benefit did not last. When most forces had relaxed their pension requirements to allow the constable to retire after twenty-five years' service on approximately two-thirds pay, men left the force at, or around, the age of 50. In the higher ranks, however, this was not the case. Men who were promoted were naturally tempted to leave with as high a pension as possible. Since their work did not entail doing night duty on the beat in winter weather, to take the main cause of poor health in constables, they were able to remain until they had reached the maximum salary for their grade, and then continue for a further three years in forces where the pension was assessed on the average wage of the last three years in service. In most cases the scales for inspector and superintendent were spread out over five years, but eight was not unknown. This situation, combined with the fact that some forces had age limits which did not allow a superintendent to retire before the age of 60 or 65, meant that opportunities for promotion were slowly blocked, the average age of senior officers rose and promotion tended to be strictly according to seniority or accusations of favouritism followed.[3] By 1919 it was clear that avenues for promotion had become almost completely blocked in many forces. The retention of senior officers in the war had been a final blow. In Lancashire 40 per cent of the superintendents (ten out of twenty-four) had between forty and forty-eight years' service and

---

[1] The differential between wage rates for skilled and unskilled work was still significantly large, though falling, even at the end of the period. It does not appear to have broken down until after 1918. See A. L. Bowley, *Wages and Incomes in the United Kingdom since 1860*, Cambridge, 1937, p. 44.

[2] T. A. Critchley, *op. cit.*, p. 155.

[3] Desborough Report, Part II, Minutes of Evidence, p. 191; 1920 Cmd. 874, xxii. It is clear that strong feelings existed in Liverpool over alleged favouritism in promotions.

in the Metropolitan police most superintendents were in their twenty-ninth or thirtieth year of service.[1]

This slow stagnation of promotion opportunities occurred at a time when the proportion of senior ranks was actually falling (see Table II.6). It is not surprising that discontent built up in many forces and, together with increasingly inadequate pay after 1903 and the harsh discipline, led to widespread discontent.

*Number of forces*

The number of forces declined as the total strength of the police grew. The majority of forces continued to be small by modern standards, and remained isolated one from another, but the very smallest were eliminated over the period.

TABLE II.7

**Total number of forces, total establishment and total population per policeman for census years**

|  | *Total No. forces* | *Total establishment* | *Total population '000* | *Population per policeman* |
|---|---|---|---|---|
| 1861 | 233 | 20,488 | 20,066 | 979·4 |
| 1871 | n.a. | 26,604 | 22,712 | 853·7 |
| 1881 | 224 | 31,596 | 25,974 | 822·0 |
| 1891 | 185 | 39,198 | 29,003 | 739·9 |
| 1901 | 187 | 44,705 | 32,528 | 727·6 |
| 1911 | 188 | 54,314 | 36,070 | 664·1 |

SOURCE: *Inspector(s) of Constabulary and Annual Abstracts of Statistics.*

Despite constant pressure from H.M. Inspectors, there was only a limited number of amalgamations after 1860. More was done by legislation. In 1877 the Municipal Corporations (New Charters) Act laid down that no newly incorporated borough could have a separate police force unless its population was at least 20,000. It was of course only a preventive measure, but positive steps were taken in 1888. Under the Local Government Act which set up county councils and reorganized the county administration, all boroughs with under 10,000 inhabitants had to merge their police forces with the surrounding county. The act reduced the number of forces from 231 to 183.

The advantages of amalgamation were economy, efficiency and

[1] *Ibid.*, p. 175 and p. 47; 1920 Cmd. 874, xxii.

flexibility. In nearly all cases it was cheaper to police a small borough as a division of a county than to have a separate force. Where the county already had a police station in the borough (a common occurrence in, for example, Lancashire), duplication of buildings ceased on amalgamation. Larger forces were able to deploy men with greater flexibility, particularly in times of public unrest. The small forces had frequently to call in outside help during the disorders of 1909 to 1913, but they could not be compelled to amalgamate.[1]

The isolation of many forces is illustrated by the lack of, or weakness in, inter-force co-operation. The Home Office and H.M. Inspectors from the first advocated mutual aid agreements, but had no powers of compulsion. As late as 1912, the Home Office sent out a circular containing model agreements.[2] The agreements which did exist were frequently only concerned with finance. Matters of police command were left for arrangement when a case arose. In 1890 the rule that all constables, when borrowed for use outside their own area, had to be specially sworn in, was waived in certain circumstances, but it continued as a general principle until 1919.

*Movement between forces*

The various forces therefore tended to develop in isolation though there was a certain amount of mobility at the top and bottom levels of the command structure. Superintendents transferred to become assistant chief constables or chief constables, and of course commanding officers moved from small to large forces. At the other end of the scale, constables who were not hoping for promotion had every incentive to move to the boroughs that were paying the highest wages, thus causing a recruiting problem for the counties. In 1877 a committee rejected a proposal which would have enabled men who changed forces to take their pension rights with them. The committee considered that the concession would encourage mobility which was already too high.[3] Men who transferred on promotion were normally allowed to count half

[1] J. M. Hart, *The British Police*, London, Allen & Unwin, 1951, p. 36.
[2] *Inspectors of Constabulary, 1912*, No. 2 District, p. 57; 1913 (76), lii.
[3] *Report from the Select Committee on Police Superannuation Funds*, p. viii; 1877 (158), xv.

their previous service as pensionable, but it was not until 1906 that the regulations were altered to make pensionable service fully transferable between force and force—and then only if the transfer was approved in writing by the chief constables concerned.

*Number of police*

The total number of police grew at a faster rate than population during the period and, with few setbacks, has continued to do so ever since. The Inspectors were from the first particularly concerned with the size of establishments and they appear to have been more successful in persuading authorities to raise numbers than they were in some other respects, such as improving the state of police lock ups. The police grant was never actually withheld after 1890, but in the 'sixteen years or so before 1900' the threat was used on average at least once a year.[1] One of the most difficult problems was to persuade the police authorities of rapidly growing boroughs that establishment and expenditure must keep pace with the increase in population. Sheffield even lost its grant between 1862 and 1863 because the force fell below the minimum considered necessary by H.M. Inspector.[2] The Inspectors were most successful when dealing with counties. A county chief constable who was generally a 'gentleman', and possibly an ex-officer, could speak to the police authority on equal terms, and with the Inspector's support, make his case for more men or money. Borough chief constables were usually in a much weaker position. They were more closely controlled by the watch committee and any increase in police expenditure had a direct political impact on the councillors via the rates, instead of being cushioned by the lump sum method of financing local services used in the counties.

*Conclusion*

Two major features stand out in any survey of the history of the police service during the nineteenth and early twentieth centuries. The first is the change in the status of the policemen, and the

[1] J. Hart, 'The County and Borough Police Act, 1856', *Public Administration*, Vol. XXXIV (1956), p. 410.
[2] T. A. Critchley, *op. cit.*, p. 130.

second is the lack of change in police organization. The police increased steadily in numbers, both in absolute terms and in relation to population. From unpopular beginnings they established themselves as an essential feature of British civilian life. Their pay and working conditions improved. The average constable, though paid little more than an agricultural labourer in the 1850's, had become the equal of a skilled worker by the 1890's. By the beginning of the twentieth century a policeman had a secure job, a fair chance of a pension and paid holidays and sick leave. Few other occupations could offer such advantages in the days before the welfare state. A decline set in after 1900 when the rising cost of living eroded the value of police pay and the rate of promotion slowed down. The resulting tensions culminated in the police strike of 1918 which sparked off the next great period of reform described in Chapter III.

In contrast to the changes in the conditions and status of the constable, the most striking feature of the national organization of the police was its stability. The sharp distinction between county and borough forces that was established between 1829 and 1840 when the different forces were set up, remained. Even the system of inspection instituted by the Police Act 1856, though important, had only limited success in enforcing common standards. Working conditions, pay scales and even uniforms continued to vary widely between forces. Of course changes occurred; the smallest forces disappeared, the command structure altered as more complex duties demanded more men in the supervisory ranks, the average size of force increased and specialized departments became more common. After 1900 the most advanced forces began collecting and exchanging information on fingerprints and the operational methods of criminals. However, policing continued to be essentially a local activity, organized in small units with little contact between forces. Co-operation between neighbouring forces was reserved for emergencies. The police could, with fairness, be described as a conservative organization and were to remain so for many years to come.

# III

# The Inter-War Years[1]

THE police service changed less during the inter-war years than did many other aspects of British life. A major reason for this relative stability was that new developments in police methods needed money, and, like other public services, the police suffered from economies in government spending. More sweeping changes occurred after the second world war when the police were faced with the combination of altered social conditions and an acute manpower shortage.

## The Desborough Committee

The two reports of the Desborough Committee published in 1919 and 1920, and their acceptance virtually intact, set the tone for the following years. The new order, embodied in the Police Act of 1919 and the Regulations of 1920, did not alter the organization or basic character of the police service. It did, however, raise the economic, and thus the social, status of the average policeman far above anything he had previously achieved. At the same time it laid down the framework which was vital if common conditions of service, co-operation between forces and progress towards scientific methods of policing were to become a reality.

The Committee was set up to deal with a very serious situation. The position outlined in the previous chapter, with wide variations in pay and conditions of service and police earnings increasingly falling behind the national average, had been intensified by the war. In December 1917 the police authorities had been allowed to give non-pensionable cost of living bonuses in order to off-set the rise in the cost of living, but the rates varied and, particularly in the counties, pay had become quite inadequate.

[1] Much of the information in this chapter is derived from Sir A. L. Dixon, *The Home Office and the Police between the two World Wars*, Home Office (unpublished), 1966.

The Desborough Committee received evidence of policemen who were quite genuinely unable to live on their earnings.[1]

The war had added a great many duties to the normal work of the force, such as the registration of aliens, enforcement of the black-out, protection of vulnerable points and co-ordination of measures for air raid warnings. At the same time many experienced and active constables had joined the services and the work load of those left behind increased. Even in 1914 the Police Weekly Rest Day Act of 1910 had not been implemented in a large number of forces and all attempts to bring it in were cancelled during the war. Leave was limited or completely stopped and some members of the senior ranks did not have a day off in years.[2] Promotion slowed down almost to a standstill in some forces. It is no wonder then that there was widespread discontent in the service, and that the Police and Prison Officers' Union, which had been active since the turn of the century was gaining members, especially in the larger forces. Discontent came to a head in August 1918 when, to quote Sir Leonard Dunning, 'an organized attempt to seduce the police from their duty met with a regrettable amount of success'.[3]

This strike, by those responsible for maintaining peace and good order at home, coming at a time when the country was still at war, led to immediate action. The strike was confined to the Metropolitan police, but the committee set up to look into the matter of police pay recommended two new scales, the higher one for the Metropolitan and similar forces and the lower one for the rest of the country. They were, however, only an interim measure and in March 1919 the Desborough Committee was set up. It produced its first report in record time four months later. The Committee appears to have been influenced by two major considerations. First, the police were in real poverty because earnings had not kept pace with the war-time rise in the cost of living. Second, they were impressed with the evidence they received on the complex and responsible nature of police work. And, of course, though it is not mentioned, the shock of the Metropolitan police strike may also have influenced them. Their report may be seen as a conscious attempt to put police work on a more professional

[1] Desborough Report, Part I, Appendix II, pp. 24–9; 1919 Cmd. 253, xxvii.
[2] Desborough Report, Part II, p. 220; 1920 Cmd. 874, xxii.
[3] *Inspectors of Constabulary, 1919*, p. 3; 1920 (91), xxii.

A.S.I.M.—4

footing, and to raise the status of the policeman in society. The Report recommended pay increases of approximately 40 per cent for constables and sergeants and left a corresponding rise for the higher ranks to be negotiated later. The Desborough pay scales not only ended all comparison between the wages of the police and the agricultural labourer (as was explicitly intended), they also put the constable at a level which was still, even in 1924, approximately 27 per cent above the national average wage.[1]

The Desborough Reports also made useful progress towards ending the nineteenth-century isolation and separatism which was a feature of many forces. Chief constables had become accustomed during the war to acting under the direction of the Home Office and the Committee recommended that the machinery for inter-force co-operation which had come into being should be strengthened. The first District and central conferences of chief officers were held in 1918 with the main aim of improving co-ordination of war measures. On the men's side there was no comparable official national organization. However, the Police and Prison Officers' Union had gained many members during the war (the figure was said to be over 90 per cent in Birmingham).[2] The Union, though actively discouraged, or at best barely tolerated by the higher ranks, found an outlet in the representative boards which were set up after 1914. They were designed to allow the men to put forward their views and were paralleled by similar organizations in the munitions factories and other branches of industry. The representative boards were not compulsory and varied in effectiveness. Some such as Liverpool, where the Union was strong, were able to have men whom they considered had been unfairly passed over promoted to sergeant.[3] The Desborough Committee was clear that channels of communication between the Home Office and all ranks of the force should be established, but it left the details to be negotiated after it had reported. As a result the Police Council and the Police Federation were set up under the Police Act 1919.

[1] C. Clark in *The National Income 1924–31*, London, Macmillan, 1932, p. 58, puts the average earnings for men in 1924 at 56s. A. L. Bowley in *Studies in the National Income 1924–1938*, Cambridge, 1942, p. 62, puts the average wage at 54·4s. The lowest police pay (70s.) is calculated as a percentage of the national average wage, estimated to be 55s.

[2] Desborough Report, Part II, p. 298; 1920 Cmd. 874, xxii.

[3] *Ibid.*, pp. 193–4; 1920 Cmd. 874, xxii.

*The Police Council and the Police Federation*

The Police Council was a national body,[1] designed to represent all aspects of the police service. It had no executive power but was intended to advise the Home Secretary on police matters. The bodies represented were the chief officers, the superintendents, the 'lower ranks' of the police, the police authorities and the Home Office. The police representatives were divided between counties, boroughs and the Metropolitan and City of London forces, and the police authorities were similarly divided, with the Receiver of the Metropolitan police representing the police authority of the metropolis. The seven representatives of the police authorities were at first heavily outnumbered by representatives from the police service, but their membership was later increased to twelve. The lower, or federated ranks as they came to be called, were also separately organized on a national scale by the Police Federation. The Federation was to some extent a compromise. It was officially recognized but its powers were circumscribed. It was prohibited from associating itself with any outside group and policemen were debarred from joining any trade union. The Federation was also limited in the matters it could discuss. Individual cases of pay and discipline were outside its competence, but matters of general principle could be discussed and the Federation was allowed to make representations direct to the Home Secretary. The organization was divided into district conferences, committees and branch boards for each rank which united to form the Joint Central Committee of the Police Federation. The Joint Committee elected delegates to the Police Council. Similar systems prevailed for chief officers and the superintendents, though the Metropolitan superintendents refused to join, maintaining that there was no comparison between their rank and the same designation in provincial forces.

The Police Council, composed as it was of chief officers, other ranks and local and central government representatives, was a surprising development in a body which had previously been as autocratic as the police. (For example, the Committee on the Police Weekly Rest Day in 1908 had not received evidence from any members of the lower ranks who were actually serving at the

[1] It was limited to England and Wales, but a representative of the Scottish Office could attend.

time. It was also clear from the replies of some chief constables that they had little communication with their rank and file.'[1]) The war had, however, changed many things and the 1918 police strike had underlined the danger of suppressing grievances. One of the main issues in the strike had been the right to join a union. Clearly at a time when trade union leaders were associated in the public mind with communism, or at least revolution, no government committee was likely to countenance a police union, and many policemen themselves appear to have been against an organization which had the right to strike.[2] On the other hand union members felt they had been cheated by the restrictions placed on the Police Federation by the 1919 Police Act and their agitation led to a second strike in 1919. This strike was best supported in London but extended to Liverpool, Birmingham, Birkenhead and to three other forces. In the changed conditions of peace and a more contented service, the strike was firmly suppressed. All the men who took part were dismissed and never reinstated.

## Home Office Powers and the Exchequer Grant

The new advisory structure of Police Council and Police Federation was complemented by greater Home Office powers to regulate individual forces. The Exchequer grant which had, until 1918, only covered half the cost of pay and uniforms was put on a new footing. The old conditions of payment which related to efficiency in point of numbers and discipline were replaced by a new stipulation that the pay and conditions of service in the force must be approved by the Home Secretary and that the force must be fully and properly administered. In addition the Home Office was able, for the first time, to withhold all or part of the grant for any length of time (as was done in 1938 when Derby County refused to contribute to the regional police laboratory). Thus the scope of Home Office control was widened. The Desborough Committee went still further. It recommended that the grant should continue to cover half the whole cost of the police, including pensions, but that it should be paid on condition that a force

[1] *Report of the Select Committee on the Police Weekly Rest Day*, Minutes of Evidence, p. 106; 1908 (353), ix.
[2] Desborough Report, Part II, pp. 295, 298; 1920 Cmd. 874, xxii.

complied with the Police Regulations drawn up by the Home Secretary. The first regulations were made under the Police Act 1919. There were few aspects of police work which were not brought within the scope of the Regulations; they included the government of the force, mutual aid between forces, pay, allowances, clothing, expenses and conditions of service. The police authorities also received detailed instructions setting out the classes of expenditure that qualified for a grant. The definitions were particularly important in the field of capital expenditure.[1]

The new developments combined greater powers for the Home Office in enforcing uniform standards with far better communications throughout the service. Together, they allowed new ideas to spread and common practices to grow up.

It would be unrealistic to suggest that isolation and conservatism in forces was thus ended, and the Home Office brought into close touch with the views of the police authorities and the service as a whole, but the situation was radically altered. When the move for regional services came there was a foundation to build upon. Local differences of course remained, as they still do, but the national framework of police administration was no longer designed to encourage and perpetuate them.

*The general economic situation between the wars*

The development of the police service cannot be considered without reference to the economic difficulties of the inter-war years. Unemployment grew from 1921 onwards and never fell below 8 per cent of the insured labour force until 1939. Serious financial crises occurred in 1922 and 1931. There has been controversy over the degree and duration of hardship in the country as a whole during these years.[2] Unemployment may have dominated the political scene, but the cost of living fell from 1922 till 1936,[3] and, for those in employment, real wages rose steadily until the second

[1] The grant system was changed in 1929 when all police grants whether from assigned revenue or other sources were amalgamated into a single Exchequer grant. At the same time the certificate of efficiency was dropped from the conditions. These changes had little direct effect on the police.

[2] See for example H. W. Richardson, *Economic Recovery in Britain*, London, Weidenfeld and Nicolson, 1967.

[3] A. L. Bowley, *Wages and Income in the United Kingdom since 1860*, Cambridge, 1937, p. 30.

world war. Motor vehicles revolutionized transport and the number of private cars increased sixfold. However from the point of view of the police, one of the most important factors was the government's attitude to the economic situation. The accepted economic theory of the day held that in times of unemployment or financial crisis, government spending should be cut in order to balance the budget. Particularly in 1922 and 1931 anti-waste campaigns flared up and the Press called loudly for reductions in spending. The police service, where the levels of pay and most other expenditure were largely within the control of the central government, naturally suffered more than some other branches of the economy where theory could not be so easily put into practice. Table III.1 shows changes in expenditure on the police and in total government spending, excluding defence. A drop occurred after the first world war and there was then little improvement until 1935. Police expenditure of course declined during the financial crises and, as might be expected, spending on capital works showed the greatest fluctuations. Despite the constant complaints and shortages of finance which held up much-needed developments in the twenties and thirties, expenditure on the police as on other social services increased as a proportion of total government spending during the inter-war years. The per capita figure remained constant, however, except for a slight rise at the beginning and end of the period.[1] After the war government spending was at a far higher level than ever before and the police share had fallen steeply.

*Police pay*

The history of police wage awards during these years clearly illustrates the way in which national economic difficulties impinged on police finances (see Table III.2). The police had been in a relatively poor position in relation to the national average in 1914, and their basic pay scales remained unchanged until 1918. They, like other workers, were granted bonuses to offset the rising cost of living. In 1917 the bonus was increased from 7s. to 12s. in most forces, but it was insufficient and was in any case non-pensionable. Pensions were therefore still calculated on the basis

[1] A. T. Peacock and J. Wiseman *The Growth of Public Expenditure in the United Kingdom.* London, O.U.P., 1961, Tables A–15 and A–16.

## TABLE III.1

### Total local authority expenditure on the police (1920-49)†

| | Current £m | 1920-21 =100 | From rates £m | 1920-21 =100 | From government grants £m | 1920-21 =100 | Capital £m | 1920-21 =100 | Total current & capital £m | 1920-21 =100 | Total government expenditure (minus defence)* £m |
|---|---|---|---|---|---|---|---|---|---|---|---|
| 20-21 | 20·8 | 100 | 10·1 | 100 | 9·5 | 100 | 0·1 | 100 | 20·9 | 100 | 1072·4 |
| 21-22 | 21·3 | 102 | 10·6 | 105 | 9·4 | 99 | 0·1 | 90 | 21·3 | 102 | 1159·5 |
| 22-23 | 18·9 | 91 | 8·6 | 85 | 8·9 | 93 | — | 6 | 18·9 | 91 | 1008·6 |
| 23-24 | 18·8 | 90 | 8·8 | 87 | 8·7 | 91 | — | 7 | 18·8 | 90 | 890·3 |
| 24-25 | 19·1 | 92 | 9·0 | 89 | 9·1 | 96 | 0·1 | 76 | 19·2 | 92 | 896·1 |
| 25-26 | 20·1 | 96 | 9·6 | 94 | 9·6 | 101 | 0·1 | 123 | 20·2 | 96 | 938·3 |
| 26-27 | 21·0 | 101 | 10·1 | 99 | 10·1 | 107 | 0·2 | 227 | 21·2 | 102 | 972·7 |
| 27-28 | 21·1 | 102 | 10·3 | 101 | 10·1 | 106 | 0·2 | 248 | 21·4 | 102 | 975·8 |
| 28-29 | 21·4 | 103 | 10·3 | 101 | 10·3 | 108 | 0·3 | 336 | 21·7 | 104 | 969·6 |
| 29-30 | 21·7 | 104 | 10·5 | 103 | 10·4 | 110 | 0·4 | 390 | 22·0 | 105 | 983·3 |
| 30-31 | 22·3 | 107 | 10·9 | 108 | 10·6 | 111 | 0·2 | 249 | 22·5 | 108 | 1025·6 |
| 31-32 | 22·3 | 107 | 10·8 | 107 | 10·6 | 112 | 0·2 | 221 | 22·5 | 108 | 1058·1 |
| 32-33 | 21·5 | 104 | 10·7 | 106 | 10·1 | 106 | 0·2 | 189 | 21·7 | 104 | 1027·6 |
| 33-34 | 21·5 | 104 | 10·6 | 105 | 10·3 | 108 | 0·1 | 146 | 21·7 | 104 | 953·6 |
| 34-35 | 22·3 | 107 | 10·9 | 108 | 10·7 | 113 | 0·2 | 254 | 22·6 | 108 | 942·0 |
| 35-36 | 23·9 | 115 | 11·8 | 116 | 11·5 | 121 | 0·4 | 412 | 24·3 | 116 | 976·6 |
| 36-37 | 24·7 | 119 | 12·1 | 120 | 11·8 | 125 | 0·9 | 909 | 25·5 | 122 | 1003·8 |
| 37-38 | 25·3 | 123 | n.a. | | 12·3 | 130 | 1·1 | 1,177 | 26·4 | 126 | 1048·8 |
| 38-39 | 26·1 | 125 | n.a. | | 12·7 | 133 | 1·3 | 1,399 | 27·4 | 131 | 1118·0 |
| 39-40 | 31·0 | 149 | n.a. | | 16·2 | 170 | 1·2 | 1,296 | 32·3 | 154 | — |
| 40-41 | 34·0 | 163 | n.a. | | 18·7 | 197 | 0·8 | 846 | 34·8 | 166 | — |
| 41-42 | 37·4 | 180 | n.a. | | 21·0 | 221 | 0·2 | 241 | 37·6 | 180 | — |
| 42-43 | 37·5 | 180 | n.a. | | 21·6 | 227 | 0·2 | 187 | 37·6 | 180 | — |
| 43-44 | 36·1 | 173 | n.a. | | 20·6 | 217 | 0·1 | 122 | 36·2 | 173 | — |
| 44-45 | 34·9 | 168 | n.a. | | 19·6 | 207 | 0·1 | 78 | 34·9 | 167 | — |
| 45-46 | 35·1 | 169 | n.a. | | 17·7 | 186 | 0·1 | 85 | 35·2 | 168 | — |
| 46-47 | 36·1 | 174 | n.a. | | 17·3 | 182 | 0·3 | 313 | 36·4 | 174 | 3059·0 |
| 47-48 | 41·1 | 197 | n.a. | | 19·4 | 204 | 0·7 | 722 | 41·8 | 200 | 3284·0 |
| 48-49 | 44·2 | 212 | n.a. | | 21·3 | 224 | 1·5 | 1,530 | 45·6 | 218 | 3522·0 |
| 49-50 | 48·6 | 233 | n.a. | | 23·5 | 247 | 2·4 | 2,486 | 50·9 | 245 | 3703·0 |

† The table refers to financial years.
* A. T. Peacock and J. Wiseman *The Growth of Public Expenditure in the United Kingdom*. London, [Ox]ford University Press, 1961, Tables A—5 and A—7.
[SO]URCE: *Annual Abstracts of Statistics*.

of the old wage scales which were so inadequate that the bonus amounted to 25 per cent of pay for the lower ranks. There were, of course, housing and family allowances, but it was clear that before 1919, police wages were barely sufficient to maintain respectable living standards. Table III.2 shows the increases in wages granted during the short space of time from the beginning of 1918 to the end of 1919. The scales shown refer to the metropolis and many forces, particularly the counties, paid less before the Desborough recommendations were implemented.

TABLE III.2

**Increases in police pay scales (1918–19)**

|  | Basic weekly pay scale shillings | Non-pensionable bonus shillings | Total shillings | % increase |
|---|---|---|---|---|
| July 1918† | 30–40 | 12 | 42–52 | — |
| September 1918† | 43–53 | 12 | 55–65 | 31 |
| Desborough 1919* | 70–90 | — | 70–90 | 27 |

† Metropolitan scale.          * National scale.

SOURCE: Home Office.

The pay awards which the police gained in 1919 had to last them for nearly thirty years. There was a brief rise in 1922 but after that the high scales fixed by Desborough came under constant attack. At first, however, the war-time rise in the cost of living continued in 1919 and 1920, and the government was still pursuing what has since been termed an inflationary policy.[1] Expenditure on the police grew (see Table III.1), and the value of the Desborough pay scales had been eroded even in their first year of existence. The Police Council called for a review of the scales and as a result the Home Office recommended the police authorities to pay a cost of living bonus. However this phase was short-lived. By April 1920 the first signs that the boom was over were appearing. Unemployment grew steadily, the cost of living fell and the bonus ended in September 1920. Not all police authorities had paid it even when the cost of living had been at its peak and the rates of payment had varied. The logical next step was, however, to reduce wages as the cost of living fell. This the Police Federation resisted even though prices fell steadily until 1935.[2] The deteriorating economic situation led to the appointment of the Geddes Committee in 1921. Its three reports, known as the 'Geddes Axe' recommended widespread cuts in public expenditure. The target (as revised) for economies in police expenditure was £1,800,000, to be achieved mainly by reducing establishments and cutting wages. Naturally few connected with the service were willing to see the improvement in morale which had followed the Desborough Report so quickly undermined. The

---

[1] C. L. Mowat, *Britain Between the Wars*, London, Methuen, 1956, p. 25.
[2] A. L. Bowley, *Wages and Income in the United Kingdom since 1860*, Cambridge, 1937, p. 30.

compromise which was accepted by the Police Council involved a 2½ per cent cut in pay, and deductions from rent allowances which ranged from 3s. 6d. for constables to 7s. 6d. for superintendents. Charges were imposed in forces where houses were provided. The virtual cessation of capital expenditure which followed the Geddes Reports is shown in Table III.1. Other expenditure also fell. At first the police authorities were asked to reduce strength by leaving 5 per cent of vacancies unfilled, but in March 1923 the target was raised to 7 per cent.

All these measures were, of course, stated to be temporary but their duration depended on an improvement in the economic position which did not occur to any great extent. The Desborough Committee was recalled in 1923 to review the level of police remuneration, but when it reported the following year it was against any change while conditions remained so uncertain. In 1925, however, the Lee Committee produced a report which was accepted by the government and the Police Council. The Geddes cuts in pay and allowances were replaced by a 2½ per cent increase in deductions from pay. This was used to bring contributions to the pension funds up to 5 per cent of pay. The measure was unpopular with the Police Federation but it answered many critics who complained at the high cost of police pensions. Table III.3 shows the expenditure on wages and salaries and the effect of these and later measures on the total.

TABLE III.3

**Expenditure on police wages and salaries (1920–21 to 1938–39)**

| | £000 | | £000 | | £000 |
|---|---|---|---|---|---|
| 1920–21 | 13,423 | 1926–27 | 13,745 | 1932–33 | 14,093 |
| 1921–22 | 14,695 | 1927–28 | 13,999 | 1933–34 | 13,351 |
| 1922–23 | 14,925 | 1928–29 | 13,905 | 1934–35 | 12,882 |
| 1923–24 | 13,619 | 1929–30 | 13,939 | 1935–36 | 13,378 |
| 1924–25 | 13,396 | 1930–31 | 14,128 | 1936–37 | 14,202 |
| 1925–26 | 13,456 | 1931–32 | 14,265 | 1937–38 | 14,580 |
| | | | | 1938–39 | 14,757 |

SOURCE: *Annual Reports of H.M. Inspectors of Constabulary.*

The next crisis followed the slump in America in 1929. It did not immediately affect Europe, but by 1931 conditions in Britain were once more very serious. In accordance with the accepted economic doctrine of the day a reduction in spending was called for. The May Committee was set up to diagnose the country's economic condition and recommend a cure. It produced a report which called for drastic cuts, particularly in unemployment benefits, the armed services and the police. The pay of the police was to be cut by 12½ per cent in two annual instalments. This was modified after the threat of reduced pay had caused a mutiny in the Navy at Invergordon. The government decided that no cuts would exceed 10 per cent. This large decrease in pensionable pay was naturally not acceptable to the police service. As a compromise, flat-rate deductions ranging from 5s. to 6s. 9d. a week for all ranks earning less than £250 a year and of 5 per cent for the rest were made in 1931 and 1932, but the scales of pensionable pay, and so of pensions, were not altered for serving members of the force.

At the same time, however, pay for new recruits was reduced for the first three years of service and a committee was set up to look into the matter of pensionable pay. It recommended a scale for constables starting at 62s. instead of 70s. and rising to the Desborough maximum of 90s. after twelve years instead of ten. The new scale was also subject to the emergency flat-rate deductions. It remained in force alongside the Desborough scale until 1945 when both were replaced by a new scale. These measures left approximately £100,000 of the target savings to be found by economies in administration. Expenditure was accordingly cut back in many fields (see Table III.1 for the effect on totals), but only for a few years. By 1936 the economic recovery was well under way and the government felt able to relax its objections to new financial commitments. The process was soon accelerated by the growing realization that war with Germany was inevitable, and that the preparations required an increase in police strengths. The flat-rate deductions from pay were halved in 1935 and abolished the following year.

### Police strength and size of force

The economies in expenditure, of course, had their effect on the total strength of the police. Although recruiting was curtailed only in 1922 and 1923, the prevailing economic climate made most police authorities reluctant to enlarge their forces significantly. As a result the overall ratio of police to population became increasingly unfavourable until 1935 (see Table III.4). The table is based on the actual number of policemen serving at any one time, not on the official establishment. This accounts for the poor figure in 1949 when the strength of the force was reduced by a total of 12,140 vacancies. At the same time, as Tables III.4 and III.5 show, there was a slow movement towards greater standardization in the size of forces and in their individual ratios of police

TABLE III.4

**Population per police constable in England and Wales (1921–49)**

|  | Total actual strength | Population 000* | Population per policeman |
|---|---|---|---|
| 1921 | 59,520 | 37,887 | 637 |
| 1922 | 57,350 | 38,158 | 665 |
| 1923 | 56,220 | 38,403 | 683 |
| 1925 | 57,070 | 38,890 | 681 |
| 1930 | 59,250 | 39,806 | 672 |
| 1931 | 59,670 | 39,952 | 670 |
| 1932 | 59,320 | 40,201 | 678 |
| 1933 | 58,900 | 40,350 | 685 |
| 1934 | 58,850 | 40,467 | 688 |
| 1935 | 59,230 | 40,645 | 686 |
| 1939 | 63,980 | 41,460 | 648 |
| 1949 | 60,190 | 43,785 | 727 |

* All population totals are estimates given in the Registrar-General's *Statistical Review of England and Wales* with the exception of 1921 and 1931 which are census figures.

SOURCE: *Annual Abstracts of Statistics* and *Annual Reports of H.M. Inspectors of Constabulary.*

to population. Table III.5 refers to the actual numbers in each force and shows that, in spite of the slow growth of total establishment, there was a general tendency towards larger forces. In 1921, half the forces had less than 100 men, while by 1949 the proportion had dropped to a sixth. The number of very small forces (with 25 men or less), had been halved by 1939 and they were virtually eliminated within the next ten years. The greatest increases were in the groups of forces with 151 to 200 men (eleven in 1921, fifteen in 1939 and nineteen in 1949), and with 500 to 1,000 (from seven in 1921 to fifteen in 1949). Table III.6 shows the variation between forces in the ratio of population to police. It is clear that the national average, ranging as it did from 601 to 700 people per constable throughout the period, was heavily weighted by the low ratios in the conurbations, e.g. the Metropolitan police with under 400 inhabitants per man. However, forces showed a general tendency to move towards the average.

In 1921, 50 per cent of the county forces had a ratio of one policeman for every thousand or more inhabitants, in 1939 it was 20 per cent and by 1949 only 5 per cent. At the other end of the

TABLE III.5

**Size of police forces in England and Wales (1921–49)**

| Total strength | 1921 | 1925 | 1930 | 1935 | 1939 | 1945 | 1949 |
|---|---|---|---|---|---|---|---|
| 0–25 | 19 | 18 | 14 | 14 | 10 | 6 | 1 |
| 26–50 | 25 | 26 | 26 | 24 | 21 | 17 | 1 |
| 51–75 | 27 | 26 | 27 | 27 | 24 | 20 | 4 |
| 76–100 | 19 | 20 | 20 | 20 | 17 | 15 | 13 |
| 101–150 | 27 | 27 | 27 | 28 | 29 | 24 | 27 |
| 151–200 | 11 | 10 | 10 | 11 | 15 | 15 | 19 |
| 201–300 | 18 | 20 | 20 | 19 | 18 | 15 | 14 |
| 301–400 | 13 | 12 | 13 | 12 | 14 | 12 | 14 |
| 401–500 | 8 | 8 | 6 | 9 | 10 | 10 | 11 |
| 501–1,000 | 7 | 7 | 7 | 9 | 13 | 13 | 15 |
| 1,000+ | 9 | 7 | 9 | 6 | 8 | 10 | 8 |
| Total | 183 | 181 | 179 | 179 | 179 | 157 | 127 |

The table excludes the City of London and Metropolitan police.

SOURCE: *Annual Reports of H.M. Inspectors of Constabulary.*

TABLE III.6

**Population per police constable in county and borough forces in England and Wales (1921–49)**

| Population per constable | Number of forces Counties 1921 | Boroughs | Number of forces Counties 1930 | Boroughs | Number of forces Counties 1939 | Boroughs | Number of forces Counties 1949 | Boroughs |
|---|---|---|---|---|---|---|---|---|
| 401–500 | — | 1 | — | 1 | — | 2 | — | 3 |
| 501–600 | — | 4 | — | 3 | — | 17 | 3 | 22 |
| 601–700 | 2 | 27 | 2 | 29 | 6 | 37 | 10 | 30 |
| 701–800 | 2 | 41 | 3 | 35 | 15 | 44 | 25 | 16 |
| 801–900 | 7 | 37 | 12 | 42 | 10 | 20 | 9 | 1 |
| 901–1,000 | 16 | 13 | 14 | 10 | 15 | — | 5 | — |
| 1,001–1,100 | 10 | 2 | 12 | 1 | 3 | 1 | 2 | — |
| 1,101–1,200 | 9 | — | 5 | — | 7 | — | 1 | — |
| 1,201+ | 12 | — | 10 | — | 2 | — | — | — |
| Total forces | 58 | 125 | 58 | 121 | 58 | 121 | 55 | 72 |

The table excludes the City of London and Metropolitan police.

SOURCE: *Annual Reports of H.M. Inspectors of Constabulary.*

scale the provincial boroughs had a ratio of one man for every 700 inhabitants or better in 25 per cent of forces in 1921, and by 1939 the figure had risen to 75 per cent. The general trend throughout the inter-war years was therefore, towards smaller differences between force and force, both in size and in the ratio of police to population.

The changes were however unevenly distributed. Table III.7 shows that the counties suffered least from reductions in strength in times of crisis and grew fastest when conditions improved. The London forces showed the opposite tendency and the Metropolitan and the City of London police, which in 1921 were larger than the total of either county or borough forces, had by 1949 a strength of only 16,358 policemen and women (establishment 21,060) as opposed to 25,027 (29,021) in the counties, and 17,873 (21,718) in the boroughs.

TABLE III.7

**Changes in the numbers of police (1921–49)**

| | Counties 1921 (18,027) = 100 | Boroughs 1921 (19,370) = 100 | London and Metropolitan 1921 (22,121) = 100 | England and Wales 1921 (59,518) = 100 |
|---|---|---|---|---|
| 1921 | 100 | 100 | 100 | 100 |
| 1922 | 96 | 96 | 97 | 96 |
| 1923 | 96 | 95 | 93 | 94 |
| 1925 | 98 | 97 | 93 | 96 |
| 1930 | 102 | 101 | 96 | 99 |
| 1931 | 103 | 102 | 97 | 100 |
| 1932 | 102 | 101 | 96 | 99 |
| 1933 | 102 | 101 | 95 | 99 |
| 1935 | 105 | 103 | 92 | 99 |
| 1939 | 120 | 115 | 91 | 107 |
| 1949 | 140 | 95 | 75 | 101 |

SOURCE: *Annual Reports of H.M. Inspectors of Constabulary.*

*Police organization*

Changes in numbers were accompanied by changes in the pattern of command. Tables III.8 and III.9 show that there was a tendency for the command structure of the different types of police force to approach more nearly to a common pattern. The fall in the proportion of upper ranks in the county forces was related to the Desborough recommendation that the work of different ranks should be standardized. The rank of superintendent embraced a wide range of responsibility (a left-over from the previous century), and, as uniformity was established, a number of posts were abolished. The command structure in the Metropolitan police stands out as different from either the counties or the boroughs. In 1921 the Metropolitan superintendents refused to join with provincial men on the grounds that their responsibilities were far greater than in other forces. The low proportion of senior

### TABLE III.8

**Proportions of the police force in each rank (1921–49)**

| | Chief Officers and assistants | Super-intendents | Inspectors all grades | Sergeants | Constables | Total actual strength 100% |
|---|---|---|---|---|---|---|
| *Counties* | | | | | | |
| 1921 | 0·4 | 2·4 | 3·5 | 13·9 | 79·8 | 18,030 |
| 1925 | 0·4 | 2·4 | 3·6 | 14·2 | 79·4 | 17,730 |
| 1930 | 0·3 | 2·2 | 3·6 | 14·1 | 79·8 | 18,360 |
| 1935 | 0·4 | 2·0 | 3·5 | 13·8 | 80·3 | 18,880 |
| 1939 | 0·3 | 1·8 | 3·9 | 13·7 | 80·3 | 21,780 |
| 1949 | 0·3 | 1·8 | 5·2 | 15·6 | 77·1 | 25,280 |
| *Boroughs* | | | | | | |
| 1921 | 0·8 | 0·6 | 4·5 | 12·6 | 81·6 | 19,370 |
| 1925 | 0·7 | 0·7 | 4·6 | 12·9 | 81·2 | 18,750 |
| 1930 | 0·6 | 0·7 | 4·3 | 12·4 | 82·0 | 19,610 |
| 1935 | 0·6 | 0·7 | 4·2 | 12·4 | 82·1 | 20,040 |
| 1939 | 0·6 | 0·7 | 4·5 | 12·1 | 82·2 | 22,340 |
| 1949 | 0·5 | 0·9 | 5·9 | 15·5 | 77·2 | 18,340 |
| *Metropolitan and City of London* | | | | | | |
| 1921 | 0·1 | 0·2 | 3·0 | 13·3 | 83·4 | 22,120 |
| 1925 | 0·1 | 0·2 | 3·3 | 14·5 | 81·9 | 20,590 |
| 1930 | 0·1 | 0·2 | 3·3 | 14·2 | 82·2 | 21,280 |
| 1935 | 0·1 | 0·2 | 4·6 | 14·2 | 80·9 | 20,310 |
| 1939 | 0·1 | 0·2 | 5·1 | 14·6 | 80·0 | 20,070 |
| 1949 | 0·1 | 0·9 | 5·0 | 18·7 | 75·3 | 16,570 |

SOURCE: *Annual Reports of H.M. Inspectors of Constabulary.*

ranks would suggest that they were at least partly justified. The London forces also differed in that they had a higher proportion of sergeants. The figures for 1949 were distorted by the very high number of vacancies in all forces (see p. 85) and especially in the Metropolitan police.

Table III.9 is based on the same data as Table III.8 but shows the percentage increase or decrease in each rank as compared with 1921. The first column shows that the absolute number of higher ranks in the counties and boroughs changed very little, but that in comparison with the growth of the forces as a whole, the proportion of senior positions was reduced. The extent of the reduction is obscured in the borough forces by the number of vacancies in 1949. The London forces, which had such a low proportion of men in the highest ranks in 1921, did increase their number, but not to any great extent until 1949 when a certain amount of re-grading took place. The counties started out with a very large number of superintendents (423) and had reduced them to 360 by 1935. A slight rise in numbers occurred in the following years. The main augmentation to the command structure took place in the ranks of inspector and sergeant. This was

TABLE III.9

**Changes in the proportions of men in each rank**
**1921 = 100**

| | Superintendents and above | Inspectors all grades | Sergeants | Constables | Total actual strength |
|---|---|---|---|---|---|
| *Counties* | | | | | |
| 1921 = 100% | 500 | 630 | 2,500 | 14,830 | 18,030 |
| 1930 | 91 | 104 | 104 | 102 | 102 |
| 1939 | 91 | 134 | 118 | 120 | 120 |
| 1949* | 99 | 210 | 158 | 136 | 140 |
| *Boroughs* | | | | | |
| 1921 = 100% | 270 | 870 | 2,450 | 16,220 | 19,370 |
| 1931 | 97 | 98 | 99 | 102 | 101 |
| 1939 | 102 | 115 | 111 | 116 | 115 |
| 1949* | 100 | 124 | 116 | 90 | 95 |
| *Metropolitan and City of London* | | | | | |
| 1921 = 100% | 50 | 680 | 2,940 | 18,790 | 22,120 |
| 1931 | 102 | 103 | 103 | 95 | 96 |
| 1939 | 134 | 149 | 100 | 87 | 91 |
| 1949* | 312 | 123 | 105 | 68 | 75 |

* Including women police.

SOURCE: *Annual Reports of H.M. Inspectors of Constabulary.*

a development which would be expected as police work became more complicated and more supervision was needed. The fall in the number of Metropolitan inspectors in 1949 reflects the re-grading of the ranks of superintendent and inspector after 1948. As might be expected, the main changes both in strength and command structure occurred in the counties and London where population changes were also most marked.

*Capital expenditure*

Changes in the distribution of population also affected the police at local level during the inter-war period. Many of the older police stations were in areas where they were no longer needed or where smaller buildings would have been sufficient. At the same time there were too few stations in the suburbs and in the growing villages near large towns. In the country stations were often needed near the main roads where traffic, and in particular, accidents, generated a growing volume of work, but many country stations were in villages away from the main routes.

The buildings themselves were out of date. The old police stations, even the headquarters, allowed little room for office space, but space was increasingly needed. The telephone, in particular, allowed easier communication within forces, but its most important contribution was as a means of contact with the public. As more calls were made, a larger office staff was needed to record incoming information. More paper work, especially on motoring offences, more complicated methods of recording crimes and registering criminals and more statistical returns to the Home Office all added to the pressure.[1] As the standard of amenities for workers in industry rose there was a growing demand in the police for space for canteens, relaxation and recreation, though the need for better conditions only really became acute after the second world war.[2]

The desirability of new buildings or extensions to old ones was recognized, but capital works, though eligible for a Home Office grant in most cases, were the responsibility of the local authority. The various restrictions on new projects in particular after the Geddes Reports (see Table III.2) affected all police authorities

[1] *Inspectors of Constabulary, 1932,* p. 5; 1932–33 (46), xv.
[2] *Inspectors of Constabulary, 1948*; 1948–9 (160), xix.

and slowed down development. There was a steady increase from 1935–36 until the outbreak of war. Capital expenditure (£1·3m.) was ten times as great in 1938–39 as it had been in 1933–34. However there was no guarantee, even in times of prosperity, that an individual police authority would undertake building works. Some forces modernized their buildings while some did not. A number of long-term schemes which were begun as the economic climate improved in the thirties were interrupted by the war. For example the Metropolitan police began a large-scale rebuilding of bad section houses, replacement of obsolete stations and a long-term programme for providing married quarters in 1934, after Lord Trenchard had found conditions in many buildings deplorable.[1] The scheme was expected to cost £3·5 millions spread out over six to seven years, but by 1938 it was behind schedule and the cost had already risen by £2 million. Like so many other schemes it was overtaken by the war and stations and houses condemned in 1934 were still in use in 1949.

*New equipment and methods*

The difficulty over buildings was repeated in many different guises. The Home Office and the Inspectors had no power to compel the use of new equipment or to insist on more than minimum standards. As late as 1936 the Inspector noted that the use of modern equipment depended on the interest of the chief constable concerned. He went on to say 'there are still forces, some of moderate size, where there is no provision within the force for the taking of a photograph'.[2] The Home Office could, and did, send out exhortatory circular letters offering advice and guidance but it would take direct action only on a very limited range of matters. Some forces, however, under energetic chief constables pioneered new methods, and the system of consultation helped to spread the results.

The rate of change, as measured by new methods and new equipment, therefore varied from force to force. All forces had telephone communication throughout the period, but some small

---

[1] Lord Trenchard was Commissioner of the Metropolitan police from 1931 to 1934 and was responsible for a large number of changes including the Hendon Police College, the introduction of cadets, improved sports grounds and better methods of recording crime.

[2] *Inspectors of Constabulary, 1936*, No. 2, p. 15; 1936–37 (75), xiv.

stations were still without a line, and most forces might well have made more effective use of the phones they had. For example, in 1925 the Inspector condemned the practice of using policemen for carrying messages and called for more private telephone systems to be installed, so freeing men for genuine police work. Teleprinters came into use towards the end of the thirties but were not general until after 1945.

### Civilians

Increases in the amount of telephone and office work led to the employment of civilians. The growth in their numbers was very slow, but by the 1930's they were employed in departments dealing with traffic offences, and for catering purposes by many of the larger forces. The Metropolitan police began recruiting clerical officers by open competition on the civil service pattern in 1930, and by that time the Traffic Offences Branch was almost entirely staffed by civilians. Cadets, boys appointed as clerks with the possibility of a police career when they reached the age of 20, were first appointed in the late 1920's. By 1939 they numbered about 500. The other main field of civilian employment was in specialized departments. For example, the Metropolitan police set up a solicitors department in 1935 which was staffed by civilians. The regional forensic science laboratories were also pioneered by scientists who came in most cases from outside the service. There was a great deal of scope for employing civilians, but little progress was made until the manpower shortage after the second world war. As late as 1938 the Inspector was advocating the use of civilians instead of policemen for cleaning stations.[1] In 1945 the number of civilians in the Metropolitan police was in the region of 2,400 of whom 500 were women. This represented 4 per cent of the total establishment, but was an understatement of the total as it excluded certain members of the Receiver's staff. Numbers rapidly increased and reached about 4,000 by 1949.

### Mobility

There were other fields where more progress was made, one being the use of motor vehicles for general work (as opposed to mobile

---

[1] *Inspectors of Constabulary, 1938,* No. 3, p. 22; 1938–39 (83), xiv.

traffic patrols which were subsidized by the Home Office and are dealt with below). The Inspectors were not especially concerned with the number of vehicles in any force, and they do not appear to have collected national totals until the 1950's. There were, however, early experiments in motorizing beats, particularly in London, and the number of vehicles in service grew steadily. In 1936 the Metropolitan police had 500 vehicles and by 1939 the number had risen to 800. A fall took place during the war, but by 1949 the total had reached 1,050. One-third of these were motor cycles.

*Inter-force co-operation and finance*

The development of regional and national police activities was very slow. It was limited first by finance. The central government was unwilling to pay more than half the cost of the police, and local authorities did not wish to spend money on anything which would not be a direct benefit to their own forces. However the need for services which only the largest forces could afford, or make economic use of, was increasingly recognized. Most forces were too small to provide adequate training, crime records, wireless communication or forensic science facilities, to mention the most important fields. The thirties were a time of prolonged discussion and some planning, but little action. The real impetus was given first by the war, and then by post-war difficulties which made it increasingly impossible for small forces to survive unaided.

One case where the problem of finance was overcome at a relatively early stage was the Road Fund Grant for traffic patrols. The Road Traffic Act of 1930 set aside part of the Road Fund to pay for the provision, depreciation and running costs of about 1,000 vehicles for police traffic patrols. The grant was assessed according to the number of vehicles (cars and motor cycles) needed for traffic patrolling or for detecting offences connected with motoring. The numbers varied from 36 for Lancashire and the West Riding to 3 for small counties and 1 for small boroughs. Some of the smallest boroughs did not qualify at all. In 1932 four county forces and a few boroughs had not joined the scheme, indicating how slowly some forces moved, even when little financial outlay was involved. The second centrally financed scheme was the 'Courtesy Cops' experiment in 1937. Two areas, one in the North West and the other in London and Essex, were chosen for pilot projects. The central government agreed to pay the cost of 800 additional men and their vehicles for experimental extra traffic patrols. The project took some time to get under way and its full effects could not be assessed before it ended with the outbreak of war.

*Training*

Training was one field in which co-operation between forces developed early, but only on the basis of local bi-lateral agreements. A national or regional administrative and financial framework had to wait until 1946. During the inter-war years there was growing recognition of the need for training, particularly in specialized fields. Even the ordinary constable had to know more, as the body of relevant law increased. The large forces had enough recruits to run regular classes but in smaller forces there was less scope for formal instruction. Birmingham had provided training places for recruits from neighbouring forces for many years and some others did the same. The Metropolitan police had provided a few places on specialized courses even before 1920, but a system for specialized training does not appear to have developed until much later.

The shortage of men capable of holding high rank was another major problem. In 1930 an advanced course for chief constables and senior officers from Britain and overseas was held by the Metropolitan police and in 1933, after the failure of the Home Office's own attempt at a national centre for advanced training, the Hendon Police College was set up by Lord Trenchard. The courses at the College were designed to fit young men from inside and outside the service, 'officer material', for the highest ranks. The first courses lasted for twelve months but by 1938 the length had been increased to two years. The value of the College to the police service was never really tested, as it was closed on the outbreak of war before its full effect could be felt. The College aroused opposition because, by admitting men from outside the service, it broke the tradition that all police promotion should be from the ranks. On the other hand, it stood for an enlightened attitude to command and men who had passed through the College were appreciated in their forces.[1]

The success of the scheme is still a matter of controversy, but it is worth noting that the first two Chief Inspectors of Constabulary, Sir Joseph Simpson,[2] and a high proportion of chief constables in the late fifties and sixties had all passed through the College.

Other developments at Hendon were less controversial. The Police Driving School was established by 1934. Some places for provincial officers were provided, but the School came into prominence in 1937 when a sudden increase in the number of advanced drivers was called for by the Courtesy Cops scheme. The provincial driving instructors were trained at Hendon and then set up schools in their own forces. Another development in training was the Wireless School, also at Hendon, which was opened in 1936 at a time when wireless communications were by no means universal.

One of the most important advances was, however, in the field of detective training. The Metropolitan police courses had been open to men from other forces since 1918, and a number of larger boroughs had their own training arrangements, but there was no attempt to standardize courses. A committee on detective work and procedure which was set up in 1933 advocated more detective training.[3] Although it did not report until 1938, its discussions had considerable influence and as a result, detective training centres offering eight-week courses for constables were set up in Wakefield and Hendon in 1936. Senior courses for

[1] Mr H. R. Pratt, Chief Constable of Bedfordshire and Luton, in a private communication commented that, '. . . the rank and file of the Metropolitan Police accepted the trained students from Hendon and welcomed them as a long needed innovation. I was a Constable in the Metropolitan Police from 1934 to 1937, during the first three years of the existence of the Police College; the facts were that many senior officers in the Force were bad leaders, were not prepared to advise and help junior ranks, but those that came from Hendon concentrated on welfare, guidance and help, and their presence was greatly welcomed. Opposition to Hendon came, in the main, from very senior officers, who disapproved of younger men gaining an advantage they had not had themselves.'

[2] Commissioner of the Metropolitan police from 1958 to 1968.

[3] The committee did not report until 1938, but its deliberations appear to have had considerable influence in police circles during the five years in which it sat. See *Report of the Departmental Committee on Detective Work and Procedure*; 1939 Non-Parl. Home Office.

sergeants followed in 1937 and the next year a third school was opened in Birmingham.

By the end of the thirties most forces had become convinced of the need for some training at least to be undertaken on a co-operative basis. Many had developed their own arrangements in the absence of any national framework. The groundwork for the development of standardized regional training arrangements and the establishment of a national police college was thus laid in the inter-war years, widespread progress was however, delayed until 1946.

### The Special Services Fund

Regional and national activities, on more than the very limited scale already described, were made possible by the development of the Special Services Fund. The Fund grew primarily out of the need for forensic science laboratories. During the inter-war years Britain lagged behind the Continent in developing scientific aids to detection. Certain enterprising chief constables set up their own laboratories, with the support of the local police authority, but in general the police remained ignorant of forensic science. The most advanced work in this field in 1933 was being done by the Nottingham City Police laboratory. The Chief Constable, Captain A. Popkess, had established the laboratory with the co-operation of staff from Nottingham University, and it was already providing a regional service to the neighbouring forces on an informal basis. In Sheffield, also with the co-operation of the University, a laboratory had been set up and in Cardiff there was a similar venture where a beginning had been made in specialized work on handwriting. The Committee on Detective Work and Procedure set up in 1933, was definitely in favour of more forensic science facilities but it was clear that they would have to be organized on an inter-force basis. The first move was the appointment of an Adviser on Scientific Aids at the Home Office in 1934. His salary, paid out of Home Office funds, represented the beginning of the Special Services vote.

The next step was to establish regional laboratories. There were two important considerations. The first was to get co-operation between the police and the qualified staff who ran the laboratories, and the second was finance. The Scientific Aids

Adviser proved successful in the first, but the second was more difficult. The attempt to set up a Police College with local authorities contributing part of the cost had failed in 1930. By the end of the thirties the economic outlook was better and the Treasury was willing to shoulder part of the cost. It was agreed that the Nottingham laboratory should be taken over by the Home Office. All its expenses would be paid by the Exchequer for the first few years of operation. If, and only if, the experiment was proved a success, the forces in the region would begin contributing 50 per cent of its cost. Their shares were to be assessed on the basis of their establishment. The laboratory was taken over in 1936 and in 1938 the neighbouring police authorities were asked to contribute. All did so except Derby county. The Home Office then proceeded, with creditable decisiveness, to make up the contribution by witholding part of Derby's police grant. No further difficulties over contributions to regional services were encountered. Other laboratories soon followed. The first was Birmingham, officially opened in 1938, then Cardiff, Preston and Wakefield. The complete regional system was delayed by the war and other laboratories were not brought into the Special Services Fund until 1946.[1]

As with so many other projects, the war interrupted further plans for the Special Services Fund. The police authorities agreed in 1938 to pay half the cost, assessed on the basis of their establishments, and the scope of the fund was extended to cover wireless

## TABLE III.10
### The Special Services Fund 1939 and 1947
### Estimated expenditure

|  | 1939 £ | 1947 £ |
|---|---|---|
| Forensic Science Laboratories | 10,620 | 55,000 |
| Wireless | 19,500 | 265,100 |
| Crime Clearing House | 10,000 | — |
| District Training Centres | — | 416,000 |
| Police Dogs | 500 | — |
| Miscellaneous | — | 500 |
|  | 40,620 | 736,600 |

SOURCES: Sir A. L. Dixon, *op. cit.*
Civil Estimates, 1947–48 Class III; 1946—47 (48–III) XVII.

[1] Sir A. L. Dixon, *op. cit.*, p. 180.

services, crime records and training as well as laboratories. Table III.10 shows the estimates which were agreed for 1939 and the huge expansion that occurred after the war.

## Wireless

In pre-war years, the other important fields were wireless communications and crime records. Experiments with wireless began in 1923 in the Metropolitan police, but only a few forces were able to use the available types of equipment successfully. The main difficulty was caused by the shortcomings of medium-wave transmission. There were some exceptions. For example Nottingham City had successfully developed wireless vehicles, the transmitter in Newcastle was providing what almost amounted to a regional service for Tyneside, and Lancashire and Brighton were pioneering pocket sets, but national coverage was long delayed. Few forces could afford the equipment or had the technical expertise and ingenuity which were needed in the early days. However, once the Special Services Fund came into being in 1939, the way was clear for regional developments. The Nottingham Police wireless station was again the first to be taken over by the Home Office, and in 1940 became the first Wireless Depot. Other regional depots were set up during the war. Technical progress slowly made radio telephony a practical proposition for all police forces. After the war high frequency replaced medium wave transmission and the coverage was gradually extended. The main post-war difficulty appears to have been shortage of money. The police wireless system did not have priority and complaints of insufficient equipment and poor maintenance by Home Office depots were rife. In 1952 the grant was even cut in response to an economy drive.[1] Complete national coverage was not achieved until the sixties.

## Crime records

In the field of crime records even less was actually achieved. It was agreed that as criminals became more mobile there was a case for centralizing and standardizing records of crime and criminals. Wakefield, the headquarters of the West Riding

[1] *Inspectors of Constabulary, 1952*, p. 16; 1952–53 (216), xvi. *Inspectors of Constabulary, 1954*, p. 16; 1954–55 (50), vii. *Inspectors of Constabulary, 1955*, p. 16; 1955–56 (203), xxvi.

Constabulary, had been operating a crime index which extended to neighbouring forces since the beginning of the century, and in the interests of efficiency many other forces had begun to do the same. The advantages of a standard national system were obvious. The problems were what system (the Metropolitan police was the only force which maintained any national records covering the whole country, and their method was not favoured by all), and how the considerable clerical work involved was to be financed. After much discussion, money was voted in 1939 for regional crime clearing houses under the Special Services Fund. The war then delayed action and nothing was done until 1949.

*Social changes*

The developments in police work and organization outlined above took place against a background of social change and stress in society. The changes were not all in the same direction but most brought problems for the police. Table III.11 below illustrates some of the major changes which affected the police.

TABLE III.11

**Vehicles, unemployment and crime (1921-49)**

| | Private cars | All motor vehicles (incl. cars) | Percentage unemployed | Indictable crimes known to police | Persons convicted non-indictable crimes |
|---|---|---|---|---|---|
| | (1) | (2) | (3) | (4) | (5) |
| 1921 | — | — | 15·6 | 103,258 | 419,330 |
| 1922 | 314,769 | 952,474 | — | 107,320 | 421,793 |
| 1925 | 579,901 | 1,509,786 | 11·2 | 113,986 | 499,177 |
| 1930 | 1,042,258 | 2,217,609 | 16·2 | 147,031 | 499,173 |
| 1935 | 1,477,000 | 2,581,000 | 14·4 | 234,372 | 689,574 |
| 1939 | 2,034,000 | 3,157,000 | 7·9 | 303,771 | 557,825 |
| 1949 | 2,258,000 | 4,113,000 | 1·2 | 459,869 | 523,563 |

Sources:
Col. (1) *Annual Abstract of Statistics.*
(2) 1922–30 excludes tramcars and trade licences.
(3) A. T. Peacock and J. Wiseman *The Growth of Public Expenditure in the United Kingdom*, Oxford University Press, London, 1961, p. 159. Table A–4.
(4) *Criminal Statistics.* Number of crimes known to the police. England and Wales only.
(5) *Criminal Statistics.* Total number of persons convicted of non-indictable offences. England and Wales only.

*Traffic*

The first two columns show the increase in the number of motor vehicles, and in particular of private cars, during the period. Complaints about the increasing amount of work caused by traffic were voiced at regular intervals from 1921 onwards.[1] Policemen were expected to be on point duty at awkward or busy junctions in town and country. In 1927 the Inspector noted that in many places there were not enough men for patrol work and that the main reason seemed to be the priority given to traffic.[2] In the following years traffic lights were generally introduced, and in 1929, the Inspectors looked forward to greater freedom for the police now that they had to spend less time on traffic control. There may have been some slight relief but as Table III.11 shows, the increase in the number of cars continued at about 100,000 a year even during the depression in the early thirties.

The Road Traffic Acts also increased the volume of work. The 1930 Act relieved the police of enforcing the speed limit but insurance offences alone caused a huge extra burden of paper work. The need to verify particulars of drivers from all parts of the country resulted in an unprecedented rise in the amount of information which had to be supplied to other forces. The Road Traffic Act of 1934 did nothing to reduce the volume of police work, and it added a modified speed limit as well. A survey in the Metropolitan police in 1935 showed that the equivalent of one-sixth of the uniformed force was engaged on traffic work every day.[3] The number of vehicles continued to increase until the outbreak of war. By 1938 there had been a 370 per cent increase over 1922. The war, however, checked the trend. The number of vehicles with licences current fell to 1,544,000 in 1943, and after the war restrictions on petrol and difficulties in the industry slowed the return to pre-war rates of growth. By 1949, however, the pre-war peak had again been passed.

[1] *Inspectors of Constabulary, 1921*, No. 1, p. 5; 1922 (5), x.

[2] *Inspectors of Constabulary, 1927*, No. 2, p. 10; 1927 (130), xi.

[3] The survey showed that 642 officers were employed exclusively on traffic and that part-time traffic work accounted for the equivalent of 2,389 full-time officers. *Commissioner of the Police of the Metropolis, 1935*, p. 48; 1935–36 Cmd. 5165, xiv.

*Labour problems*

The third column of Table III.11 shows the percentage of unemployment. The problem was not acute immediately after the first world war but the numbers out of work increased rapidly during 1921. The peak level of unemployment, 22·1 per cent of the insured work force, was reached in 1932, but the rate fell below 9 per cent in only one year (1927). Demonstrations, strikes and lockouts were frequent and all added to the work of the police. The most famous was of course the General Strike of 1926. The strikers were, on the whole, very orderly, but to quote C. L. Mowat, 'it is, of course a fable that there was no violence during the general strike; it is true there was no loss of life'.[1] Outbreaks of violence occurred in many large towns, Glasgow, London, Doncaster and Liverpool, to name only a few. The police, however, behaved with restraint, and the success of carefully planned measures for co-operation between forces encouraged those who favoured regional organization. Apart from the General Strike, there were hunger marches and demonstrations in 1922 and the long-drawn-out miners' strike later in the decade. In the thirties the south enjoyed a certain amount of prosperity, but in the nineteenth century industrial areas of the north and Wales, unemployment became a way of life for many. The police were involved mainly in dealing with demonstrations, breaking up rival factions of the unemployed, preventing coal thefts in the mining areas and containing minor crime.[2] There appears to have been little fear that the police would side with the class from which most of them came, against the middle classes. Such a fear had been voiced in the early years of the century when the Police Union was strong,[3] but after the Desborough Committee Report it appears to have died away.

*Crime rates*

The crime figures in the last two columns of Table III.11 highlight the problems of the police. Non-indictable crimes, with the exception of traffic offences, increased at approximately the

---

[1] C. L. Mowat, *Britain between the Wars*, London, Methuen, 1956, p. 317.
[2] C. L. Mowat, *Britain between the Wars*, London, Methuen, 1956, p. 486.
[3] Desborough Report, Part II, p. 163; 1920 Cmd. 874, xxii.

same rate as population. Indictable crimes on the other hand showed a serious rise in absolute numbers, and even more per head of the population. New methods were needed. As Lord Trenchard said in 1932, 'the rough and ready methods of fifty years ago are unsuitable today. The criminal has become more skilful, more mobile and more scientific, and the methods of dealing with him must not only keep pace, but get ahead of him.'[1]

## The work load

The police in the inter-war years therefore faced a situation in which the increase in road traffic was diverting men from ordinary duties and causing a staggering rise in clerical work,[2] crime was on the increase and a significant proportion of the population was living in enforced idleness. At the same time police numbers were not keeping pace with population. Clearly the amount of work which the individual policeman and the service as a whole were expected to perform was rising far faster than total expenditure on the force. Some changes were needed if the situation was not to get unmanageable. However, since many of the proposed changes were expensive, progress was slow. In 1939 when a variety of schemes were at last getting under way all normal measures were abandoned in the face of the war-time emergency.

## Post-war developments

The war first of all brought about an increase in the strength of the regular police, but as time passed an increasing number were called up and the force had to manage with auxiliaries. As in the first world war police duties and Home Office control were both extended, but again most of the emergency administrative machinery was dismantled when peace came. In 1945 recruitment and retirement had been virtually at a standstill for four years and the manpower shortage was severe. Older men retired in large numbers and the service was faced with the combination of an unprecedented number of recruits and an unusually low proportion of experienced men. Some sort of inter-force co-

[1] *Commissioner of the Police of the Metropolis, 1932*, p. 7; 1932–33 Cmd. 4294, xv.
[2] The Metropolitan Police Survey in 1935 showed that one hour of traffic work outside the station on average generated two hours of paper work inside.

operation over training was essential. First to come were the District Recruitment Boards in 1945. Their aim was to make sure that all acceptable recruits were employed even if they were not taken by the force of their first choice. The District Training Scheme followed in 1946. All recruits were trained away from their forces at hastily established centres, many in temporary accommodation. This relieved the individual forces of finding the time and men for training and ensured greater standardization. The training was done by police officers seconded from the forces of each District, but the large classes meant that fewer men were needed than if each force undertook its own training.

The other major development in co-operative training, the Police College, was also a post-war venture. Attempts to set up a national police training centre for higher ranks had failed in the thirties. The main reasons were the unwillingness of either central or local government to provide finance, and opposition by the Police Federation. After the war local authorities had accepted the idea of regional services and were used to sharing with the Home Office. The financial obstacles to setting up the College thus no longer existed and the need for training men for command was as great as ever. The objections of the Police Federation were largely met by restricting attendance at the College to serving policemen who had been recruited in the normal way. The College was founded in 1948 in temporary quarters and began running courses for newly promoted Inspectors and Superintendents. It is important as the first national, as opposed to regional, police venture which was supported by local police authorities.

*Conclusions*

The Desborough Committee set up after the police strike of 1918 resulted in far reaching changes. Pay and conditions of service were standardized throughout the country. The establishment of the Police Council for the first time allowed regular consultations between policemen of all ranks, the Home Office, and the police authorities. The lower ranks achieved a national organization—the Police Federation. Although individual forces retained their traditions and independence, it became possible to speak of the police as a unified service.

The Desborough pay scales gave the constable a wage which was approximately 30 per cent above the national average wage for men. Despite the falling cost of living and the economic crises the Police Federation were able to keep the scales in being, at least nominally. The actual level of pay was reduced by 'temporary deductions' imposed in 1921 and 1931, and as national wages rose the differential created by the Desborough award decreased. However in 1939 the police were still relatively well off. By 1945 the situation had changed. Police wages were barely above the national average and even the large award made in 1949 on the recommendation of the Oaksey Committee was soon overtaken by rising national wages. The advantages of a police career in terms of status and security were perhaps greatest during the inter-war years when the possibility of unemployment and poverty was so great.

The police were, however, subjected to severe strains between the wars. Recruitment was limited by the need for economy and the number of police failed to keep pace with the rise in population. At the same time the police had to deal with disturbances among the unemployed, with rising crime rates, an increase of 350 per cent in the number of vehicles on the roads and a growing volume of traffic law and paper work. Faced with these changes the gap between the most advanced and the most conservative forces grew. Photography and other scientific aids, motor transport and good communications were necessary for some forces, but in others the methods of the nineteenth century were still adequate.

The central government became increasingly associated with the new developments. At first, with the introduction of the Police Regulations and central machinery for negotiating pay, government influence was largely regulatory. Towards the end of the thirties, however, a great many constructive decisions were taken by the Home Office and the national associations. Co-operative arrangements for specialized training, laboratories and wireless services came into being between 1936 and 1939. They were financed jointly by the police authorities and the central government. After the war, in response to the unprecedented influx of recruits, the arrangements were extended to cover recruitment and general training. The Police College which was the first national, as opposed to regional, police venture was opened in 1948. The realization that financial contributions to regional services were worthwhile and indeed essential for efficient police work, was perhaps the most outstanding characteristic of the period. After 1949 this trend towards two tiers of police organization, local and regional, continued in response to the changing demands made on the service.

# IV

# The Post War Period—1950–65

FROM 1950 to 1965 the pace of change in the police force quickened. By the beginning of the period the second world war and its aftermath were no longer the dominant features in national life. Post-war reconstruction was almost complete and the new conditions, so different from those that followed the first world war, were beginning to be regarded as normal. For the police, this meant a growing realization that the manpower shortage had come to stay and a slow modification of the beat system to meet the change. The well-tried expedient of extending beats so that men covered more ground less thoroughly, either on foot, by cycle, motor cycle or car, became widespread. Gradually, however, the new methods, which were pioneered in a few forces, spread. Generalizations must, of course, be treated with reservation when applied to so many separate organizations as the police forces of England and Wales, but it is fair to say that there was growing specialization and division of labour in the service. Greater mechanization, once the motor industry recovered from the war, gave far more flexibility and a new freedom to experiment with different methods of policing. The increase in private motoring resulted in a huge expansion of police traffic patrol work. Later the coming of motorways made inter-force co-ordination of traffic patrols essential and new methods were developed to deal with highly organized mobile criminals.

Communications improved, though slowly. Radio communication became really feasible for the first time and covered the whole country by the early sixties. Facsimile transmission of material such as fingerprints came in during the early sixties and at the end of the period the full possibilities of personal radios for individual policemen on the beat were at last being realized. Forensic science did expand but it was seriously hampered by lack of funds and qualified staff. In the sixties, as the crime rate continued to rise and detection rates fell in nearly all forces

Criminal Investigation Departments were expanded and there was a new emphasis on crime prevention and public relations. The volume of statistics and other material demanded by the individual criminal record offices, the Home Office and the Ministry of Transport grew, but all this information was not fully used. Its relevance and usefulness for policy decisions were beginning to be realized by the end of the period, but the main developments in the scientific application of statistical information to police work occurred after 1965.

*Cost*

All these changes were accompanied by a huge increase in expenditure. As always, however, by far the largest share of the total bill for the police continued to go on wages, salaries and pensions. The increase was necessary to keep pace with inflation (see Table IV.3). Other expenditure also increased at a slightly faster rate. Capital investment, despite the increase in equipment and vehicles used by the police, was still largely confined to buildings. In the early fifties investment in police housing predominated but towards the end of the period new administrative buildings and police stations took a growing share. These changes are described in more detail in the following paragraphs.

Table IV.1 shows the growth of gross national expenditure in England and Wales. The second column shows total current and capital spending by public authorities, excluding defence. It covers all spending by central and local government bodies except for defence expenditure, which made up a varying percentage of the total (from 20 per cent in 1952 to 15 per cent in 1963). Defence has been excluded in order to concentrate on spending which was influenced by home rather than international conditions, though of course exact separation is never possible. Total police spending, computed in national accounting terms[1] is shown in the final column. All three items increased greatly over the period, though

[1] The aim of the national accounts is to make certain that no item of expenditure is counted more than once in the final total. For the police this means that central government grants to local police authorities are counted as local expenditure and only the Central Services and a few other special grants appear as central government spending on the police. The income of local authorities whether from other authorities in payment for police services, or from other sources is deducted from the total.

A.S.I.M.—6

part of the increase must, of course, be discounted as it is due to the change in the value of money following inflation. Gross national expenditure rose by 163 per cent, public spending (excluding defence and transfers) by 202 per cent and the cost of the police service by 256 per cent. In other words the country devoted a greater proportion of its resources to the police in 1965 than in 1950.[1]

TABLE IV.1

**Changes in national expenditure (1950–65)***

| | Gross national expenditure | Total public expenditure (excluding defence) | Total police expenditure (current & capital) |
|---|---|---|---|
| | £m. | £m. | £m. |
| 1950 | 10,449 | 3,325 | 54·9 |
| 1951 | 11,535 | 3,649 | 63·4 |
| 1952 | 12,471 | 3,815 | 69·3 |
| 1953 | 13,408 | 3,986 | 72·1 |
| 1954 | 14,171 | 3,971 | 73·9 |
| 1955 | 15,108 | 4,414 | 81·5 |
| 1956 | 16,394 | 4,854 | 92·9 |
| 1957 | 17,375 | 5,395 | 95·3 |
| 1958 | 18,143 | 5,765 | 102·5 |
| 1959 | 19,036 | 6,215 | 107·7 |
| 1960 | 20,263 | 6,574 | 120·3 |
| 1961 | 21,683 | 7,285 | 136·1 |
| 1962 | 22,657 | 7,670 | 145·7 |
| 1963 | 24,059 | 9,398 | 161·7 |
| 1964 | 25,865 | 8,976 | 173·2 |
| 1965 | 27,505 | 10,048 | 195·2 |

* Percentage increase 1950–65

| 163 | 202 | 256 |
|---|---|---|

All figures refer to England and Wales. Cols. 1 and 2 have been reduced by 11 per cent from the totals for the United Kingdom.

SOURCES: *National Income and Expenditure*, London H.M.S.O. and Central Statistical Office (unpublished).

The conditions that allowed these developments were in marked contrast to those that prevailed in the inter-war years. In 1950 most reminders of war-time stringency were fading away and the Korean War boom was beginning. Nearly all war-time measures,

---

[1] It should, however, be noted that expenditure on all social services went up during the period and the police were not alone in recording such a large increase.

such as controls on raw materials, had been removed by 1953 and restrictions on building were finally abolished in 1954. The expected slump had not taken place. Full employment and inflation were the post-war order. In the inter-war years unemployment averaged 10 per cent, with peaks at over 20 per cent of the insured labour force. The cost of living fell from 1922 to 1936. In marked contrast, after 1946 unemployment averaged under 2 per cent and never rose above 3 per cent in a full year. The cost of living rose from 81 points in 1952 to 115 in 1964.[1] There were no cuts in government expenditure to match the measures taken in the thirties. From the police point of view the recurrent setbacks occasioned by balance of payments crises and stop-go government economic policies had far less effect. Wage increases were delayed and arbitrators awarded less than the Police Federation demanded on many occasions but there were no cuts. Police building was held up from time to time (for example in 1954), by checks on local authority spending, and, perhaps most important of all, the development of central services, in particular radio communications, was slowed by shortage of funds. Though they occasioned much heart-burning at the time, none of these measures could compare with the inter-war cuts in wages, long delays in spending and inability to put new ideas into effect.

*Central and local government expenditure*

Table IV.2 shows the breakdown of police expenditure, again in national accounting terms. The great predominance of local authority spending over central services stands out. Even the growing importance of the central contribution in the sixties has done little to alter the balance. Expenditure under all heads has increased by approximately 200 per cent or more, with the fastest increase towards the end of the period. This is particularly true of the central services where government initiative was slow at first and salaries were a smaller proportion of total expenditure. The headings 'current expenditure on goods and services' and 'fixed capital formation' are dealt with in greater detail in the tables that follow. The largest component in 'goods and services'

[1] London and Cambridge Economic Service; *The British Economy—Key Statistics 1900–1964*, London, The Times Publishing Co. Ltd., 1965, Table C, p. 8. 1958 = 100.

TABLE IV.2

**Expenditure on the police in England and Wales (1950–65)***

| | Local authorities | | Central government | | Total |
|---|---|---|---|---|---|
| | Current expenditure on goods and services | Fixed capital formation | Current expenditure on goods and services | Fixed capital formation | |
| | £m. | £m. | £m. | £m. | £m. |
| 1950 | 49·1 | 5·0 | 0·7 | 0·1 | 54·9 |
| 1951 | 55·8 | 6·8 | 0·7 | 0·1 | 63·4 |
| 1952 | 60·4 | 8·1 | 0·7 | 0·1 | 69·3 |
| 1953 | 63·2 | 8·1 | 0·7 | 0·1 | 72·1 |
| 1954 | 66·1 | 7·0 | 0·7 | 0·1 | 73·9 |
| 1955 | 72·7 | 8·0 | 0·7 | 0·1 | 81·5 |
| 1956 | 84·3 | 7·6 | 0·9 | 0·1 | 92·9 |
| 1957 | 87·9 | 6·2 | 0·8 | 0·4 | 95·3 |
| 1958 | 95·0 | 6·0 | 1·2 | 0·3 | 102·5 |
| 1959 | 100·2 | 6·0 | 1·2 | 0·3 | 107·7 |
| 1960 | 111·8 | 6·9 | 1·3 | 0·3 | 120·3 |
| 1961 | 125·6 | 8·7 | 1·2 | 0·6 | 136·1 |
| 1962 | 134·0 | 10·0 | 1·2 | 0·5 | 145·7 |
| 1963 | 147·8 | 11·8 | 1·5 | 0·6 | 161·7 |
| 1964 | 156·9 | 14·0 | 1·6 | 0·7 | 173·2 |
| 1965 | 175·8 | 16·3 | 2·0 | 1·1 | 195·2 |
| Percentage increase 1950–65 | 258 | 226 | 186 | 1,000 | 256 |

\* The statistics refer to financial years.

SOURCE: Central Statistical Office (unpublished).

was salaries, but all establishment costs, rents and transport costs, etc., are included. New purchases of vehicles, radios, and scientific and other equipment come under the heading 'fixed capital formation', but by far the most important item was building (see Table IV.15). From 1952 to 1956 the largest share (over £4m.) went to police housing, but after 1961 expenditure on police stations rose steadily, reaching over £8m. in 1965. Central government capital formation was accounted for mainly by extensions to district training centres and forensic science laboratories.

*Salaries and wages*

Wages, salaries and pensions consistently averaged about 70 per cent of the total cost of the police. The sums shown in Table IV.3 represent the total wage bill of the police service. They include

## TABLE IV.3

### Expenditure on police salaries and pensions (1950–65)*

| | Local authorities | | | | Central government | | Total salaries £000 | Total police expend. £m | L.A. salaries at constant strength† |
|---|---|---|---|---|---|---|---|---|---|
| | Salaries £000 | % total spending | Pensions £000 | % total spending | Salaries £000 | % total spending | | | |
| 1950 | n.a. | — | n.a. | — | n.a. | — | n.a. | 54·9 | n.a. |
| 1951 | 34,400 | 54 | n.a. | — | 390 | 1 | 34,790 | 63·4 | 38,350 |
| 1952 | 37,900 | 55 | n.a. | — | 430 | 1 | 38,330 | 69·3 | 41,240 |
| 1953 | 38,600 | 54 | 11,390 | 16 | 430 | 1 | 39,030 | 72·1 | 41,370 |
| 1954 | 41,800 | 57 | 11,770 | 16 | 470 | 1 | 42,270 | 73·9 | 44,750 |
| 1955 | 46,200 | 57 | 12,630 | 16 | 500 | 1 | 46,700 | 81·5 | 49,360 |
| 1956 | 55,200 | 59 | 13,990 | 15 | 590 | 1 | 55,790 | 92·9 | 57,620 |
| 1957 | 57,400 | 60 | 14,710 | 15 | 640 | 1 | 58,040 | 95·3 | 58,270 |
| 1958 | 60,900 | 59 | 15,990 | 16 | 690 | 1 | 61,590 | 102·5 | 60,660 |
| 1959 | 62,700 | 58 | 17,260 | 16 | 750 | 1 | 63,450 | 107·7 | 61,470 |
| 1960 | 73,900 | 61 | 17,680 | 15 | 790 | 1 | 74,690 | 120·3 | 71,750 |
| 1961 | 84,900 | 62 | 17,540 | 13 | 1,000 | 1 | 85,900 | 136·1 | 80,550 |
| 1962 | 90,500 | 62 | 18,120 | 13 | 980 | 1 | 91,480 | 145·7 | 82,880 |
| 1963 | 96,140 | 59 | 21,310 | 13 | 1,110 | 1 | 97,250 | 161·7 | 85,760 |
| 1964 | 104,500 | 60 | 22,330 | 13 | 1,220 | 1 | 105,710 | 173·2 | 91,420 |
| 1965 | 112,850 | 58 | 23,340 | 12 | 1,500 | 1 | 114,360 | 195·2 | n.a. |

* The statistics refer to financial years.

† This column is obtained by adjusting actual local authority expenditure on salaries according to a volume index provided by the Central Statistical Office. The index is weighted according to the salary scales and number of men in each rank with 1958 taken as 100.

SOURCES: Ministry of Housing and Local Government, *Local Government Financial Statistics*; *Civil Appropriation Accounts* and Central Statistical Office (unpublished).

the pay of civilians and also all payment of allowances over and above basic rates of pay, e.g. detective duty allowances and rent allowances. The figure given for pensions is the amount paid out to members of the service who have retired, minus the pension contributions of serving members of the service.[1]

The table shows the division between the central and local government salary bills. Until the end of the financial year 1964–65 all pensions were paid by local police authorities. Under the Police Act 1964 the central government became responsible for the pensions of police officers on central duties. The sum was negligible (£3,000 in 1965) and has been included under central salaries.

Pension payments more than doubled during the period for which figures are available but their share of the total fell slightly. This would be expected in a period when rising wages were combined with an expanding force and when the proportion of policemen (as opposed to civilians who retire later) in the force was falling (see below p. 78). The relative fall in total pension payments was intensified by the high number of men who resigned before reaching pensionable age (see Table IV.10 below). There were more men who resigned voluntarily without a pension than who received one in every year except three from 1945 to 1965.

Central salary payments were made to the Inspectors of Constabulary and their staff and, under the Special Services Fund, to the staff of the Police District Training Centres, the Police College, the laboratories and the wireless depots. The largest share went to the District Training Centres but salary payments to laboratories and wireless depots rose fastest (over 300 per cent), reflecting the increase in their activities. The cost of the Inspectorate rose steeply in 1963 when the number of Inspectors increased to nine, one for each police district and the head of the Home Office Police Research and Planning Branch.

For the sake of completeness the cost of the Home Office departments that administer the police should be included under central expenditure. The data is, however, incomplete. The number of senior administrative staff remained virtually unchanged until 1964, but salaries rose. (For example the starting

---

[1] For those familiar with normal national accounting practice, this method of calculating pension contributions may seem unusual. It applies to the police and fire services.

salary of an Assistant Secretary was £1,500 in 1950 and £3,500 in 1965). At the same time there was an expansion in the number of professional staff connected with the police. The establishment of scientific officers grew, especially after the Police Research and Planning Branch was set up in 1963. In 1965 it had a total staff of thirty of whom nine were scientific officers and nine seconded policemen.

The final column in Table IV.3 shows the change in local police authority salary payments when weighted according to the total size and structure of the force. The index used takes into account changes in the numbers in each rank and is based on the strength of the force in 1958. It shows how much of the growth of the salary bill was accounted for by rising earnings and how much by an increase in the number of policemen. Thus, although total salary payments rose by 230 per cent over the period, wage increases accounted for a rise of only 140 per cent. The remaining 90 per cent was accounted for by the growth of numbers.

The level of police pay in relation to the national average bore little comparison with the favoured conditions that prevailed in the nineteen twenties. The police found their status relative to the average manual worker much reduced at the end of the war, but there were no strikes and no Desborough Committee. A small award was made in 1946 and the Oaksey Committee in 1949 did give the service a substantial rise in pay, but it, like other subsequent increases, was soon overtaken by the rise in national average wages. Between 1959 and 1960 the maximum rate of pay went up by 31 per cent. Table IV.4 compares the maximum and minimum pay of constables with the index of national average wages. Average earnings, which are higher than average wage rates, are frequently used to draw unfavourable comparisons with police pay.[1] But earnings, which include overtime pay, bonuses and other extras should correctly be compared with police pay and allowances. However, since there are no reliable statistics giving the full value of allowances, this comparison has never been made. The most important benefit enjoyed by the police was free housing or rent allowance. In 1960 the Royal Commission estimated that it was worth £112 a year on average.[2] By 1965 it

---

[1] *Royal Commission on the Police*, Minutes of Evidence, Day 1, Appendix III, p. 73.

[2] *Royal Commission on the Police*, Interim Report, p. 40; 1960–61, Cmnd. 1222, xx.

## TABLE IV.4

### Movements in police pay compared with the national average wage index (1950–65)

| | Constable's pay per annum | | | | National weekly wage rate Index* |
|---|---|---|---|---|---|
| | Max.† £ | Index | Min. | Index | |
| | April 1958 = 100 | April 1958 = 100 | £ | April 1958 = 100 | April 1958 = 100 |
| 1950 | 420 | 60 | 330 | 66 | 64 |
| 1951 | 505 | 73 | 400 | 78 | 68 |
| 1952 | 505 | 73 | 400 | 78 | 74 |
| 1953 | 505 | 73 | 400 | 78 | 77 |
| 1954 | 550 | 79 | 445 | 87 | 81 |
| 1955 | 550 | 79 | 445 | 87 | 86 |
| 1956 | 640 | 92 | 475 | 93 | 92 |
| 1957 | 660 | 95 | 490 | 96 | 97 |
| 1958 | 695 | 100 | 510 | 100 | 100 |
| 1959 | 695 | 100 | 510 | 100 | 103 |
| 1960 | 910 | 131 | 600 | 118 | 105 |
| 1961 | 910 | 130 | 600 | 118 | 109 |
| 1962 | 940 | 135 | 620 | 122 | 112 |
| 1963 | 965 | 139 | 635 | 125 | 115 |
| 1964 | 965 | 139 | 635 | 125 | 121 |
| 1965 | 1,105 | 159 | 700 | 137 | — |

* Index for weekly wage rates for adult males in manufacturing industry. *The British Economy, op. cit.*, Table C, p. 8.

† This does not take into account long service increments after 17 and 23 years.

SOURCES: Calculated from the *Royal Commission on Police 1960 Interim Reports; Minutes of Evidence Day 1.* Appendix I p. 19 (1960–61 Cmnd. 1222, XX).
Reports of the Commissioner of the Police of the Metropolis for the years 1960–65.

appeared to have doubled in London[1] and to have increased, but less dramatically, in most other forces. Other allowances were for detective or plain clothes duties, boots, bicycles and cars. However, even if the value of all these allowances could be calculated, police recruiting literature generally gave prominence to rates of pay rather than total earnings, and increases in pay have frequently been justified partly on grounds that they would attract recruits.[2] Table IV.4 shows that basic police pay increased at

[1] *Commissioner of Police of the Metropolis, 1965*, p. 33; 1966–67, Cmnd. 3052.

[2] *Inspectors of Constabulary, 1946*, p. 6; 1946–47 (134), xxiii, and *Commissioner of Police of the Metropolis, 1954*, p. 8; 1955–56 Cmd. 9471, xxvi,

much the same rate as the national average for all wage earners in manufacturing industry between 1950 and 1965. The police were, in fact, slightly ahead in most years. The maximum pay for constables has also increased faster than starting pay, giving greater benefits for long service. Two points must, however, be made. First the police had come, in the inter-war years, to expect their pay to be considerably higher than the national average. Second, as mentioned above, police pay was frequently compared with average earnings. In 1950 average earnings in manufacturing were £400 and in 1964, £960.[1] The police, or at least the substantial proportion with at least ten years service, clearly earned more than the national average when their allowances were taken into account, but equally clearly they did not earn very much more. The differential was considered by many to be too small and was aggravated by other social changes. With full employment the security of the police service no longer meant the difference between a steady job and the fear of the dole, paid holidays soon became general and the health service and national insurance reduced the value of free medical attention, sick pay and a pension. The disadvantages of police life, however, remained. No wonder, therefore, that many resigned, especially in periods when wage increases lagged behind the national average.

*Strength of the police service*

Table IV.5 summarizes the main changes in the numbers of police officers and civilians over the last century. Numbers as such are an unreliable guide to the amount of police cover available to the population as they are greatly affected by changes in working conditions. For example, the working year of the constable has, in theory at least, been reduced by almost exactly a hundred days since 1861, and by nearly fifty days since 1945. Meanwhile there have been substantial increases of population and, as we have already shown, of the major forms of work such as crime and traffic.

We have made such allowances as seem possible in calculating the figures of Table IV.5. The detailed bases of the calculations are described in full in Appendix B.1, but it should be mentioned that we have counted only the actual strength of the service, and

[1] *The British Economy Key Statistics 1900–1964, op. cit.*

## TABLE IV.5
### Police service man hours (1861-1965)*

| Year (1) | Population '000 (2) | Total no. police officers (3) | No. of police officers (adjusted for sickness) (4) | Hours worked by police officers '000 (5) | per 1,000 population (6) | Total no. of civilians (7) | No. of civilians (adjusted for sickness) (8) | Hours worked by police service (including civilians) '000 (9) (as in col. 5) | per 1,000 population (10) (as in col. 6) |
|---|---|---|---|---|---|---|---|---|---|
| 1861 | 20,006 | 20,489 | 19,870 | 62,948 | 3,146 | — | — | " | " |
| 1871 | 22,712 | 26,005 | 25,219 | 79,894 | 3,518 | — | — | " | " |
| 1881 | 25,974 | 30,904 | 29,844 | 93,203 | 3,588 | — | — | " | " |
| 1891 | 29,002 | 38,283 | 36,970 | 113,461 | 3,912 | — | — | " | " |
| 1901 | 32,528 | 43,463 | 42,138 | 114,278 | 3,513 | — | — | " | " |
| 1911 | 36,070 | 51,203 | 50,000 | 135,200 | 3,748 | — | — | " | " |
| 1921 | 37,887 | 60,709 | 58,693 | 140,863 | 3,718 | — | — | " | " |
| 1931 | 39,948 | 60,492 | 58,577 | 140,585 | 3,519 | — | — | " | " |
| 1938 | 41,460 | 63,800 | 62,098 | 149,035 | 3,595 | — | — | " | " |
| 1949 | 43,758 | 60,418 | 57,763 | 133,086 | 3,040 | 4,774 | 4,645 | 142,934 | 3,264 |
| 1951 | 43,745 | 62,629 | 59,690 | 137,526 | 3,144 | 6,023 | 5,860 | 149,949 | 3,428 |
| 1961 | 46,071 | 75,798 | 73,367 | 169,038 | 3,669 | 12,515 | 12,177 | 194,853 | 4,229 |
| 1965 | 47,763 | 84,425 | 81,503 | 163,658 | 3,426 | 19,093 | 18,577 | 197,394 | 4,133 |
| *Adjustment for regular overtime in 1965* | | | | | | | | | |
| 1965† | 47,763 | 84,425 | 81,503 | 173,438 | 3,631 | 19,093 | 18,577 | 207,174 | 4,337 |
| Difference due to regular overtime | | | | 9,780 | 205 | | | 9,780 | 204 |

* Man hours in this table include hours worked by women. The basis on which this table was compiled is described in full in Appendix B.
† The second set of figures for 1965 allows for regular overtime.

we have reduced this to allow for sickness. We have assumed a nine-hour working day until the end of the nineteenth century, and eight hours after that. The number of working days are derived from the Police Regulations for 1921 onwards, and from accounts of working conditions for the earlier period. A small adjustment has been made to allow for the greater leave entitlement of ranks above that of constable and for long service. We have also related our totals to the size of the population. As it is well known that regular overtime is still a feature of service in certain forces we have made an additional set of estimates for 1965 which take this into account, and which allow us to show its overall effect.

The table distinguishes between the hours worked by police officers and by the police *service*—that is including civilians (except for those employed by the Receiver of the Metropolitan police), cadets and traffic wardens. Figures for strengths were taken from the Reports of H.M. Inspectors of Constabulary.

Column 5 shows how the number of police officers increased fairly steadily up till 1921 but then, with minor fluctuations, remained relatively unchanged for thirty years. The last fifteen years, however, have seen the most rapid growth in the history of the service. The number of hours worked by police officers has, in the main, increased, but less steadily. The effects of increased numbers have tended to be partially offset by improved working conditions. The reduction in hours was not so apparent following the Police (Weekly Rest Day) Act of 1910 as might have been expected. This was partly because many forces did not implement the Act until after the first world war, and partly because the strength of the service increased quite substantially in the first twenty years of the century.

After the second world war working conditions improved rapidly. Annual leave was increased by six days in 1946; six further days were granted for public holidays in 1948. In 1955 the standard working week was cut from forty-eight to forty-four hours and in 1964 it was again cut to forty-two hours. The shift system cannot, however, be easily modified in a service which has to give twenty-four-hour protection to the public, and the changes in hours were achieved by adding to the number of rest days per month. In forces where the manpower problem was severe, the shorter week could not be introduced. In 1961 54 per

pent of the police had been granted the forty-four-hour week,
26 per cent had a partial grant (usually meaning a forty-six-hour
week) and 26 per cent were still working forty-eight hours.[1] These
figures applied only to the provincial forces as the Metropolitan
police were still working the old week in 1965. Where the extra
rest days could not be granted men were paid a regular overtime
wage. Even in 1957 the danger of this practice in bringing about
differential salary scales between forces was realized,[2] but it helped
to pave the way for the 'manning up allowances' which were
reluctantly introduced in January 1966 to enable forces that were
severely under strength to offer higher pay than the rest. So far
(March 1968), such allowances have only been paid to members
of the London forces.

The improved conditions achieved after the second world war,
however, resulted in a sharp fall in the number of hours worked
by police officers. This meant that, in relation to population, the
number of hours was lower than at any previous period. The
position improved rapidly after 1949 as the number of police
officers increased, but deteriorated again by 1965, once more as
a result of better conditions. Notwithstanding this it must be
recognized that in the 1960's total hours worked by police officers
were substantially greater than in earlier years.

Population increases have tended to nullify some of the increase
in hours, but even so the figures for the 1960's were not much
lower than those for the inter-war years, particularly when it is
realized that the increased employment of civilians meant that
police officers should have had more time available for public
duties.

Civilians have been omitted from the calculations for the pre-
war years. Before 1919 virtually none were employed. A few cooks,
cleaners and female gaolers were encountered in large forces and
civilian clerks were occasionally taken on, but most of the latter
transferred to the police. The use of civilians, particularly in large
city forces grew slowly, but there are no figures for the total
number employed. It seems unlikely that there were more than

----

[1] *Inspectors of Constabulary, 1961*, p. 7; 1961–62 (220), xx.

[2] *Inspectors of Constabulary, 1957*, p. 7; 1957–58 (218), xvii. 'If this (48-hour week with extra pay) is allowed to continue for any length of time, it will be tantamount to a departure from the principle of standard conditions of service and might have an unfortunate effect on the contentment of the service.'

2,000 including cadets even in 1939, and far fewer in 1931. The same may be said of women police, whose numbers actually fell after 1920, and in 1939 only 246 were employed in the whole country.

One of the major post-war changes, in fact, was the increased contribution of women police officers and civilians. The women police were to some extent an indication of growing specialization within the force.[1] Though acting as ordinary police constables and undergoing the same basic training as the men, they tended to be employed more on work involving women and children. The contribution of civilians cannot be omitted from any consideration of police work in the post-war years and by the nineteen fifties they had become an integral part of the force. Not only did they perform many of the duties which had taken up the time of attested constables in the past—station cleaning and clerical work —but they also fulfilled many functions without which modern police work would be impossible—for example radio telephonists, scientists and fingerprint specialists. In many forces the number of civilians grew much faster than the total number of police. This was particularly true of the Metropolitan police, where there were most police vacancies and relatively few civilians were employed in the immediate post-war years. The early post-war totals for civilians were, however, artificially reduced because the staff employed by the Receiver, many on financial and administrative work, were not shown in the Metropolitan returns of civilian staff. In 1954 they numbered 2,620. The work of the Receiver's office was partly paralleled by work performed for the police by local authority departments. In some police authority areas the pay of the force was entirely the responsibility of the County or Borough Treasurer's office and in others police transport came under the local authority garage, just as certain vehicles, mainly vans, were the direct responsibility of the Receiver. All comparisons of the number of civilians employed by different forces have therefore to take into account these differences of organization.

The contribution made by civilians can be shown by comparing the right- and left-hand halves of Table IV.5. It will be seen that numbers increased to 19,000 by 1965, and they made a difference of 33·7 million hours in the total worked by the service. This

[1] The work of women police is discussed in Chapter IX.

increased the hours per thousand of the population by 707, so that the totals for the 1960's were the highest ever, 1965 being 4,133.

The contribution of systematic overtime should not, however, be overlooked. Our calculations show that it amounted to nearly ten million hours in 1965 and, when related to population increased the number of hours per thousand by 205. Important though this was, however, it was still a relatively small proportion (5·6 per cent) of the overall total.

The great increase in police man-hours per thousand population should not, of course, be taken to indicate a simple increase in police protection since the Victoria era. The massive increase in crime and traffic, even since 1939 (see Table IV.6) meant that modern police work bore little comparison with that of the past. Not only did manpower have to be increased, but more money had to be spent on the equipment and training necessary to increase the efficiency of the individual policeman.

TABLE IV.6

**Crimes and traffic 1950–65 (England and Wales)**

|  | Indictable offences known to the police | Non-Indictable offences— persons found guilty | Private cars '000 | All vehicles '000 |
|---|---|---|---|---|
| 1950 | 461,435 | 564,844 | 2,258 | 4,414 |
| 1955 | 438,085 | 627,591 | 3,526 | 6,412 |
| 1960 | 743,713 | 871,730 | 5,526 | 9,440 |
| 1965 | 1,133,882 | 1,149,613 | 8,917 | 12,939 |

SOURCE: *Annual Abstract of Statistics.*

*Distribution and size of forces*

The overall numbers of the police increased and at the same time there was a marked redistribution of effort. In 1921 the total force was evenly divided between London, the Boroughs and the Counties, with London slightly in the lead. By 1965 the situation was as shown in Table IV.7. The London forces shrank to barely a quarter of the total strength and the Counties rose to approximately 45 per cent.

The dichotomy between county and borough forces was no longer as meaningful in terms of the type of criminal or the work

## TABLE IV.7

### Strength of the police (1950-65)

| | Counties | | Boroughs | | London | | Total | |
|---|---|---|---|---|---|---|---|---|
| | Total forces | Police only | Total forces | Police only | Total forces | Police only | Service | Police |
| 1950 | 29,630 | 26,850 | 20,730 | 19,140 | 17,250 | 16,920 | 67,610 | 62,910 |
| 1955 | 33,330 | 29,180 | 22,190 | 20,310 | 21,340 | 16,630 | 76,860 | 66,120 |
| 1960 | 37,820 | 32,250 | 25,280 | 22,640 | 23,210 | 17,950 | 86,310 | 72,840 |
| 1965 | 46,530 | 38,000 | 31,620 | 26,920 | 26,900 | 19,510 | 105,050 | 84,430 |
| Percentage increase | | | | | | | | |
| 1950-65 | 57 | 41 | 53 | 41 | 56 | 15 | 55 | 34 |

SOURCES: Based on data from the *Reports of H.M. Inspectors of Constabulary and of the Commissioner of Police of the Metropolis.*

encountered. Organizational differences, however, remained. To give an example; there was little point in drawing up detailed plans for putting up road blocks at short notice in a borough force where a fast car could make a getaway outside the police area in five minutes or less, but in a county thirty or even more minutes might be needed and radio patrol cars would have time to set up road blocks.

Over the period 1950 to 1965 there was very little reduction in the number of forces. The real developments in this field took place after 1966. The size of individual forces, measured in terms of the total number of police and civilians, grew. The smallest forces with less than a hundred men disappeared (Table IV.8). Borough forces continued to be small. Eighty-three per cent had a strength of four hundred men or less in 1950, and the figure was still 55 per cent in 1965. The county forces had always been larger on average and they increased in size during the period, partly through amalgamations. Only half had five hundred men or less in 1950 and by 1965 the share had fallen to barely a quarter.

### Recruitment and wastage

It is obvious, therefore, that a great deal of progress was made during the fifties and early sixties, but the success has been obscured by the inability of so many forces to recruit up to their full establishments, by the problem of premature wastage and by failure to stem the rise in crime rates. The three questions of recruitment, wastage and establishment were closely interlinked

## TABLE IV.8

### Size of police forces (all employees) (1950–65)

| | Counties | | | | | Boroughs* | | | |
|---|---|---|---|---|---|---|---|---|---|
| Size of force | 1950 | 1955 | 1960 | 1965 | Size of force | 1950 | 1955 | 1960 | 1965 |
| 0–100 | 6 | 1 | — | — | 0–100 | 4 | 2 | 1 | — |
| 101–200 | 9 | 9 | 6 | 1 | 101–200 | 39 | 36 | 30 | 19 |
| 201–300 | 6 | 5 | 6 | 4 | 201–300 | 11 | 13 | 18 | 22 |
| 301–400 | 4 | 5 | 6 | 7 | 301–400 | 6 | 8 | 5 | 9 |
| 401–500 | 8 | 6 | 4 | 2 | 401–500 | 3 | 3 | 8 | 6 |
| 501–600 | 5 | 5 | 4 | 5 | 501–600 | 3 | 3 | 2 | 4 |
| 601–700 | 5 | 5 | 4 | 3 | 601–700 | — | 1 | 1 | 2 |
| 701–800 | 3 | 5 | 5 | 3 | 701–800 | 3 | 2 | 3 | 2 |
| 801–900 | 1 | 2 | 4 | 5 | 801–900 | 1 | 1 | — | 2 |
| 901–1,000 | 1 | 1 | 2 | 2 | 901–1,000 | — | 1 | 1 | 2 |
| 1,001 + | 7 | 8 | 10 | 16 | 1,001 + | 4 | 4 | 5 | 6 |
| Total | 55 | 52 | 51 | 48 | | 72 | 72 | 72 | 72 |

\* Including City of London and Metropolitan police.

SOURCE: *Annual Reports of H.M. Inspectors of Constabulary.*

and difficult to disentangle. In the early years recruiting difficulties received most publicity, but in the sixties, voluntary resignations (wastage) came to be seen as the real problem. Undoubtedly it was financially the most important as money spent on training was almost completely wasted when men resigned early. Table IV.9 shows the net loss and gain for the provincial police forces in each year from 1950 to 1965. The final column shows the persistent failure to recruit up to establishment. Faced with this situation, the Home Office was for many years reluctant to approve large increases in establishment for forces that were severely under strength. In 1964, however, on the recommendation of the Royal Commission on the Police 1960–62, the policy was changed and forces were asked to calculate 'realistic establishments'; hence the increase in the percentage of vacancies even though 1965 was a good year for recruiting. The position in the metropolitan police was virtually the same, though net losses occurred in rather more years.

The table shows a net loss in three years and negligible gains in two more. The large city forces had the greatest difficulty in attracting sufficient recruits. The failure of enough suitable recruits to come forward was frequently blamed on low rates of pay, and it is perhaps significant that the years in which pay increases were introduced were among those which recorded net losses (see Table IV.4). In 1951 and 1955 the pay increases were made in August and September respectively and at that time the police statistical year ended in September. The increases therefore had no effect on recruitment or resignations in the year in which they were awarded. In 1960 the connection is less obvious because although the 31 per cent increase was back-dated to September 1960 it was not, in fact, awarded until February 1961. Both the 1960 and 1964 awards, which were substantial, had a marked effect on the net gain in the following years. The actual numbers recruited in any one year were also influenced by a variety of other factors, such as changes in the length of National Service, rates of pay in the armed services and the number of cadets who reached the age of 19.

Although the total number of recruits was never less than 3,000 in a year, there was little progress in manning up to establishment. Efforts were made to widen the pool of potential recruits. Many forces dropped height standards, some to the Home Office minimum of five feet eight inches, while others such as the Metropolitan

TABLE IV.9

**Recruitment and wastage in provincial police forces (1950–65)**

| r | Net loss | Net gain | Joined during year | Proba-tioners | Left during the year | | | Total | Vacancies in establish-ments % |
| | | | | | Resigned without pension/gratuity | Pensioned or given gratuity | Other reasons or died | | |
|---|---|---|---|---|---|---|---|---|---|
| 0 | — | 2,419 | 5,225 | 816 | 446 | 1,447 | 97 | 2,806 | 11·2 |
| 1 | 148 | — | 3,399 | 1,072 | 708 | 1,665 | 102 | 3,547 | 12·6 |
| 2 | — | 2,482 | 4,769 | 699 | 472 | 1,008 | 108 | 2,287 | 7·9 |
| 3 | — | 576 | 3,526 | 917 | 670 | 1,237 | 126 | 2,950 | 7·6 |
| 4 | — | 234 | 3,502 | 850 | 858 | 1,453 | 107 | 3,268 | 8·0 |
| 5 | 465 | — | 3,488 | 915 | 1,188 | 1,746 | 104 | 3,953 | 10·1 |
| 6 | — | 1,763 | 4,148 | 716 | 584 | 954 | 131 | 2,385 | 8·4 |
| 7 | — | 1,435 | 4,176 | 834 | 710 | 1,057 | 140 | 2,741 | 7·0 |
| 8 | — | 1,132 | 4,113 | 876 | 677 | 1,275 | 153 | 2,981 | 6·0 |
| 9 | — | 872 | 4,747 | 1,054 | 920 | 1,715 | 186 | 3,875 | 5·1 |
| 0 | 372 | — | 3,101 | 996 | 1,115 | 1,213 | 149 | 3,473 | 6·7 |
| 1 | — | 2,409 | 4,457 | 780 | 541 | 543 | 184 | 2,048 | 4·4 |
| 2 | — | 2,116 | 4,737 | 802 | 641 | 842 | 336 | 2,621 | 3·8 |
| 3 | — | 1,500 | 4,771 | 728 | 617 | 1,555 | 371 | 3,271 | 5·0 |
| 4 | — | 850 | 4,948 | 860 | 832 | 1,764 | 642 | 4,098 | 8·7 |
| 5 | — | 2,694 | 6,558 | 793 | 921 | 1,272 | 877 | 3,863 | 11·0 |

SOURCE : *Annual Reports of H.M. Inspectors of Constabulary.*

A.S.I.M.—7

police allowed some relaxation on eyesight and even on occasion accepted men with glasses. There is no direct evidence of a change in educational standards, but it is perhaps significant that the Police Federation complained of the low level of educational tests in 1960.[1] Advertising was also tried. In 1955 police authorities' expenditure on advertising became eligible for a 50 per cent grant, and in 1962 the Home Office launched a national campaign. There is no direct evidence of the success of advertising but the Home Office estimated that 14 per cent of appointments were directly attributable to the national campaign. Individual forces continued to advertise, but their expenditure varied enormously and appeared to have little relation to the number of recruits.[2] The central campaign also continued and cost £200,000 in 1965.

There was, however, a further aspect of recruitment which caused concern, namely that although the number of pupils leaving school with general certificates of education was going up each year, the police were not getting their fair share of the better educated. At a time, therefore, when police work was becoming increasingly complex and the volume of law relevant to the police was constantly mounting, the police were no longer as able to recruit from the more educated sections of the community. Police cadets were the exception to this general rule. They joined the force, generally at the age of 16 and spent their time assisting the police (mainly with clerical work), and in various forms of training and community service. The exact nature of their duties and the amount of time spent on further education and training varied from force to force, but in all they were encouraged to work for the Ordinary and Advanced level certificates of education. By the time they were 19 and eligible to become probationary constables a high proportion had at least one G.C.E. pass. In 1965 the proportion with one G.C.E. pass was 79 per cent for ex-cadets and 38 per cent for men recruited directly into the provincial police forces. The first analyses of premature wastage also showed that men who had been cadets were less likely to resign before reaching pensionable age, and as a response the number of cadets has been

---

[1] *Royal Commission on the Police*, Minutes of Evidence, Day 3, p. 172.

[2] *Estimates*, Sel. Cttee. 1st Report. Appendix 2, pp. 284–99; 1966–67 (145). E.g. Glamorgan spent £560 for a recruitment of 117, or just under 10 per cent of establishment, while Newcastle-on-Tyne spent nothing on advertising and recruited 80 men (11 per cent).

progressively increased. It was agreed that they should not form more than half the total number of recruits in any one year but in fact only the West Riding took more than 30 per cent in 1965. The objection to cadets most frequently voiced was that they had no experience of work outside the police and so were likely to lack the wide range of experience and sympathy with the general public which were expected of the British police. There is, however, no empirical evidence on this point. After 1965 even greater efforts were made to attract better educated men and women into the police and incentives to graduates were extended. There is some evidence that these measures were successful. In 1966 the Select Committee on Estimates reviewed the question and concluded that, if possible, more cadets should be recruited, though not more than 40 per cent of recruits should be ex-cadets.[1]

The improvement in recruiting after the second world war led many to expect that vacancies would soon be reduced to pre-war levels. This, however, did not occur.

The real problem was then identified as one of resignations by serving policemen.[2] The bare statistics of resignations are shown in Table IV.9 divided between probationers and the rest. The number of probationers who resigned to some extent reflected poor selection of recruits, but although the resignation rate might have been expected to rise when recruiting became difficult this in fact did not happen, and the rate actually fell during the sixties. The recruits who left during the first two years of service represented a heavy loss in financial terms. There are no published data breaking down resignations into periods within the two years of joining, but most completed the initial training course of thirteen weeks (resignations or dismissals during the course averaged 4 per cent or less). On the other hand resignation of all probationers ran at 21 per cent of recruits during the period and for these the cost of the thirteen weeks' residential training at a District Training Centre was a complete loss to the service. Probationers also spent further time on training, both residential and in their own forces, and this too must be counted a loss on resignation.

The gravest problem was, however, the resignation of policemen in mid-career. The most serious losses, in organizational

[1] *Estimates*, Sel. Cttee. 1st Report, p. xx; 1966–67 (145).
[2] *Commissioner of Police of the Metropolis, 1958*, p. 11; 1958–9 Cmnd. 800, xviii.

terms, were men with five to fifteen years' service—those who should be at once highly trained, experienced and active. Their contribution to the force could not be measured merely in terms of financial investment in training, or outlay on pay, because so much police work depends on actual experience in the job for success. Obviously a profession suffers both in efficiency and morale if experienced men who should be training new entrants are leaving before their time. Losses of experienced men averaged 1 per cent of actual strength in the provinces and 3 per cent in London.[1] On the face of it, this seems a low rate of separation, but the numbers ran at over half of those who retired on pension and averaged 24 per cent of all those who left. It has been suggested that since this is no higher than the normal rate of turnover to be expected in any firm or industry, it is not a cause for concern.[2] Police training is, however, relatively expensive when compared with what is normal in industry. Every trained constable has received a total of four months' residential training in police work at a district training centre, has probably attended other short courses, and has had a varying amount of instruction in his own police force. All this training is highly specific to police work and has very little relevance, apart from developing character and self-confidence, to any other job. In the past it was assumed that very few men would resign voluntarily, so the cost of training would not be wasted. In this the police were similar to the armed forces. Concern over the loss of trained men is a reflection of changed conditions. For many the police service is no longer a lifetime commitment. Part of the change was, of course, a result of full employment and rising wages which made mobility easier and increased job expectations. The disadvantages of this change have, of course, been intensified by the rising costs of training. The Select Committee on Estimates received evidence that in 1966 the cost of wastage was running at £1·6 millions a year for probationers alone.[3]

The other main source of wastage was the number of police pensioned. The basic trend was determined by past recruitment

[1] Rates for women police were very much higher, but they form a negligible proportion of the total.

[2] *Royal Commission on the Police*, Interim Report, p. 32; 1960–61 Cmnd. 1222, xxi.

[3] *Estimates*, Sel. Cttee. 1st Report, p. 237; 1966–67 (145).

and the number leaving was expected to rise after 1970 when the heavy intake of men who joined straight after the war had passed through the service. On the other hand the actual number of men leaving in any one year varied according to recent pay awards. After the Oaksey Committee had recommended that a pension should be assessed on the average pay of a constable's last three years of service, many chose to stay on for an extra two or three years after each major pay award. As a result the numbers pensioned in 1951 and 1963 and 1964 were well above average. Pensions continued to be a heavy item of expenditure (see Table IV.3), but after 1961 although an officer qualified for a half-pay pension after twenty-five years' service, it could not be paid until he reached the age of 50. The length of time a man might be pensioned was still very long, a fact dramatically illustrated by the Commissioner in 1954. He reported that the Metropolitan police was still paying pensions to five ex-officers whose ages ranged from 96 to 103, and that the oldest had joined the force in 1879.[1]

Once the gravity of the problem of premature wastage was realized some effort was made to counteract it. Research into the reasons was continuing in 1967[2] but the problem was by no means simple. The first studies suggested that poor pay, domestic problems associated with hours of work and education of children, and poor man-management were the main reasons for resignation. All were of course closely connected with one another. Pay and, in principle, hours were agreed nationally and so were not within the control of individual police officers, or even forces, but man-management most certainly was. At a time of social change when class differentials were to some extent breaking down, the old-fashioned disciplinary attitudes of many police officers were becoming anachronistic. The nearest parallel to conditions of service in the police would be the armed services, but they did not make the same demands on the rank and file for initiative in crises, and tact in day to day dealings with members of the public. In an attempt to spread modern techniques the Metropolitan police began courses in man-management for officers from all ranks with assistance from the Regent Street Polytechnic in 1965. Senior

---

[1] *Commissioner of Police of the Metropolis, 1954,* p. 8; 1955–56 Cmd. 9471, xxvi.
[2] Home Office: *Police Manpower, Equipment and Efficiency* (Taverne Report), H.M.S.O., 1967, p. 22.

officers first attended courses run by the Royal Institute of Public Administration in 1963, and the Police College devoted much time to administration and techniques of command from its inception. Further developments took place after 1965,[1] but a solution to the problem of wastage appeared to depend on a reorganization of police methods combined with acceptance of a higher rate of turnover than was normal in the past.

*Establishment*

The discussion of recruitment and wastage leads to the question of establishments which ultimately determine the number of vacancies that the force has to fill.[2] Two important considerations arise. The first is the idea of 'realistic establishments', and the second the whole method of deciding the correct establishment under modern conditions. When it became clear that vacancies were not going to be quickly filled after the war, the Home Office which sanctioned all increases in establishment, adopted a policy of discouraging large increases for forces which were seriously under strength. As a result, the conurbations particularly, had fewer vacancies on paper than they would have had if their establishments had been allowed to keep pace with the growth in population. Realistic establishments, as opposed to those which had been previously thought capable of achievement, began to be calculated and adopted after 1964.

It was undoubtedly essential that if the real police needs of the country were to be assessed the number of policemen should be calculated with as much accuracy as possible. The question however then arose as to how many men were actually needed. The strength of the police force was originally calculated on the basis of the population, size and rateable value of the area to be protected. The intensity of coverage was then left to the judgement of the police authority advised by the chief constable. The Inspectors attempted to see that comparable standards were

[1] Taverne Report, pp. 126–9.

[2] Police strength refers to the actual numbers of police officers in a force, establishment or authorized establishment is the number of police officers which constitutes the maximum strength which a force is permitted to reach. An establishment for each force is approved by the Secretary of State on the recommendation of the police authority. Civilians are excluded. See *Royal Commission on the Police*, Interim Report, p. 20; 1960–61 Cmnd. 1222, xx.

maintained all over the country. The growth of indoor police work had long ago distorted this simple pattern. Men for specialist work in the C.I.D. and traffic patrols could always be found. As a result the shortage of men was heavily concentrated in the beat patrols and they tended to be looked down on by their colleagues. While mechanization and improved communications continued to be used mainly to extend the area which one man could patrol on his beat, there was little prospect of a new approach to the problem of calculating establishments. However as the manpower shortage came to be seen as a more or less permanent feature, the potentialities of modern means of transport and communications for a completely new approach to providing police protection for the public, began to be realized. It is clear that a better equipped force can give equal or better service with fewer men.[1]

*Civilians*

The term 'establishment' as used in the preceding paragraphs, therefore, had a special and restricted meaning. It did not refer to the number of employees in any police force, but only to the attested constables. In the past there could be no objection to the practice, but as the number of civilians working for police authorities grew, it introduced a measure of distortion and possible misunderstanding. Policemen and women alone could not have dealt with all the extra work that has fallen on the police since Victorian times, even given the increase in their numbers shown in Table IV.5. By employing civilians a force was able to keep expenditure at a reasonable level and improve the service it gave the public.

The Oaksey Report in 1949[2] recommended more general use of civilians and in the following year the Home Office sent out a circular letter backing up the recommendation. The number employed increased rapidly (see Tables IV.5 and IV.7) in total, but was very unevenly distributed between forces. Table IV.10 gives the percentage of civilians in the largest forces in 1950 and 1965. Although the overall number of employees had increased in the later year the variation between forces was still almost as great as it had been fifteen years earlier. Even in the largest forces

[1] Taverne Report.
[2] *Report of the Committee on Police Conditions of Service Part I and Part II*, 1948-49 Cmd. 7674, Cmd. 7831, xix.

therefore there was still a great deal of scope for employing civilians on work which they had been found perfectly capable of performing satisfactorily to the general benefit of the public service. (See also Chapter IX.)

TABLE IV.10

**Proportion of civilian employees in large forces***
**(1950 and 1965)**

*1950*

| Counties | | Counties | | Boroughs | |
|---|---|---|---|---|---|
| % civilians | | % civilians | | % civilians | |
| Cheshire | 7 | Lancashire | 5 | Liverpool | 4 |
| Durham | 10 | Staffordshire | 18 | Manchester | 7 |
| Essex | 10 | Yorkshire W.R. | 8 | Birmingham | 4 |
| Kent | 16 | | | | |
| | | *All counties* | 8 | *All boroughs* | 7 |

*1965*

| Counties | | Counties | | Boroughs | |
|---|---|---|---|---|---|
| % civilians | | % civilians | | % civilians | |
| Cheshire | 8 | Lincolnshire | 10 | Bristol | 17 |
| Devonshire | 16 | Nottinghamshire | 11 | Liverpool | 20 |
| Durham | 21 | Staffordshire | 23 | Manchester | 19 |
| Essex | 16 | Surrey | 13 | Newcastle-upon-Tyne | 18 |
| Gloucestershire | 13 | Warwickshire | 15 | Birmingham | 19 |
| Hampshire | 15 | Yorkshire W.R. | 21 | Leeds | 14 |
| Hertfordshire | 18 | Glamorganshire | 15 | | |
| Kent | 23 | | | | |
| Lancashire | | *All counties* | 15 | *All boroughs* | 14 |

* Forces with over 1,000 employees

SOURCE: Based on data from *H.M. Inspectors' Reports.*

The increase in the number of civilians was the result partly of an expansion in the fields in which they were already employed and partly of their use in a much wider variety of jobs than in the past. Cleaning and catering had for long been entirely civilianized except in small country police stations, and with larger forces, more police stations and improved canteen facilities, more people were needed.

In clerical and communications work the advantages of employing civilians became increasingly clear. Much of the work was repetitive and did not call for any high degree of skill, training or specialized knowledge of police work. The main argument against using civilians was that the experience gained in all branches of police work was part of a constable's training and fitted him for promotion. As the manpower shortage continued and the cost of a constable in terms of pay and investment in training rose, most forces found it more rational to increase the number of civilian employees. Where necessary they could be supervised by a serving policeman and, being frequently employed on the same scales as local authority clerical officers, the wage bill was very much lower than it would have been for a corresponding number of policemen. The most notable progress was made in the C.I.D. where much of the huge volume of written work was taken over by stenographers. The Metropolitan police, for example, began detailed studies of how civilians could relieve the C.I.D. of indoor clerical work in 1961.[1] There was, however, still a great deal of scope for extending the use of typing pools, stenographers and dictating equipment to all forms of report writing. In 1966 there were still forces where constables typed their own reports.[2] Eyewitnesses could also attest that in 1965 there were still many men who found it quicker to write out reports in careful longhand, rather than use a typewriter for which no constable was trained as part of his duty.[3]

As communications work increased, in particular as the number of telephone calls and teleprinter messages went up, the number of civilian telephonists also grew. There was a distinction between ordinary switchboard work and radio and emergency communications. When modern switchboards were installed (and the Home Office began an advisory service on installation in 1962), less specialized police knowledge was needed for the job, but in many forces the communications room, the nerve centre of the force was still manned entirely by policemen. Not only were radio messages sent out and received there, but emergency calls came in and also calls from burglar alarms wired directly to police headquarters. These alarms had grown in popularity over the years. For example, there were 3,956 in the Metropolitan police area in 1955 and 15,129 at the end of 1965. Much time was wasted in answering false alarms. (In 1965 only 897 out of 39,767

---

[1] *Commissioner of Police of the Metropolis, 1961*, p. 9; 1961–62 Cmnd. 1765, xx.
[2] Taverne Report, p. 79.
[3] See also *Inspector of Constabulary, 1964*, p. 50, 'The immobilising of patrol cars for lengthy periods while drivers sit in police offices writing in longhand or typing reports is today unjustifiable' (1964–65 (251)xxi).

calls were the result of genuine attempted break-ins, but each had to be treated as a real emergency.) The responsible nature of the work made it essential that there should be very careful police supervision of all these operations even in forces where some civilians were employed. In some forces also, civilians did not work night shifts and policemen took over their duties after normal working hours.

Apart from such general work which had always been done, but which grew in complexity and volume as the scope of modern police operations increased, there were new developments on which civilians could be employed. Among these were the recording and classification of traffic accidents, coding and punching cards for the Home Office statistical returns on crime, and the development of *modus operandi* and similar record systems in forces which had previously had little or none.

In the sixties there was an expansion in the number of civilians with technical qualifications. The regional wireless service was maintained by Home Office employees, but the staff had always been small. In the fifties when cuts were made, it fell from 180 to 150 but after 1960 it rose again and reached 278 in 1965. Other technically qualified civilians worked in police garages, and as the number of vehicles increased so did the maintenance staff. The forensic science laboratories registered a big increase in percentage terms but still employed so few as to have little effect on the total (84 in 1950 to 140 in 1965).

The aspect of civilianization which was perhaps most obvious to the public was the institution of traffic wardens. They were first introduced in 1960 and between 1962 and 1965 their numbers grew from 456 to 2,396. They were intended to assist the police in dealing with the tedious and time-consuming work of controlling car-parking and so free constables for other duties. Instead they widened the scope and efficiency of police work by undertaking a duty which the police had been forced, by pressure of work, virtually to abandon. Control of vehicles became much more efficient but constables gained little time for non-traffic work. It was not until the second Functions of Traffic Wardens Order in 1965 enabled them to direct traffic that the wardens could relieve constables of point duty and so free them for other activities. Further developments in the use of traffic wardens were again more likely to improve general police efficiency in regulating the growing volume of traffic than to free constables for other work.[1]

Civilians were able to make their greatest contribution in large forces where the administrative, clerical and specialized departments could be centralized. In practice, however, even though most of the largest forces had more than the average proportion of civilians, there were very wide variations in numbers (see Table IV.10). More use could have been made of them in almost all forces in 1965, but their increase in numbers was accompanied by new problems. In the first place the forces that were most seriously under strength, and therefore had most need of civilians to free constables for active police work, were those where the recruitment of civilians was almost as difficult as the recruitment of constables. The Metropolitan police, for example, found it hard to fill vacancies at both clerical and professional levels.[2] In 1960 there were eight vacancies for solicitors in the Solicitor's Department and the prospects of recruiting up to establishment were poor.[3] Staff shortages in the Department were again mentioned in 1964.[4] Although, therefore, there was an incentive to civilianize in the conurbations the progress achieved was not always as great as in some county forces.

The other difficulty arose from the nature of civilian employees, other than domestic and catering staff. At first they were predominantly female clerical workers who had the advantage of needing little or no training and no time off other than the usual holidays. They therefore often worked effectively longer hours than the police and were paid considerably less. However, as civilians came to do more varied work, some of it responsible and some demanding relatively high qualifications, changes were necessary.

The larger forces could introduce a career structure and make arrangements for training. The Metropolitan police had been recruiting executive grade officers direct from the Civil Service Commission competition since before 1953 and were able to introduce a measure of promotion for traffic wardens as early as

[1] Taverne Report, pp. 41–2

[2] *Commissioner of Police of the Metropolis, 1955*, p. 21 and *Commissioner of Police of the Metropolis, 1964*, p. 13; 1955–56 Cmd. 9786, xxvi. 1964–65 Cmnd. 2710.

[3] *Commissioner of Police of the Metropolis, 1960*, p. 38; 1960–61 Cmnd. 1440, xx.

[4] *Commissioner of Police of the Metropolis, 1964*, p. 47; 1964–65 Cmnd. 2710.

1963. In other forces specialists such as fingerprint experts could look forward to some advancement within the force, but for most the only chance of promotion was to transfer to another department within the local authority, thus depriving the police of their experience. Even so, it seemed certain that the financial advantages of replacing policemen by civilians wherever the work allowed would continue to be well worth the effort involved in reorganizing the departments concerned.[1]

*Structure of command*

The question of promotion and supervision of civilians leads on to the subject of the command structure of the force as a whole. Under the traditional system the main function of both sergeants and inspectors was to supervise, with the grade of inspector being determined by the number of his subordinates. Command, in the sense of initiating new developments and forming policy was the province of superintendents and chief officers. Under the more flexible systems of policing which were being slowly introduced from 1946 onwards, all ranks had more scope for initiative and, in particular, sergeants had to make decisions on where and how to deploy their men. The changes were, however, very slow to spread and even by 1967 were still the exception rather than the rule. A new command structure was coming into being, but as Table IV.11 shows there was little basic change in the period under discussion. The proportion of upper ranks to constables had never been higher but this was partly a reflection of the number of vacancies. (All vacancies were assumed to occur in the lowest ranks, because it was always possible to find men to fill the higher ranks, cf. the situation in the specialized departments mentioned on p. 91 above.)[2] The main changes were that the proportion of superintendents in the county forces fell, thus bringing them closer into line with the national average. The numbers in the London forces, on the other hand, increased dramatically, almost entirely on account of a reorganization in the Metropolitan police in 1953 which doubled the number of superintendents. The proportion of inspectors, after remaining constant for most of the

---

[1] Taverne Report, pp. 28–43.

[2] In actual fact there were a few vacancies for sergeants also. In 1965 they amounted to 1,050 or 6 per cent of all vacancies.

## TABLE IV.11

### Proportion of the police force in each rank (1950–65)

| | Chief officers & assistants | Super-intendents | Inspectors (all grades) | Sergeants | Constables | Total actual strength = 100% |
|---|---|---|---|---|---|---|
| *Counties* | | | | | | |
| 1950 | 0·3 | 1·5 | 5·4 | 15·2 | 77·6 | 26,850 |
| 1955 | 0·3 | 1·4 | 5·6 | 15·3 | 77·4 | 29,180 |
| 1960 | 0·3 | 1·3 | 5·9 | 15·3 | 77·2 | 32,250 |
| 1965 | 0·3 | 1·2 | 6·8 | 16·2 | 75·5 | 38,000 |
| % increase 1950–65 | 10 | 14 | 79 | 51 | 37 | 41 |
| | | | | | | |
| *Boroughs* | | | | | | |
| 1950 | 0·4 | 1·0 | 4·8 | 15·0 | 78·8 | 19,140 |
| 1955 | 0·4 | 0·9 | 5·8 | 15·0 | 77·9 | 20,310 |
| 1960 | 0·4 | 1·0 | 5·9 | 14·8 | 77·9 | 22,640 |
| 1965 | 0·4 | 0·9 | 6·2 | 15·7 | 76·8 | 26,920 |
| % increase 1950–65 | 12 | 41 | 82 | 48 | 37 | 41 |
| | | | | | | |
| *Metropolitan and City of London* | | | | | | |
| 1950 | 0·1 | 0·8 | 5·0 | 18·3 | 75·8 | 16,920 |
| 1955 | 0·2 | 1·5 | 5·1 | 17·9 | 75·3 | 16,630 |
| 1960 | 0·1 | 1·3 | 5·3 | 17·6 | 75·7 | 17,950 |
| 1965 | 0·1 | 1·3 | 5·6 | 20·5 | 72·5 | 19,510 |
| % increase 1950–65 | 27 | 96 | 28 | 30 | 10 | 15 |

SOURCES: Based on data from *Reports of H.M. Inspectors of Constabulary and of the Commissioner of Police of the Metropolis.*

period, increased rapidly in the provincial forces after 1962. In London, however, there was little increase and the absolute total even fell from 1956 to 1958. The traditionally higher proportion of sergeants in London was still maintained although the rate of increase was very much lower than in the provinces.

*Promotion*

The main change for the better in the field of promotion was that the system of examinations for sergeant and inspector was finally centralized. The Oaksey Committee had recommended the change in 1949 but agreement on a satisfactory system could not be reached. Finally in 1956 it was agreed that the Secretary of State should appoint a Police Promotion Examinations Board to work in consultation with the Civil Service Commission. The first examinations to be set and marked centrally were held in February 1958. Success in the examinations, which were divided into two parts—educational and police subjects—qualified a man or woman for promotion but did not ensure that they actually reached the higher rank. In many small forces promotions were so infrequent that few had bothered to qualify.[1] Various other measures in the sixties, however, opened the way to promotion for the ambitious. A new police regulation in 1962 allowed a man to change forces without the written permission of his chief officer, and the number of transfers increased.[2] Before the change the transfer of constables had been rare and of sergeants and inspectors almost unknown[3] but under the new regulations men could move to forces where the promotion prospects were good. In 1964 the minimum length of service required to be served before promotion to sergeant was cut from five to four years. Finally in 1965 chief constables were required to advertise one in three of all posts of chief inspector and above, a measure which was expected to have wide repercussions throughout the service. Further arrangements for accelerating promotion have been introduced since 1965.

Even though the structure of command in the police was little altered on the surface, changes were taking place in the nature of the force. The trend was towards a more highly qualified, more specialized body of men and women and was the result of better training. This improvement was the great achievement of the period.

*Training*

The organization of the various forms of training is complex. Two main types are involved. In the first place there is mass training which may take up a greater or lesser amount of time but which should touch virtually every member of the force. Most training of this nature was done in the District Training Centres. Ideally it should include general training in police subjects and law,

[1] *Inspector of Constabulary, 1965*, pp. 25–6; 1966–67 (90).
[2] *Inspector of Constabulary, 1964*, p. 17; 1964–65 (251).
[3] *Inspectors of Constabulary from October 1958 to December 1959*, p. 10; 1959–60 (257), xx.

driving, and frequent refresher courses to keep serving policemen up to date and interested in their work. Secondly there is more specialized training. Some is designed to enable men to work in specialized departments, such as the C.I.D., and some to develop special skills which are useful to the whole force but are not needed by all members. Examples are the command courses at the Police College, organization and management training and crime prevention.

The work of the District Training Centres accounted for well over 60 per cent of all training. Its volume is ultimately determined by the number of recruits and as long as the turnover of serving policemen remains high a large proportion of the training effort must be devoted to introductory courses. Recruit training also continued throughout the two probationary years, though its intensity varied from force to force. Local training of this nature was not recorded. Similarly, refresher courses for serving constables were not recorded but it seems certain that much more could have been done. The Chief Inspector noted in 1964 that although local force training for recruits was generally satisfactory, there was still room for great improvements in refresher courses for senior constables.[1] Ideally the work of the Driving Schools should come under the heading of general training, with the possible exception of the advanced course. The Driving Schools ran ordinary driving courses, refresher courses and an advanced course intended for traffic patrol officers. All lasted from four to six weeks. The shortage of places was so great that only police who had to drive in the course of their duties could be sent on the ordinary courses and in 1965 there were still some members of traffic patrols who had not been on an advanced course.[2]

The most important of the specialist courses were concerned with crime detection and prevention. The detective training schools ran courses of ten weeks at two levels. There were also courses for scenes of crime officers, crime prevention and aids to the C.I.D. The latter were organized locally. Like the driving schools the detective training establishments could not keep up with the demand for places and much needed reforms in the curriculum could not be put into practice while the pressure of work remained so great.

[1] *Inspector of Constabulary, 1964*, p. 27; 1964–65 (251).
[2] *Ibid.*

The courses given at the Police College were reorganized in 1961 after the College had moved to its permanent headquarters at Bramshill in Hampshire. The new courses included one for constables judged suitable for accelerated promotion to sergeant and above, known as the Special Course, and a Senior Staff Course designed to fit men for the highest ranks. Courses for those promoted, or about to be promoted, to Inspector and Superintendent continued but were reorganized and improved. All courses placed emphasis on techniques of command, administration and man-management. Since 1960 new developments have taken place in these important fields. The Metropolitan police began courses in man-management in 1963, as already mentioned. Small numbers of officers began attending administration, and organization and methods courses in the same year.

### The cost of training

The District Training Centres for recruits and the Police College for advanced courses were treated as central services financed by the Home Office. Half their cost was recovered from the local police authorities whose contributions were calculated according to the size of their establishments. Then there were regional and national co-operative training arrangements between forces which qualified for a 50 per cent police grant in the normal way. The driving schools, the detective training centres at Wakefield, Birmingham and Hendon, the crime prevention courses run by Staffordshire and the forensic science courses at various centres were examples of such joint arrangements. Some of the large forces also ran courses mainly for their own members but admitted a few men from outside. An example was the specialist course on the work of the Stolen Vehicles Investigation Branch run by the Metropolitan police.[1] Finally there was local training conducted by individual forces. In 1959 the Home Office agreed that force training officers should attend courses for potential instructors free of charge to their parent forces in order to encourage local training. The variety of activities covered by these different arrangements was very wide and there was no complete record even of training received under co-operative agreements.

There are two main ingredients in the cost of training. The

---

[1] *Commissioner of Police of the Metropolis, 1961*, p. 75; 1961–62 Cmnd. 1765, xx.

first is the amount spent on running the various training establishments. The second is the cost of sending men on courses. Information on the cost of training is available for the central services, but is not entirely satisfactory. The data on capital expenditure and depreciation was too unreliable to use, so the following figures are all under-estimates. Table IV.12 which is based on the annual estimates of central government current expenditure shows that the cost of the Police College has risen steadily in almost every

TABLE IV.12

**Current expenditure by the central government on police training (1950–65)\***

| | District training centres | | | Police college | | |
|---|---|---|---|---|---|---|
| | Salaries £000 | Other £000 | Total £000 | Salaries £000 | Other £000 | Total £000 |
| 1950 | 215·6 | 235·6 | 415·2 | | | |
| 1951 | 183·9 | 215·7 | 399·6 | 44·1 | 55·6 | 99·7 |
| 1952 | 223·3 | 236·8 | 460·1 | 47·0 | 43·3 | 90·3 |
| 1953 | 214·0 | 239·9 | 453·9 | 54·8 | 48·8 | 103·6 |
| 1954 | 221·2 | 236·0 | 457·2 | 56·8 | 62·8 | 118·8 |
| 1955 | 226·9 | 252·4 | 479·3 | 68·2 | 66·3 | 134·5 |
| 1956 | 257·0 | 266·4 | 523·4 | 72·0 | 76·3 | 148·3 |
| 1957 | 274·7 | 300·4 | 575·1 | 78·4 | 80·6 | 159·0 |
| 1958 | 300·3 | 300·4 | 600·7 | 83·0 | 81·2 | 164·2 |
| 1959 | 311·5 | 296·5 | 608·0 | 89·6 | 85·4 | 175·0 |
| 1960 | 321·0 | 301·8 | 622·8 | 95·7 | 95·9 | 191·6 |
| 1961 | 391·0 | 303·0 | 694·0 | 99·6 | 86·3 | 185·9 |
| 1962 | 435·0 | 297·0 | 732·0 | 114·0 | 72·0 | 186·0 |
| 1963 | 443·0 | 305·0 | 748·0 | 119·0 | 95·0 | 214·0 |
| 1964 | 507·0 | 334·0 | 841·0 | 136·0 | 90·0 | 226·0 |
| 1965 | 576·0 | 464·0 | 1,040·0 | 141·0 | 94·0 | 235·0 |

\* Statistics refer to financial years.

SOURCE: *Civil Estimates.*

year of its existence, but that District Training Centres showed little increase from 1950 to 1955. Since then they too have risen in cost, though by 130 per cent as opposed to nearly 150 per cent for the Police College over the years 1950 to 1965. This represents only the cost of running the establishments and of pay for permanent staff and seconded police instructors, and not the total cost of training. Each man or woman on a course was not available for police work in his own force, but was still paid a full salary. In consequence the cost of training should include all payments made to members of the force during the times when they were

A.S.I.M.—8

not on active duty. Travel allowances should also be included but there was no reliable way of calculating the sum involved. Table IV.13 shows the estimated cost of training in 1960 and 1965 at the central service institutions when trainees' salaries are included. A comparison with the relevant years in Table IV.12 shows that while current expenditure increased by 60 per cent the total cost of training was up by 70 per cent. Salary payments to staff and recruits at the District Training Centres showed the greatest increase (nearly 80 per cent). Although total costs rose substantially, the number of men trained also went up. In other words expenditure per man-day increased much more slowly than total cost. The District Training Centres registered an increase of 17 per cent in current expenditure per thousand man-days and the Police College only 5 per cent. The latter figure is a remarkable achievement at a time of rising prices.

TABLE IV.13

**Estimated cost of training in district police training centres and the police college (1960 and 1965)**

|  | District training centres | | | Police college | | |
|---|---|---|---|---|---|---|
|  | All salary payments | Other current | Total | All salary payments | Other current | Total |
|  | £000 | £000 | £000 | £000 | £000 | £000 |
| 1960 | 881·3 | 301·8 | 1183·1 | 260·9 | 86·3 | 347·2 |
| 1965 | 1581·5 | 464·0 | 2045·5 | 444·9 | 103·0 | 547·9 |

SOURCES: Based on data from *Annual Reports of H.M. Inspectors of Constabulary* and *Civil Estimates*.

There are no published data on the cost of other forms of training, but some idea of the impact of recorded training on total police time is given in Table IV.14. The average number of days spent on training each year rose from ten to twelve days for each policeman or woman. In other words the time spent on training amounted to more than the time which would be lost if a five-day week were introduced. It must also be realized that the figures given in Table IV.14 are an under-estimate since all short local courses are excluded. Statistics of the time spent on training were only available from 1960 onwards, but there is little doubt that even by then there had been a considerable advance on 1950.

## TABLE IV.14
### Police training (1960–65)

|      | Av. no. of days training | District training % total | Police college % total | Detective % total | Driving % total | Other % total | Total no. man-days = 100% |
|------|------|------|------|------|------|------|------|
| 1960 | 9·9  | 64 | 9 | 10 | 17 | —  | 719,000 |
| 1961 | 10·1 | 66 | 9 | 9  | 17 | —  | 763,340 |
| 1962 | 10·2 | 67 | 7 | 9  | 17 | 1  | 802,230 |
| 1963 | 11·0 | 65 | 9 | 9  | 16 | 1  | 883,940 |
| 1964 | 11·2 | 62 | 9 | 11 | 17 | 1  | 912,030 |
| 1965 | 12·0 | 64 | 8 | 12 | 15 | 1  | 1,016,150 |

SOURCE: Based on data from *Annual Reports of H.M. Inspectors of Constabulary.*

Table IV.14 would suggest that the police were approaching the limit in the amount of time they could give to training without loss of efficiency. On the other hand the introduction of new techniques and new equipment clearly demanded more training. The most obvious need therefore was to cut down on recruit training and use the time and money saved to improve the qualifications of serving members of the force. This, however, could not be done until wastage and vacancies were reduced to manageable proportions. The other line of attack was to alter the content of training, particularly for recruits. In 1965 the emphasis was very definitely on basic law and police procedure, much of which had to be learnt by heart. Refresher courses were similarly designed to bring serving officers up to date on new legal developments. With the advent of personal radios the individual policeman could always ask headquarters for information on points of law and so needed to know less himself. There was therefore potentially more time available for training men in the new techniques to enable them to use more sophisticated equipment.

The overall police manpower situation was, however, by no means as bad as adverse publicity and the number of vacancies might have suggested at any time during the period. There were more policemen and more civilians than ever before and the opportunities for training at all levels of the force had never been so good. These improvements were accompanied by more and better equipment which allowed new methods of policing to be developed and increased the efficiency of existing practices. The main trends in equipment and police investment in buildings are outlined in the following paragraphs.

*Capital expenditure*

Capital expenditure is shown in greater detail in Table IV.15. Central spending was relatively low and almost all went on buildings. The services provided by the central government were training, wireless facilities and forensic science laboratories. The Police District Training Centres and the Police College were residential establishments capable of accommodating over a thousand men at any one time. They were, except for the Police College which was opened a year later, set up in 1947, but many were in temporary premises or had temporary extensions attached and the provision of permanent buildings continued throughout the period. Other capital expenditure was on laboratory buildings and scientific and radio equipment.

Local authority investment also concentrated on building, a definition which included the acquisition of land. Plant was of very little importance even in 1965 and spending on vehicles was similarly static from 1951 to 1958.

*Building*

Police building was mainly financed by local government (see Table IV.15). Central expenditure was rarely as much as 1 per cent of the total. Only the figures for total expenditure on the central services are available, as the estimates for each individual service were found too unreliable to use. Delays in the acquisition of land, grant of planning permission or arrival of stores meant that estimates were either too high, or, at other times, too low on account of rising costs. It is clear, however, that the largest proportion of central investment in building went to the Police District Training Centres. This was especially so in 1952 and 1953 when it became possible to replace some of the make-shift premises which had been hurriedly run up to cope with the post-war inflow of recruits. Between 1958 and 1961 there was heavy expenditure on the Police College which moved from temporary quarters into a renovated Jacobean mansion in Hampshire.

Local authority spending was divided between police housing and other building. Until 1960, if the price of land is left out of the calculation, the cost of new housing exceeded that of other building. In 1965 the number of police houses in England and

## TABLE IV.15

### Capital expenditure in England and Wales on police services (1951-65)*

| | Central government | | Land | Dwellings | Other new building | Local authorities | | Total expenditure | Less Sales | Total capital formation |
|---|---|---|---|---|---|---|---|---|---|---|
| | Buildings | Total fixed capital formation | | | | Plant | Vehicles | | | |
| | £000 | £m | £000 | £000 | £000 | £000 | £000 | £000 | £000 | £000 |
| 1951 | 53,930 | 0·1 | 1,029 | 2,440 | 2,662 | 168 | 711 | 7,010 | 174 | 6,836 |
| 1952 | 116,840 | 0·1 | 974 | 4,394 | 2,003 | 188 | 732 | 8,291 | 242 | 7,849 |
| 1953 | 122,830 | 0·1 | 1,124 | 4,407 | 2,010 | 125 | 704 | 8,370 | 192 | 8,178 |
| 1954 | 62,610 | 0·1 | 1,153 | 4,234 | 1,681 | 73 | 560 | 7,701 | 218 | 7,483 |
| 1955 | 58,690 | 0·1 | 1,132 | 4,148 | 2,204 | 91 | 750 | 8,325 | 190 | 8,135 |
| 1956 | 51,460 | 0·1 | 1,327 | 3,378 | 2,163 | 76 | 811 | 7,755 | 157 | 7,598 |
| 1957 | 90,430 | 0·4 | 1,014 | 3,118 | 1,374 | 143 | 787 | 6,436 | 188 | 6,248 |
| 1958 | 250,640 | 0·3 | 1,019 | 2,723 | 1,584 | 87 | 898 | 6,311 | 275 | 6,036 |
| 1959 | 316,790 | 0·3 | 937 | 2,230 | 2,078 | 121 | 955 | 6,322 | 260 | 6,062 |
| 1960 | 241,550 | 0·3 | 1,075 | 1,981 | 2,461 | 85 | 1,360 | 6,962 | 215 | 6,747 |
| 1961 | 191,250 | 0·6 | 1,603 | 2,329 | 3,456 | 197 | 1,457 | 9,042 | 430 | 8,612 |
| 1962 | 88,360 | 0·5 | 1,669 | 2,647 | 4,431 | 174 | 1,396 | 10,317 | 337 | 9,980 |
| 1963 | 131,400 | 0·6 | 2,343 | 3,244 | 5,391 | 156 | 1,544 | 12,678 | 713 | 11,965 |
| 1964 | 101,600 | 0·7 | 2,652 | 2,954 | 6,915 | 285 | 1,624 | 14,430 | 440 | 13,990 |
| 1965 | | 1·1 | 4,043 | 2,153 | 9,370 | 442 | 1,890 | 17,898 | n.a. | n.a. |

* The statistics refer to financial years.

Source: Central Statistical Office (unpublished).

Wales was approximately 39,500.[1] As would be expected most houses were in county forces (70 per cent), and 13 per cent were in the Metropolitan Police District. These totals do not include section houses in London and similar bachelor quarters in other large forces. Police houses became less popular as the proportion of home owners in the population increased and the police found that they were deprived of a chance of buying their own houses on mortgage. In the counties, however, a certain number of police houses had to be maintained so that men could be transferred from one area to another in the course of their duties. In addition, most rural police houses also served as police stations.

The main period of house building was from 1950 to 1955 when 14,500 new houses were built, with a peak of 2,590 in 1954. These were years when it was at last possible to make up for the war-time standstill on building and to rebuild the houses lost through bombing. After 1956 the number of new houses built annually declined. The Metropolitan police had met most of the need for married quarters by 1958, but was unable to do the same for section houses because they were classed as administrative buildings and had to compete for funds with projects for new police stations and offices.

Other buildings, mainly police stations, were urgently needed but did not always have priority over other local authority projects. There was a tendency for finance committees to cut the estimates made by the police authorities and building often suffered.[2] As in the inter-war years, new stations were needed to keep up with the movement of population to new towns and new suburbs. Changes in work methods demanded more space. In particular more office space and more room for communications equipment was needed. Garages and parking space were essential but often severely restricted in the old city police stations. Finally the advent of women police put an added strain on facilities which were often designed in the nineteenth century and had changed little since. In 1954 police authorities, excluding the Metropolitan police, had a programme of work estimated to cost nearly £12 million over the following five years.

[1] Institute of Municipal Treasurers and Accountants, *Police Force Statistics 1964–65* (1965), and *Commissioner of Police of the Metropolis, 1965*, p. 37; 1966–67 Cmnd. 3052.

[2] *Inspector of Constabulary, 1964*, p. 70; 1964–65 (251).

New stations had the first priority, and old ones were adapted but rarely replaced in the early part of the period. The Metropolitan police, for example, opened its first post-war station in 1955. The following year building was again restricted as an economy measure. After 1960 there was an increase in the amount spent each year and in 1965 the total went up by £2 million to over £9 million. Progress was clearly being made but the backlog of obsolescent buildings was very great and there seemed little hope of catching up for many years.

*Transport*

One of the most obvious aids to police efficiency is transport, and much progress was made in this field during the period. The growth of the police transport fleet had been steady in the thirties, but there was a drop during the war. However, by 1950 the motor industry was recovering and petrol rationing had ended. The way was open for new developments. At first it was a matter of replacing old vehicles. By 1959 the provincial forces had 67 per cent more vehicles than in 1948,[1] an increase from 5,500 to 8,650. By 1966 the total, including London, was in the region of 14,000, about 8,000 cars and vans and 6,000 motor cycles.[2]

The greatest increase occurred after 1959 (see Table IV.15 for the sharp upward turn in capital expenditure on vehicles after that year).

Table IV.16 gives a detailed breakdown of provincial police expenditure in the financial years 1958 and 1964. The purchase of new vehicles, as might be expected, went up faster than any other head of expenditure. The only other increase to rival it was the small outlay on hire of vehicles (£41,000 in 1964). Running costs which cover petrol, oil, tyres, licences, insurance and repairs increased at a slower rate. The drop in expenditure on cycles highlights the change in police methods which took place in the sixties. To quote Her Majesty's Chief Inspector, 'the pedal cycle as a means of transport for a police officer is fast becoming an anachronism'.[3] Other transport which did not actually fall in

---

[1] *Inspectors of Constabulary from October 1958 to December 1959*, p. 11; 1959–60 (257), xx.

[2] Taverne Report, p. 76.

[3] *Inspector of Constabulary, 1964*, p. 32; 1964–65 (251).

## TABLE IV.16

### Police expenditure on transport (1958 and 1964)*

Provincial forces

| | New vehicles £ | Running costs £ | Car allowance £ | Use of vehicles £ | New cycles £ | Cycle allowance £ | Other transport £ | Total (less sales of vehicles) £ |
|---|---|---|---|---|---|---|---|---|
| 1958 | 950,440 | 1,656,530 | 406,460 | 21,780 | 9,160 | 111,190 | 78,150 | 3,079,950 |
| 1964 | 1,878,440 | 2,793,050 | 638,020 | 41,480 | 6,610 | 90,090 | 102,950 | 5,307,200 |
| 1964 as % of 1958 | 198 | 169 | 157 | 190 | 72 | 81 | 132 | 172 |

* The statistics refer to financial years.

SOURCE: Home Office (unpublished).

total cost, but increased at less than half the average rate, included horses and boats.

The overall figures conceal the growing trend towards specialization in the use of vehicles which became more marked as the motorways were opened in the late fifties. However, even in 1965 the police still used a very wide variety of vehicles, partly because unco-ordinated buying policies had resulted in variegated fleets, and partly because different types of vehicle were needed for different types of work. At the beginning of the period the police had little experience of using motor transport either in conjunction with a manpower shortage or faced with the traffic conditions and the growth of organized crime which soon occurred. In the inter-war years motor transport had of course been widely used but mainly for the supervision of beat patrols and for traffic patrolling and the vehicles had not needed to be specialized. There was, therefore, a tendency to buy general purpose cars without detailed consideration of what they would be used for. However, traffic conditions were soon to become quite unlike anything encountered before the war and a different type of vehicle was needed. High-powered motor cycles and fast cars were essential for patrolling on clearways and motorways, and all had to have radio telephone equipment.

There are no detailed statistics available to illustrate these changes, partly because a definite policy had still not been evolved by 1965. Some forces used obsolete traffic patrol cars for general work though, because of the high petrol consumption, the practice was clearly uneconomic in the long run.[1] There was, however, a general swing towards motor cycles, though not all were high-powered machines. In 1938 23 per cent of all vehicles were motor cycles, by 1959, 40 per cent and by 1966 43 per cent.[2] In the Metropolitan police 52 per cent of all vehicles, well above the national average, were motor cycles in 1965.

The popularity of motor cycles was partly a reflection of the manpower shortage, it encouraged experiments with mechanized beat patrols—particularly in rural and suburban beats. The Metropolitan police, for example, began using lightweight motor cycles for patrolling outlying areas in 1956 and found the experi-

[1] Taverne Report, p. 77.
[2] *Inspectors of Constabulary from October 1958 to December 1959*, p. 11; *1959–60* (257), xx and Taverne Report, p. 76.

ment successful. The number of these motor cycles was 90 in 1957 and 228 two years later. Other forces, such as Cambridge (later part of Mid-Anglia) began using scooters. The difficulty of finding suitable vehicles which met the exacting requirements of police work was, however, greatest in the case of two-wheeled machines. They had to be extremely reliable, operational in all weathers and able to stand up to long hours of use with frequent stops and starts. In some rural beats in the north of the country scooters would have been virtually useless for part of the year. Other forces found that lightweight motor cycles did not stand up at all well to heavy police use. However, since there were no co-ordinated tests of equipment, and conditions varied so much from force to force that generalizations could be misleading, each force had to conduct its own user tests and make do with the equipment it had acquired.

The mechanization of beats did not stop at motor cycles. Various types of cars were used, either alone or to supplement foot beats, but problems arose. For example in 1963, the Metropolitan police found that radio patrol cars were spending so much time answering emergency calls that they were virtually useless for patrolling or traffic supervision.[1] A further difficulty was that by mechanizing beats, the police became so mobile that it was difficult for members of the public to attract their attention. The ground was covered, but at the cost of the contact with the public which is so essential if the police are to receive vital information and maintain good relations.

As the number of vehicles grew, however, new methods of policing, as opposed to merely mechanizing beat work, were developed. For example, some forces such as Bedfordshire and the Metropolitan police formed flying columns which could make surprise visits to an area, or suddenly double the number of policemen in a district for a week or more. The deterrent effect of such 'saturation tactics' was found to last for some time after the mobile police had been withdrawn.

The increase in the number of radio controlled vehicles allowed greater flexibility and made it possible for smaller forces to invest in more specialized types. For example, cars or vans with special equipment, such as dog vans or cars with tools for dealing with serious accidents, could not be left to roam the police area on the

[1] *Commissioner of Police of the Metropolis, 1963*, p. 8; 1963–64 Cmnd. 2408, xviii.

off-chance that they might encounter specialized work. With radio however they could join in general patrolling until a call for their specialized service was received, thus making better use of men and equipment.

As vehicle fleets grew and more expensive cars were bought, the problem of combining rational use and operational requirements became more urgent. Ideally a vehicle had to be in use at the very least sixteen hours a day (two or more shifts) if the financial outlay was to be justified.[1] On the other hand such intensive use often required very careful organization of beat work in conditions where there was in any case little room to manoeuvre because of the manpower shortage. The situation was also complicated by the problem of maintenance. Police work put considerable strain on vehicles and careful maintenance was essential, but arrangements varied in convenience and efficiency. Some forces had their own garages, mainly staffed by civilians, but others, especially the smaller forces, used the general local authority garage. When delays occurred, e.g. when a police car had to wait its turn among other local authority vehicles, operational arrangements could be upset.

To sum up, the police were in the process of transition from a predominantly pedestrian force to one in which a high degree of mobility was combined with specialized beat work designed primarily to maintain contact with the public. The detailed organization of vehicle deployment and maintenance required by those developments was still being evolved. Given the number and variety of conditions of work in British police forces it is not surprising that the process of transition was long drawn out and seemed likely to continue into the next decade.

*Communications*

There was greater progress in the use of vehicles than in the field of communications. The delays in setting up a reliable police wireless service in the years before 1950 have already been described (see Chapter III). They resulted chiefly from lack of money and insufficient technological expertise. After 1950 there was an improvement but a great deal remained to be done, even in 1967. With the exception of Lancashire, Birmingham and the

[1] *Inspector of Constabulary, 1963*, p. 54; 1963–64 (259), xviii.

Metropolitan police, all police wireless schemes were the direct responsibility of the Home Office and equipment was rented to individual forces. The same branch also provided radio communications for the fire service and the Civil Defence. In the fifties the first aim was to cover the country with a network of high frequency stations. By 1960 there was some coverage in all forces but the outlying areas of some counties were still without radio communications of any sort, and in many forces there were blank spots where the local signal was weak or unobtainable. Frequent breakdowns and slow maintenance work tended to prevent full and imaginative use being made of the equipment that existed and discouraged experimentation. There was a consequent tendency to consider radio as an unreliable and inflexible means of communication for police forces. Its development did not have high priority and in the mid-fifties the staff of the maintenance depots was actually reduced. In their annual reports for 1956 and 1957, the Inspectors drew attention to unsatisfactory maintenance work[1] but there was some improvement in the sixties.

One important development was the increase in the number of radio-telephone sets on motor cycles and in cars and vans. In 1958 there were about 400 cars and the same number of motor cycles with radio equipment. By 1965 the number was 5,000 cars and 3,250 motor cycles. There was, however, still room for further progress. The advantages of radio telephony in deploying men, meeting emergencies and increasing overall mobility are almost too obvious to need mention.

All the problems that were encountered in the development of ordinary police radio communications applied in far greater measure to personal radios. Their advantages were again obvious. They allowed a man to move freely about an area and yet be in constant communication with headquarters, whereas before he could only be contacted at certain fixed times and places. Knowledge that help could be quickly summoned gave a man greater confidence when dealing with a difficult situation. Despite the advantages, there was still in 1967 no entirely satisfactory personal radio for the police.[2] Sets were developed in Lancashire

---

[1] *Inspectors of Constabulary, 1956*, p. 17, and ditto 1957, p. 22; 1956–57 (210), xviii; 1957–58 (218) xvii

[2] Taverne Report, p. 89.

and some other forces, but were not wholly successful. Similarly, early experiments by the Home Office were not a complete success and private trials organized by manufacturers also failed to produce a perfect set. At first the sets were too large and bulky for easy use. This difficulty was overcome but there were still problems of reliability and clarity of reception. Ideally a set had to be capable of being used by beat constables in shifts for most of each twenty-four hours. Few pocket sets were designed to withstand such strenuous conditions. A force which hired sets could therefore rarely expect to have the full complement in use at any one time and, under the circumstances, they naturally tended to be used for emergencies such as searches, or for crowd control at large meetings, and not as items of day to day police equipment.

The police had, of course, developed line communications at an early date and progress continued. Private telephone systems and internal teleprinters were supplemented by inter-force tele-printer lines and telex. The number of telex subscribers was 3 in 1955 and 98 in 1965, which, with joint arrangements, gave almost complete coverage. The equipment was rented from the G.P.O. and, where a force was too small to justify an individual subscription, it either arranged for access to the equipment of a larger force or joined with a group of small forces in a co-operative scheme. Facsimile transmitting equipment was installed at the regional Criminal Record Offices in the early sixties and by 1963 all the regional offices were linked with the central Metropolitan Criminal Record Office. The system allowed high quality repro-ductions of such things as photographs and enlarged fingerprints to be quickly sent between Offices. Further research was however needed before the high installation costs of the system could be justified if it was to be used as a normal means of communication within and between police forces.

*Other central services*

The need for nationally provided police services which were beyond the financial resources of individual police authorities was recognized increasingly after 1950. Central services were not limited to wireless and training. The work begun in the inter-war years was continued and expanded (see Ch. III).

*Forensic science laboratories*

A regional laboratory had been established in each Police District by 1950 though the Metropolitan police laboratory was too short of space to function properly as a District service. It was the only one not run directly by the Home Office, but received a central government grant from 1958 onwards. Table IV.17 sets out the total current expenditure on laboratories. There was an increase of 20 per cent from 1950 to 1951, but after that the rate of growth was slower until 1961. The greatest increases occurred between 1963 and 1965, when expenditure rose by 70 per cent. The laboratories were staffed mainly by civilians and had the advantage over many other fields of civilian work in the police that there was a career structure and the opportunity to do original research work for those who could find the time. The number of

TABLE IV.17

**Current expenditure on forensic science laboratories**

|  | £000 |  | £000 |  | £000 |  | £000 |
|---|---|---|---|---|---|---|---|
| 1950* | 77·5 | 1954 | 106·7 | 1958 | 146·9 | 1962 | 200·0 |
| 1951 | 92·3 | 1955 | 113·2 | 1959 | 151·4 | 1963 | 200·0 |
| 1952 | 92·5 | 1956 | 127·6 | 1960 | 165·2 | 1964 | 262·0 |
| 1953 | 92·3 | 1957 | 141·3 | 1961 | 206·0 | 1965 | 339·0 |

* The statistics refer to financial years.

SOURCE: *Civil Estimates.*

staff increased from 84 to 140 during the period with the main expansion towards the end.

There were two main factors preventing the laboratories from being as useful to the police service as they might have been. The first was lack of money and the second the shortage of officers trained to collect scientific evidence from scenes of crime. Like other central services, they could easily have used more funds. All the laboratories were short of space and needed more staff. Work piled up and the police forces were discouraged from using the service as freely as they might because in many cases the delays were so long. The other problem was that their facilities for training scenes of crime officers were limited by the same shortages of time and space. The laboratories, however, depended on these officers for most of their material. The ordinary policeman or even detective constable was not trained to find and photograph marks and specimens and the advantage of having specially trained officers was officially recognized in 1961.[1] By 1964, it was clear that the number of clues found was very much higher wherever trained officers were available but at the same time training had to be temporarily discontinued for lack of space. The laboratories were therefore not able to make their full potential contribution to the work of the police during the period. However, one achievement was a more constructive attitude to laboratory work which spread through the service.

There were other central government contributions to the efficiency of the British police service. In long-term importance the most notable development was probably the establishment of the Police Research and Planning Branch[2] at the Home Office in 1963. The branch was staffed by seconded police officers and Home Office scientists. Their job was to evaluate police methods and equipment, publicize the most successful and evolve long-term plans at a national level. Their influence was only beginning to be apparent in 1965, but by 1966 the Select Committee on Estimates was recommending that 'the Home Secretary review the establishment of the branch with the intention of substantially increasing its size and expertise'.[3]

The other notable central development was the creation of the Regional Crime Squads. Such squads were first formed on local initiative when chief officers found that police boundaries were preventing them from dealing with highly organized mobile criminals. The Metropolitan and Provincial Crime Branch, formed in 1954, was the forerunner of the scheme. The branch was composed jointly of Metropolitan and home counties detectives and concentrated on travelling criminals. A similar organization was set up by Birmingham and the neighbouring forces in 1956. Bristol and Newcastle followed and in 1964 it was decided that there should be nine squads, one for each District. A national co-ordinator was appointed in 1965 and paid out of central funds. The scheme was regarded as experimental and the Home Office Police Research and Planning Branch set up a project for studying the methods and results of the squads. Like the various other central services and District co-operation arrangements, such as

---

[1] *Inspectors of Constabulary, 1961*, p. 20; 1961–62 (220), xx.
[2] Since retitled Police Research and Development Branch.
[3] *Estimates*, Sel. Cttee. 1st Report, p. xv; 1966–67 (145).

criminal record offices, the scheme was intended to enable the police to keep pace with modern developments without losing the advantages of their traditional organization. Individual forces could not operate efficiently in isolation when they were faced with highly organized crime or massive traffic congestion. On the other hand, a thorough knowledge of local people and local conditions was essential in order to control local crime (which had also increased over the years), and to carry out many other police activities successfully. Amalgamations were intended to eliminate the worst disadvantages of small size. A two-tiered organization of local forces and inter-force units and services was designed to enable the separate forces to function in a modern setting.

*Conclusions*

At the end of the second world war, the police service was short of men, equipment and of buildings. The period 1950 to 1965 covered the end of the post-war recovery and the beginning of far-reaching changes. The cost of the police at current prices rose by 200 per cent. All changes in expenditure were dwarfed by the steady rise in the bill for wages and salaries, which was never less than 70 per cent of the total. Police pay at a time of rising national wages was constantly under discussion, but never reached the relatively high levels of the inter-war years. In 1950 the constables' pay was slightly above the national average wage for men in manufacturing industry and it remained ahead in most years. If pay and allowances could have been compared with average earnings, the police position would probably have looked slightly more favourable, but there seems little doubt that the financial status of the police was lower than before the war.

The size of the police force increased steadily, but at the same time, holidays were extended and the length of the working week fell. In terms of man-hours the increase in the numbers was the dominant factor. By 1961 the annual number of manhours worked per head of the population had passed the nineteenth-century peak. By 1965 it was 15 per cent higher than it had been before the first world war, despite the introduction of the 42-hour week which, in 1966, was being worked by 33 per cent of constables.[1] Crime rates and vehicles per head of the population had, however,

[1] See Table VI.5.

risen even faster and the police were dealing with far more work.

Increase in manpower alone could not have met the growing pressure. Greater specialization, better equipment and training and larger units of operation were all important. Specialized traffic patrols were developed. The number of women police increased. Civilians were much more widely employed, first on general clerical and communications work, but increasingly in the specialized fields of mechanical data processing, scientific and technical work. Traffic wardens, introduced in 1960, were the most striking example of the use of civilians to extend the scope of policing. The logical development of growing specialization was the unit beat system which was in use in a few forces by 1965. It allowed an area to be policed by combinations of specialists in contrast to the old system where the beat constable had few precise duties, and specialists were on call rather than attached to any particular area.

The need for greater mobility and flexibility resulted in an increase in the number of police vehicles, particularly motor cycles, and the number equipped with radio increased even faster after 1960. The problems of police radio communications which had held up developments since the thirties were close to solution by 1965. The countryside network was completed in the sixties and work on a police personal radio was increasingly successful. The scientific side of police work developed more slowly. Laboratories were unable to expand for lack of funds and staff. Methods of storing and exchanging information improved but much remained to be done.

More training was essential to meet the increase in the technical content of police work and keep constables up to date with the growing volume of law. Recruit training continued to be the most important activity but specialized courses increased in number and scope. The Police College, detective training centres and driving schools all developed more advanced, specialized courses. Individual forces also increased the amount of time spent on training, mostly in the form of short courses on the use of new equipment or the implications of new laws.

The trend towards larger units of operation continued. By 1965, 52 out of the 125 forces had strengths, including civilians, of more than 500. It was, however, clear that policing could no longer be based entirely on local force areas. Inter-force co-operation proved essential for patrolling the motorways. Regional crime squads were set up in an effort to control highly organized mobile criminals. In the Home Office the Police Research and Planning Branch was established to undertake research and to disseminate the best existing police practice to all forces. Following the amalgamations proposed by the Home Secretary in 1966, it seemed likely that by 1970 the number of forces would have been reduced by half and the traditional beat system almost entirely replaced.

# V

# The Design of a Manpower Survey

*The general problem*

OUR previous chapters have shown how the structure of the police service was established during the middle years of the nineteenth century, and how it has since been modified. This description has been expressed primarily in terms of finance, and of manpower. Quite early in this history certain key issues began to emerge, and our story has turned on how they were handled at different times, and the consequences which followed the adoption of particular policies.

These issues have all been of a broad nature. Thus we have considered the strength of the service, its structure in terms of numbers of forces and their organization, the trend towards specialization with its implications for training and the development of the technical aspects of police work. These facets of manpower have also been related to the use of capital resources, firstly in the form of police buildings and houses, latterly more and more in the form of transport, communications and technical equipment. We have also shown how the initiative has passed to and fro between Chief Constables, Police Authorities and the Central Government.

So far we have been mainly concerned with the establishment of the service, and relatively little with the nature of the work done and the demands it has made on the manpower available. We now turn our attention to these aspects.

Police forces have many functions. We have shown how the various concerns of police work have waxed and waned at different periods. As reformed during the nineteenth century the service had as its prime aims the maintenance of public order and, by its public presence, the prevention of crime; only later did it develop its two other main activities—criminal investigation and the supervision of traffic. Other duties have accumulated—the preparation of and participation in court work, supervision of aliens, animal movements and other quasi administrative activities —while purely civil, perhaps almost social work, tasks have always been undertaken and may even be gaining in importance.

Comments on such matters often imply that one form of duty has come to take an unreasonable proportion of police time, to the neglect of other functions. For example, the Secretary of the Police Federation in a press interview said, 'Another of our big worries . . . is the time spent hanging around in courtrooms when policemen could be usefully occupied elsewhere'.[1] Similar complaints are frequently made about traffic supervision, the escorting of prisoners to remand homes, the writing of reports and so on. The fact that time so occupied seems, to the person concerned, to have achieved little, naturally generates a feeling of frustration which, in turn, is likely to lead to an exaggeration of the time involved. However, although many people have held strong beliefs about such matters they have not usually been based on more than impressions, simply because the comprehensive enquiries necessary to establish the facts on more than a local scale have not been conducted.

One of the principal aims of this research, therefore, has been to investigate the variety of duties undertaken by the police, and to estimate how effort has been distributed between them. No one can be certain how the service will develop in the future, but a rational and informed discussion of the possibilities must be based on firm knowledge of the present situation.

Although it is a commonplace that the nature of police duties has been changing, very little information has been available up to now concerning the overall pattern of work and its demands in terms of manpower, equipment and capital investment in the form of buildings. In the earlier parts of this book we have used the existing published, and in some cases unpublished, information to present a broad outline of trends in expenditure on the service as a whole, and covered certain aspects in more detail. This allowed us to isolate some specific topics, for example the development of training, but it was impossible to allocate the bulk of expenditure according to purpose or to the area of activity involved. An allocation which would do justice to the complexity of modern police work could not be made until new and more

[1] Reported in the *Daily Mail* 22 November 1965.

precise data were obtained.[1] We decided, therefore, to conduct our own surveys to obtain the necessary information.

Our main interest was in obtaining data relevant to some rather broad questions of policy. As with any organization designed to solve a variety of problems the emphasis on one aspect of police work as against another is in each force partly a matter of choice. The problems dealt with, and the amount of attention given to them, depend on how important the police perceive them to be. Sometimes, as with homicide, major robberies and so on, the problem is so serious and so public as to be unavoidable;[2] but with lesser, or more concealed, offences (particularly those of a sexual or domestic nature), the policy of a particular force, the zeal of individual officers, and indeed the sheer volume of work may be all important. Well-known examples of local policy may be cited: in 1963 the then Chief Constable of Southend on Sea announced that he did not intend to take police action against every shoplifter,[3] while in Manchester a change of policy towards the offence of male importuning led to an apparent increase in that offence from 2 cases in 1958 to 135 in 1961 and 216 in 1962.[4]

In addition to the direct influence of policy whether local or

---

[1] We are, of course, glad to acknowledge the pioneering work carried out in certain forces: the Metropolitan police, in connection with the Dixon Report on the organization of the force (unpublished) and, most notably, the surveys carried out in the Durham and Lancashire Constabularies respectively in 1948 and 1965 under the inspiration of Col. T. E. St Johnston (now Sir Eric St Johnston, H.M. Chief Inspector of Constabulary). Only the Durham survey however, appeared before our own work began. The Lancashire survey—whose results have kindly been made available by Sir Eric St Johnston—was conducted concurrently with our own. The lessons learned from these surveys are discussed below, see p. 127.

[2] Even homicide, however, may be investigated with less than zeal under certain circumstances, e.g. the murder of one negro by another in some Southern states of the U.S.A. See for example Guy B. Johnson 'The Negro and Crime' reprinted in Marvin E. Wolfgang *et al.* (ed.) *The Sociology of Crime and Delinquency*, New York, John Wiley & Sons, 1962, pp. 145–53.

[3] *The Times* reported the Chief Constable as saying: ' "There are many cases where offences of shoplifting entail trifling values and I am not prepared to prosecute at the public expense if no good purpose can be served." He said that each case reported would be investigated and if it is felt that the person will not commit another similar offence, is not a persistent offender, and the value of property is small, no further action will be taken by the police.' *The Times* 26 February 1963, p. 10.

[4] Reported in *Supplementary Criminal Statistics*.

national there is the underlying power of tradition—both of the service as a whole and of each force. The trend towards fewer forces together with the development of shared facilities, particularly training, are likely to produce more and more of a common pattern influencing all work to some extent. Nevertheless each force also has its own characteristics stemming largely from the lead given by its chief constable. One may be particularly concerned with crime prevention, one with the maintenance of public order, another with the close supervision of traffic and yet another with equipment and technical innovations. Such interests are, of course, combined in a variety of ways to produce the diversity of forces found in this country.

Our need, therefore, was to discover sufficient about the present situation[1] and its emphasis to enable us to break down the total cost of the service according to its various functions and activities. It seemed to us that any such allocation would have to be based on the fact that, for most of the post-war period, about 70 per cent of the total cost of the police service consisted of wages, salaries and pensions.[2] In short, the use of manpower was all important. Any allocation should start by ascertaining the time spent on each significant activity, and the estimate of cost should be derived from this.

We first considered whether adequate estimates could be inferred from the departmental structure of each force. Some possibilities existed in this direction as certain departments have quite specialized duties. For a number of reasons, however, a departmental classification is not sufficient. Even the specialist departments such as Criminal Investigation, Road Traffic, Dog handlers, Administration and so on, cover a range of other work which cannot be inferred from their titles, and which may involve varying proportions of their time. For example, Road Traffic departments are liable to be concerned with matters such as crime, or even accidents which have nothing to do with traffic. To label all this 'traffic work' would disguise and diminish the variety of duties encompassed.[3]

---

[1] The possibility of conducting surveys were first investigated in 1963, a pilot was undertaken in 1964 and the main sequence followed in 1965, and early 1966.

[2] See Chapter IV, p. 72.

[3] As an example of this may be cited the history of the South West Traffic

Specialization, moreover, is likely to be more extensive in larger forces, smaller ones having to involve individual officers in a wider range of activities. Above all, the bulk of each force, the officers 'on the beat' have to deal with whatever crops up during their patrols, and there is an immense range of possibilities. It seemed to us that nothing short of a field survey of the time actually spent on the different functions would give information accurate enough for our purposes.[1]

Having decided to conduct such a survey three main problems of method had to be solved: the choice of recording procedure; how to classify the work done by individuals, and how to select the sample of individuals to be surveyed. Our solutions to these problems are discussed in the next section.

## (a) *Recording procedure*

Surveys of work done by individuals involve a choice between two main methods of recording. The first consists of techniques by which each individual's activities are recorded either by an observer or by mechanical devices of one kind or another, both being external to the person observed. The second is to get the individual himself to record what he does. Each method has its pros and cons, some of a more general nature, others specifically relevant to a survey of police work.

Recording by an observer is likely to have advantages in terms of accuracy, as recording is the observer's primary duty. On the other hand his presence may affect the way the work is done. Most important of all, however, is the fact that each observer

---

experiment, in which 500 miles of road were intensively patrolled, primarily as an experiment in traffic policing. The Chief Constable of Devon and Exeter commented 'As regards crime, it is very interesting that we had 296 arrests for all causes, drunks in charge and so on, but there was quite a lot of crime dealt with by these patrols which, shall we say, we were not looking for, but it was a very useful and very valuable bonus on the scheme.' (*Estimates*, Sel. Cttee. 1st Report: Minutes of Evidence Q.916, p. 142; 1966–67 (145).

[1] The mechanics of arranging the surveys will not be mentioned at this point, except to say that they could not have been undertaken without the support of Her Majesty's Inspectors of Constabulary, the Police Department of the Home Office, the Association of Chief Police Officers of England and Wales and, of course, of the Chief Constables of the forces concerned. We are indebted to all of them for their constructive assistance.

normally can follow only one, or at most a few, subjects at a time. As our enquiry was intended to discover the broad pattern of police work, and to take some note of possible types of variation between forces of different kinds, it would need quite a large sample, or samples, of individuals. The numbers likely to be involved, therefore, ruled out the use of observers and made self-recording methods essential.

There were also strong positive reasons in favour of this decision. First, was the fact that we could get information on a far larger scale than by any other method. Second, a procedure could be devised so that the data could be recorded with a minimum of delay, thus reducing the risk of errors creeping in due to unnecessary reliance on memory. Third, such a method is peculiarly appropriate when dealing with the police. This is because the making of a written record of his work is a fundamental part of a police officer's job. To a degree quite unusual in most jobs the police officer is trained to record every significant incident in which he is involved. The extent and thoroughness of such recording are two of the features that strike the observer of police life most forcibly when he first encounters them. Provided our survey could attract the same conscientiousness, self-recording should be entirely satisfactory.

The disadvantages of self-recording are primarily that the individual is tempted to record what he thinks the research worker wants to see, and what will show him in the best light both in the research and before his own superiors. There is also scope for non-co-operation by deliberate omission, perfunctory or even inaccurate recording.

We devoted considerable care, therefore, to ensuring that the operation went smoothly. We emphasized that all we wanted was the most accurate account possible of the work of the force as a whole. We were not going to be concerned with the work of individuals, and the results would not be in a form which could be used for criticizing anyone's work. Opportunities for 'cooking the books' certainly existed, but as no one (including ourselves) knew how this could be done to best advantage the risk seemed to be minimized.

Although we started with the indispensable support of the Chief Officers of each force we thought it vital to justify and explain the research to all ranks. This was done through a briefing procedure designed to give the maximum possible number of members of the force a chance to see, hear and question a member of the research team.

Before describing the briefing procedure as such we should explain that, for a self-recording survey, we decided that the work of each force should be surveyed for a fortnight. We had to avoid too short a period, which might have been highly untypical, and too long a one, which might have imposed too great a burden on the force and led to a loss of interest and co-operation. A week would have been rather short, while a month would have been too long. Two weeks seemed a reasonable compromise.

With our limited research staff it would have been quite impossible to survey all forces simultaneously—though this might have had advantages for comparative purposes—and we decided to cover areas consecutively, often with an overlap of a week between two surveys. In the event this programme was disrupted and had to be spread over a longer period than originally planned.[1]

The surveys of the provincial forces were conducted between February and November 1965, and the Metropolitan survey was held in April 1966.[2] The procedure varied slightly from force to force depending on circumstances, in particular the amount of travelling entailed in briefing the force. A more or less common pattern rapidly evolved, and took the following form.

Each force was asked to designate a liaison officer to work with the Institute's representative. Liaison officers made all the arrangements for meetings at which members of the force could be briefed, accompanied the research worker while in the area, and usually became so well informed about the survey that they were able to deal with many queries themselves. Their help was invaluable.

Recording booklets, which included printed instructions, were dispatched to forces about ten days before the survey period was due to begin. The liaison officer then saw they were distributed to all members of the force taking part in the survey in time for them to be studied before the briefing began.

[1] Our original plans were for all the surveys to be supervised by one Research Officer, Mr J. Bradley. To our great dismay he died suddenly during the survey of the first force and subsequent arrangements had, therefore, to be improvised. The programme could not have been maintained with so little disruption had we not been able to obtain the assistance of two colleagues who took over at short notice and carried the bulk of the load.

[2] The selection of forces is discussed below, see p. 134 and Appendix C,

The exact procedure varied from force to force but essentially the briefing was divided into two phases—introductory explanation with discussion and, later, a follow up to deal with queries. Because of its crucial importance it is worth while to describe a fairly typical briefing.

All our surveys began on a Monday and lasted fourteen days. About the middle of the week before the survey was due to begin a member of the research team arrived at the force Headquarters. He would meet the Chief Constable, who would then introduce the liaison officer. The research worker's first task was to make the liaison officer fully conversant with the project and to obtain his advice on any special aspects of police work in the locality. Usually all queries were routed through the liaison officers and they soon gained enough understanding of the research to be able to handle most questions themselves.

We then held as many briefing meetings as could be arranged. These were attended by representatives of most ranks, with particular emphasis on inspectors and sergeants, as the officers most closely concerned with the rank and file. Such meetings varied in size from half a dozen up to a maximum of about 200. The research worker usually started with an introductory talk about the background of the survey, discussed how the booklet was to be completed, then answered questions and tried to deal with comments and criticisms. Most such meetings lasted between one and two hours.

All in all these were stimulating occasions. The survey was the first of its kind to be conducted by an outside organization, and some doubts as to the value of the operation were only to be expected. We felt it better that they should be expressed and openly discussed rather than be stifled and left to linger. We invited as much comment and criticism as possible over a wide range of topics. Thus we dealt not only with the details of recording, but also with how the results would be handled and, indeed, with any aspects of police life which people liked to raise. Obviously some were unconvinced, but in the main the response was most heartening.

Although such meetings were the means by which we met the largest number of men and women, they were not the only medium. In small forces, and in the rural areas of county forces, we spent much time driving round visiting officers individually and in small groups. Such occasions were shorter and less formal, but they were also more direct and concerned with the specific problems arising in each locality.

Having concluded the initial meetings the research worker then had to sit back and wait until the survey actually began. Once the booklets had been in use a few hours, say by the middle of the first Monday morning, he began to tour the force seeing as many individuals as possible. The usual form was to examine the booklets in use, to ask how officers were getting on with them, and whether any snags had been encountered.

Such tours were made at all hours of the day and night, paying particular attention to the need to cover all three shifts and officers doing as wide a variety of jobs as possible. Depending on the size of force we reckoned at this stage to meet at least a third of even the largest force individually; in smaller forces we would see almost every man and woman. Queries from the remainder would go through the liaison officer and would either be answered by him direct or passed on to the research worker.

(b) *Classification of activities*

For the purposes of recording all work done over a given period it was necessary to devise a suitable classification. This involved balancing several considerations—the need to subdivide police work in terms of the functions it was intended to fulfil and according to the area of activity involved, to isolate civil work and, generally, to provide information relevant to policy. The classification, furthermore, would have to be practical enough to be usable under ordinary working conditions.

To satisfy the criterion of practicability we believed we should produce a recording booklet which would be reasonably easy to use, and which could be carried in the breast pocket of a policeman's uniform. Other surveys of police work had, we thought, erred on the rather high proportion of time being put under some general heading such as 'miscellaneous'. While some such category is unavoidable we tried to keep the classifications relatively few in order to reduce the temptation to class too much time under 'general duties'.

Initially, therefore, we devised a recording booklet which allowed for 20 categories of activity. Through the co-operation of the Chief Constable of Bedfordshire we were able to conduct a pilot survey, which enabled us to test the classifications and also to discover what procedural problems were likely to be encountered. Various modifications were made in the light of this experience, and it was found that some classifications could easily be subdivided, so that in the end we managed to distinguish 23 types of activity. The booklet had 14 pages, each with space to record a whole day's work. All time was recorded in quarter-hour units, and where a variety of things were done during a quarter of an hour the one occupying the largest proportion of time was recorded. In addition there was space for recording certain details of interest to Chief Officers, such as the time spent in Police Stations, while the cover was used for summarizing the work of the whole fortnight.[1]

The subdividing of work according to the functions it was intended to fulfil was, from the first, one of our main aims in undertaking this research. We regarded it as fundamental to our purpose to devise a way of setting the expenditure of *all* services having any connection with crime into a common framework. Our initial formulation[2] of the idea used three main heads: Law Enforcement, Administration of Justice and the Treatment of Offenders. There was also a residual category of Civil Duties, in which we included activities which were either purely civil, or at least hardly seemed to merit the description 'law enforcement'. 'Law Enforcement' was to cover all those activities concerned with the prevention and detection of crime which preceded, in terms of time, criminal prosecutions and the work attendant upon them in each case. Thus it would include such major activities as the investigation of crimes, the preservation of public order, dealing with traffic incidents where criminal proceedings were likely, and general patrolling.

The Administration of Justice covered all activities within, or supportive of, the courts. This included not only the giving of evidence (together with relevant waiting or travelling time), but also the preparation of antecedents,[3] issuing of summonses, escort-

---

[1] The booklet is reproduced in facsimile in Appendix A.

[2] J. P. Martin and J. Bradley, 'Design of a Study of the Cost of Crime', *British Journal of Criminology*, Vol. IV, No. 6, October 1964.

[3] Statements concerning an offender's criminal record, prepared by the police and made available to the court between the finding of guilt and the passing of sentence.

ing prisoners remanded in custody (before sentence) and so on. All these activities should be treated as costs of the administration of justice, as they are essential services without which the courts could not operate.

Finally, the 'treatment of offenders'—using that phrase in a sense which does not necessarily imply therapy—covered everything done to or for an offender from the moment of sentence until his final release from any legal constraints following from that sentence. The main forms of penal treatment are outside the functions of the police, and for the purposes of this survey were likely to be relatively unimportant. Any police contribution would probably be in the running of Attendance Centres, some escort work and Juvenile Liaison work with offenders after they have been formally cautioned.

A functional breakdown of this kind, however, is only one way of analysing police activity. While reasonable as far as it goes it is not very precise and is probably more appropriate to a study covering a number of services (for which, after all, it was originally intended). It was necessary, therefore, to use other types of subdivision as well.

The alternative broad grouping of activities was in terms of what we called Areas of Operation. We distinguished four of these: traffic, crime, civil order and internal organization. They require little explanation, except perhaps to point out that they did not allow us to differentiate between, for example, different forms of traffic work such as supervision and court work. Broadly speaking all work directly concerned with traffic was included under that heading, and this included patrolling by members of traffic departments.[1]

'Crime' covered all investigations of crimes, the gathering of criminal intelligence, keeping observation on premises where there were reasons to expect a crime to be committed, court work and also the very small amount of after conviction work that was done.

Civil Order was the phrase we used to cover all work that was concerned with incidents which were unequivocally civil in nature

---

[1] The subdivision of patrolling was somewhat arbitrary. Patrol work by the traffic department was allocated to traffic, and all other patrolling to Civil Order. It is clear that men on the beat keep an eye on traffic, while equally traffic patrols may deal with pedestrians. It seemed reasonable to treat these two overlaps as if they cancelled each other out.

(for example a policeman is called to an accident where a painter has fallen off a ladder) and also public work of a general character, i.e. those parts of patrolling where no directly criminal or traffic work was undertaken. Also in this category was work specifically classified under 'public order'. This covered the handling of processions, political demonstrations, crowds at major incidents (such as fires) and so on.

Internal Organization was intended to cover those relatively domestic matters necessary simply to keep the force running— pay, pensions, housing, buying of stores and equipment and so on. Many people would describe this work as 'administration', and initially we did so ourselves, but we came to realize that in a police context this was misleading. All forces have Administration Departments, but these usually cover a far wider range of functions than such domestic matters. They may cover, for example, almost all correspondence with outside bodies of any kind, the preparation of statistics, the issuing of summonses and warrants, licensing, training and so on. The list of jobs undertaken varies from force to force. As far as possible we tried to get members of administration departments to classify their work according to what their work was concerned with, rather than give it the blanket title of administration. After the first few surveys we did this by changing the term and referring to Internal Organization.

These two breakdowns of work—according to functions and to areas of operation—while informative, do not, however, provide sufficient detail to answer more than the broadest questions. Once launched on the recording process it seemed sensible to get as much detailed information as was practicable. We subdivided, therefore, these broad groupings to cover as many other points as we could manage. This involved a number of other considerations.

The first and simplest was the need to isolate all purely civil work. This was done by having a classification entitled 'Civil Incidents' (which included all such matters as civil accidents, helping lost children and so on). Also simple to isolate were 'Private Duties'. These are the occasions when police officers are hired to operate on private premises—the most common being attendance at sporting occasions such as football matches.

Traffic work (other than court work) was divided into three categories: supervision, dealing with accidents unlikely to result in court proceedings, and dealing with incidents likely to result in proceedings. The first of these covered all forms of direct supervision, such as point duty, school crossings, directing traffic at diversions, and so on. It also included a few aspects of traffic work, which did not fit in well anywhere else, such as the escorting of wide loads, traffic planning and road safety. Incidents were divided according to whether or not they were likely to result in proceedings. This involved the officer having to judge what was likely to happen, and we asked officers simply to use their experience of such matters; no attempt was made to correct these judgements in the light of subsequent events. In practice, however, relatively little work was classified under the 'No process', i.e. no proceedings, heading and it would probably have been possible to have excluded this as a classification.

The various types of court work were divided to distinguish between Juvenile (all types of case being grouped together), Traffic (Magistrates' and Higher Courts also being combined), Civil and Coroners' and Criminal (subdivided into Magistrates' and Higher Courts). 'After-Conviction' work was simply divided according to whether it was with Adults or Juveniles.

A rather different expenditure of time constituted what in the police service is often termed *Abstractions*. This might be defined as time officially accounted for but during which the individual is not directly available for active duty. Most of this time goes on Training (including instructing), Leave, Sickness and Refreshment breaks. A very small amount of work connected with sport, often concerned with the administration of sporting events, may also be included under this heading. We separated each of these five types of abstraction.

We could not avoid some general categories, of which the two most important were patrolling and general duties. Patrolling was defined as time spent on patrol when not dealing with specific incidents, while general duties covered a variety of miscellaneous activities which could not be included elsewhere. Examples of general duties are manning switch-boards, vehicle maintenance, dealing with miscellaneous queries at the enquiry desk, supervision of other officers, giving public lectures and so on. We tried to minimize the use of such a category, but inevitably some time had to be recorded under this heading.

Finally, we should mention 'Foreign Enquiries'. Their importance is administrative, in that they represent work done on behalf of other organizations and this has some bearing on such matters as the size of police areas. They fall into three main types: enquiries for other police forces, work done for other public bodies, and replying to queries from special classes of the public, e.g. solicitors, insurance companies and so on. Work under this heading could not be subdivided according to its nature without using more space than we had available, but fortunately the total time involved was far less than expected, so that the lack of sub-division was unimportant.

Having described the classifications it might be helpful to show them in tabular form and this is done below in Table V.1.

Although such a scheme looks tidy, and has a rational basis, inevitably there are problems of interpretation. The detailed instructions issued with the booklet (in its final version) are included in Appendix A, but the problem of overlap must be mentioned here. Many activities can easily be put into a category, but in some cases more than one might seem equally appropriate. For example, if the police stop a car at night because it appears to be being driven dangerously they may find it is being used without its owner's consent, by a driver who is uninsured. Both traffic and criminal offences are involved. Similar considerations might apply in cases of sudden deaths which might be entirely civil matters, but might also involve crime.

Without going into detail, our general principles were, at the incident and investigation stage, to give priority to the element of crime (if at all applicable), while at the Court stage the same rule held unless the offender was a juvenile. The net result of this may have been slightly to underestimate the amount of work arising out of traffic situations, even if it was more correctly treated as crime.

## (c) *Selection of the sample*

Although it was fairly easy to decide to conduct a sample survey, the operation presented a number of problems. These are discussed in more detail in Appendix C, but the main considerations should be mentioned here.

A completely random sample of police officers and civilians drawn from the whole country seemed out of the question. The

TABLE V.I

Relationships between allocation of active duty by function and by area of operation

| FUNCTION | AREA OF OPERATION | | | |
|---|---|---|---|---|
| | Crime | Traffic | Civil Order | Internal Organization |
| Law Enforcement | Crime Investigations | Patrolling (Traffic Dept.) Traffic Incidents (Possible process) | Patrolling (non-Traffic) Public Order | |
| Civil Duties | | Traffic Supervision Traffic Accidents (No process) | Civil Incidents Private Duties | |
| Administration of Justice | Criminal Courts (Magistrates') Criminal Courts (Higher) Criminal Courts (Juvenile) | Traffic Courts | Civil and Coroners' Courts | |
| Treatment of Offenders | After Conviction (Adults) After Conviction (Juveniles) | | | Internal Organization |

briefing and administration of the survey would have involved almost insuperable difficulties for a small research unit, and we should have been unable to draw an accurate picture of the work of even one force.

On the other hand the fact that the police service was disciplined and highly organized allowed us to consider the alternative plan of including all members (of certain ranks) of a sample of forces. This is what we decided to do. Operating in this way we reckoned we could cover a total sample of about 10 per cent of forces and of the men and women in the service.[1]

We included all ranks likely to have jobs which were not wholly supervisory. As the work of the more senior officers is almost entirely supervisory we excluded Superintendents and above.[2] We already knew that they formed a very small proportion of the total strength, they are usually very busy and our procedure was not designed to record the nature of supervision as such, so that the results of including them might have been of doubtful value. Should we later wish to divide their salaries and allowances according to function it would, in the absence of a special survey, be quite reasonable to make the division according to the pattern of work of those under their command. Civilians whose functions were domestic were also excluded.

The selection of forces was a complex matter. The survey was planned in 1964 when there were 123 provincial forces in England and Wales, ranging in size from the small (less than 150 police officers) to the largest (Lancashire, with over 3,600 officers).[3] They varied also in other respects—degree of urbanization, stability of population, volume of traffic, volume of crime, seasonal pattern of work (particularly in seaside areas), and so on.

Although it seemed likely that some of the characteristics mentioned above would be relevant to the distribution of work in the various forces there was no evidence from which we could infer the optimum stratification, yet clearly areas varied so much that some stratification was desirable. It was decided that we should aim to sample one force from each of eleven cells repre-

---

[1] Appendix C also gives details of the sample of forces.

[2] Chief Inspectors and above in the Metropolitan police. This was largely a matter of convenience.

[3] The Metropolitan police was covered at a later stage on a rather different basis. See pages 135.6.

senting different types of force. A further complication was that some sixty-one forces were taking part in a survey of drunkenness being undertaken on behalf of the Home Office and, in order to minimize the burden on them, we were requested to exclude them from our sampling frame.

The basis of the stratification is summarized in Appendix C but the essence of the procedure was as follows: first, we treated all seaside Borough forces as a stratum in themselves, on the assumption that their work was likely to be dominated by the seasonal characteristics of the areas; second, we separated off the very large forces (Boroughs with average strengths of 800 or more, Counties with 1,000 or more); third, the remaining forces were separated into counties and boroughs, each of these in turn being divided into larger and smaller, and finally these larger and smaller forces were split according to whether they were in areas of high or low crime.[1] This process, however, left us short of the 10 per cent which we thought desirable for the size of the sample, and one larger county (Bedfordshire) was added.

Our surveys in the Metropolitan Police District were, through the force of events, conducted on a rather different basis. We had originally intended to follow the survey of the provincial forces with one in the Metropolitan Police District, but owing to the death of the research officer concerned this plan was reluctantly abandoned. However, in February 1966 the House of Commons' Select Committee on Estimates asked if it would be possible to revise our plans and, in effect, revert to our original intention of covering the force, but within the short period of four months. The Institute agreed to make the attempt in spite of the problems of fitting in so much extra work without any extension of our timetable.[2]

Owing to the size and structure of the Metropolitan police, together with the tight schedule, it was impracticable to sample the whole force. The force consisted, in September 1965,[3] of nearly 19,000 Police Officers. Of these some 3,500 were employed either

[1] This was defined as being above or below the median rate of crime per 1,000 of the population for Boroughs and Counties respectively.

[2] This represented an increase of about 30 per cent on our original workload, to be completed without any increase in the time available.

[3] These figures are based on those given in the Report of the Select Committee on Estimates. *Estimates*, Sel. Cttee. 1st Report: Memorandum submitted by the Receiver for the Metropolitan Police District, p. 48; 1966–67 (145).

in Specialist units or at Headquarters, the remainder being divided between 23 land divisions. In addition, the force employed about 6,000 civilians, divided in much the same way. A refined scheme of sampling would theoretically have been possible, but this would have involved more time and staff than were available. In order to do the survey at all it was necessary to adopt a procedure which would be administratively straightforward; it was decided, therefore, to cover in their entirety two land divisions and the Central Traffic Division, and to obtain certain data from some of the central departments. The two land divisions were selected as examples of a central and of a more varied outlying area. For the central area 'B' Division—covering Chelsea, Kensington and Notting Hill—was used, and for the outer area 'S' Division was chosen, running from Golders Green out to West Hendon and almost as far as Watford.

While in no sense based on a random sample this part of the survey covered some 1,800 Police Officers and Civilians, and included a varied selection of the work of a large metropolitan force. On the whole it seemed better to operate in this way than to make no survey at all.

(d) *Data processing*

At the end of the survey in each force the booklets were collected, checked for completeness and returned to the Institute of Criminology. At the Institute they were again checked, and various calculations were made, using spaces provided on the booklets. The information was then coded and punched on cards. The results were tabulated and summarized in a standard set of tables in the same form for each force.[1]

The sets of tables relating to each force have been the basis of

---

[1] This work was done on a Tabulator, rather than a computer; this was mainly because the time spent on tabulating was only a small proportion of the total, but partly because we were running to a tight schedule where any delay, for example, in waiting for time on a computer, would have made it impossible for us to have met the Select Committee's deadline. As it was, all the basic tables were submitted to the Select Committee at the beginning of July 1966. Subsequently, the figures supplied to the committee were corrected in various relatively minor respects, so that our final figures are slightly different from those published by the committee as Appendix G to its Report. *Ibid.*, pp. 291–317.

all the survey data used in this book. We contemplated recalculating all our results to give weighted estimates relating to all the provincial forces. When we started to do so, however (see Chapter VI, pp. 154–5), we found that almost identical results could be obtained far more simply by adding the relevant figures for the forces in the survey. In effect this gave more weight to the practices of the larger forces.

We have also expressed the results of some of our calculations in terms of what we have called Manpower Equivalents, i.e. the number of men working full time that it would take to do all the work recorded in a given category. For example, in Bristol all forms of Traffic Work combined occupied 23·5 per cent of active duty time. The Manpower Equivalent would be 298 out of the total strength of 1,270 police officers, civilians, traffic wardens and cadets.[1]

There was one important exception to this procedure. In August 1965 the Lancashire Constabulary under the command of Col. T. E. St Johnston,[2] conducted their own manpower survey. Although designed on somewhat different lines from our own its objects were similar. The results were kindly made available to us but the differences between the methods of the two surveys made it difficult for us to use the Lancashire figures.

---

[1] This is based on the total strength of the force as given in the Report of H.M. Chief Inspector of Constabulary, not on the numbers taking part in our survey.

[2] Now Sir Eric St Johnston, H.M. Chief Inspector of Constabulary.

# VI

# The Pattern of Police Work

*Overall characteristics of the sample*

THE broad characteristics of the sample of members of provincial forces obtained by the procedure described in Chapter V and Appendix C are summarized on Table VI.1, which also gives the overall totals for the provincial forces as at 31 December 1965. It will be seen that the sample had a somewhat lower proportion of civilians, very slightly smaller proportions of cadets and traffic wardens and, consequently, a rather higher proportion of police officers.

TABLE VI.1

**Characteristics of the total sample of provincial forces (1965–66)**

|  | Provincial forces at 31/12/65 | | Sample* | |
|  | No. | % | No. | % |
| --- | --- | --- | --- | --- |
| Policemen and Women | 63,901† | 81·3 | 5,916 | 86·4 |
| Cadets | 3,259 | 4·2 | 252 | 3·7 |
| Civilians | 10,438‡ | 13·3 | 606 | 8·9 |
| Traffic Wardens | 1,030 | 1·3 | 75 | 1·1 |
| Total | 78,628 | 100·1 | 6,849 | 100·1 |

\* Where provincial forces were surveyed twice, the earlier figure has been used in calculating this total.
† The figures used are those of the 'Strength for Ordinary Duty'.
‡ This figure is for whole-time civilians, excluding domestics (of whom there were 2,599).

SOURCE: *Inspector of Constabulary, 1965*, Appendix II, 1966–67 (90).

For the rest of this chapter we shall present some of the main results of the surveys. We shall consider the effective strength of the police, the total work load per person, overtime and the principal features of the work load. Later chapters will deal with more detailed aspects.

*The effective strength of the police*

The earlier parts of this book have shown how, on paper at least, the growth in the population of England and Wales has been matched by a corresponding increase in the total strength of the police (see Table IV.5). Yet for more than a decade the 'shortage of manpower' has been lamented at almost all levels of authority in police circles. One of our main tasks, therefore, is to attempt to elucidate this paradox.

The first comment must be that the total strength of any police force is a somewhat misleading measure of what it can do. Although, on occasions, it is possible to muster almost the whole of a force this can only be done for a dire emergency, or, perhaps, for a state ceremony as rare as a Coronation or Sir Winston Churchill's funeral. But such a concentration of effort is, by its very nature, self-defeating in terms of the wider aims of policing. A price has to be paid, whether in terms of overtime and extra pay[1] or, more likely and more insidious, in other tasks neglected.[2] Policemen, moreover, are in short supply; the conditions of service can no longer be quite as strict as those imposed on men of earlier generations. Rest and recreation on a scale which will stand comparison with other occupations are essential if men are to join or stay in the service, while the complexity of the job demands more specialized training. Thus, in some respects, winning the necessary battle for better conditions has also meant that the war against crime has to be fought with different weapons from those used by the overworked men of the past.

The policing of the country is also a continuous activity. Cover must be provided for twenty-four hours a day, three hundred and sixty-five days a year. Hence, the officers available at any one time normally can be only a proportion of the total strength on paper. Our first concern, therefore, must be to examine the significance of the gap between the normal strength and the average manpower available.

[1] Even political demonstrations can be quite expensive. For example *The Times* on 18 October 1963 carried the following report: 'C.N.D. BILL.— The cost of providing police reinforcements to deal with C.N.D. demonstrations at R.A.F. Marham, Norfolk, last May was £5,460. Norfolk county council is being asked to approve the expenditure.'

[2] It is well-known that certain criminals make a habit of committing offences at times when police and public attention are diverted,

The term *Abstractions* is used in police circles to denote those activities, including leave, which make an officer unavailable for active duty on a particular occasion. They are legitimate reasons for absence. In our survey we were not concerned at this stage whether members of a force got the time off to which they were entitled, but merely how many hours were counted under the various categories of abstractions. A whole day's leave, or sickness, was counted as eight hours for this purpose.

Our figures are stated in three groups. The first are the simple aggregate of the surveys of the provincial forces, thus giving an unweighted average for abstractions as a percentage of the total hours accounted for by the survey (which we have termed Potential Duty Time).[1] It is heavily influenced by the larger forces because of the numbers employed by them. Secondly, we give a weighted estimate of the overall figures for abstractions in all the provincial forces.[2] Thirdly, the figures for the Metropolitan police are presented as a simple average for the two Divisions included in the survey. It cannot strictly be argued that they are representative of the whole Metropolitan force, but it should not be assumed they are unrepresentative. The biggest differences are likely to be between divisions in the central areas and those forming the outer ring. We have one of each type so that our sample might be said to embody a rough stratification.[3] Apart from this working hours are standardized for the force, and there is a considerable movement of officers between divisions so that for

---

[1] It is all time actually worked, together with leave, sport and sickness.

[2] This involves treating each survey force as representative of its stratum and multiplying its figure for abstractions by the proportion the stratum forms of the total strength of the provincial forces. We also made direct use of the figures from the Lancashire survey.

[3] The ratio of the strength of the two divisions was almost exactly the same as that of all inner and all outer divisions respectively.

| | Strength | % | | Strength | % |
|---|---|---|---|---|---|
| B Division | 668 | 48·5 | All inner divisions | 8,654 | 48·6 |
| S Division | 708 | 51·5 | All outer divisions | 9,146 | 51·4 |
| | 1,376 | 100·0 | | 17,800 | 100·0 |

SOURCE: Research and Planning Branch, Metropolitan police.

The figures relate to a slightly different date from that of our survey and they include higher ranks, hence the slight differences,

most purposes working practices are likely to be fairly similar throughout.[1]

It will be seen from the overall totals given in Table VI.2 that the provincial forces averaged a little over 40 per cent while the Metropolitan averaged about a third. The distribution of averages among the provincial forces showed only a limited range, from 36·0 per cent to 46·6 per cent, and seven of the twelve were in a narrow band of figures between 41·2 per cent and 44·0 per cent. It seems justifiable to regard figures of this order as typical of provincial forces.

TABLE VI.2

**Abstractions from potential duty time (1965–66)**
**(force totals)***

| Force | Total hours potential duty (incl. abstractions) | Total hours abstractions | Abstractions as percentage of potential duty |
|---|---|---|---|
| Provincial (survey only) | 782,937 | 330,221 | 42·2 |
| Provincial All forces estimate | | | 42·3 |
| Metropolitan 'B' and 'S' Divisions | 157,368 | 53,126 | 33·8 |

\* Where forces were surveyed twice only the results of the first survey have been used in compiling this table.

The explanation of the extent to which some forces have low (or high) figures for abstractions may involve several factors. The two main ones are abnormal figures (either high or low) for particular forms of abstraction, e.g. training or sickness, and unusually high figures for the total hours worked.

Obviously if the time spent on abstractions remains the same and the total time worked goes up then abstractions will form a smaller proportion of the whole. Working hours may go up either in an unsystematic way, e.g. the C.I.D. puts in many extra hours on account of a murder, or systematically if, in the face of a manpower shortage (as in the Metropolitan and some other forces), extra shifts are worked as a matter of routine.

[1] The principal complication is afforded by the various centralized departments at the Commissioner's Office and the Central Traffic Division. Figures for some of those are given later when discussing the work of specialized departments. See below p. 147 ff.

In this study we are naturally concerned to examine the relationship of various characteristics of our police forces with their work, and to assess whether these relationships might have occurred by chance or whether one characteristic varies systematically in relation to another. This is generally done by the procedure known as testing for statistical significance.

Problems arise in doing this because of the small number of forces in our sample—twelve provincial ones plus, in some cases, the two Metropolitan divisions which for this purpose may be regarded as forces in themselves. The relationship between any two sets of observations can be expressed in terms of Pearson's product-moment correlation coefficient ($r$), but it is also necessary to test the statistical significance of the value of $r$. This is particularly important when the number of observations is small. Under these circumstances an appropriate test is based on Student's $t$ distribution, and this has been used wherever correlations have been calculated in this study. (For details of the method see Appendix B.2, p. 273.)

Product-moment correlations are expressed as values of $r$ which can range between $-1\cdot0$ and $+1\cdot0$. The further the value is from zero the closer the correlation, positive or negative. A positive correlation occurs when both variables move in the same direction as, for example, height and weight in human beings; a correlation is negative if the values of one variable decrease when those of the other increase.

Statistical significance is usually expressed in terms of the probability of a particular relationship occurring by chance, and the values of 5 per cent, 1 per cent and sometimes 0·2 per cent or 0·1 per cent are conveniently used for this purpose. The smaller the percentage level at which the value of $r$ is significant the more likely it is that the relationship is not due to chance.

We attempted to examine these effects further by correlating the average percentage of a force's potential duty time spent on abstractions with other variables.[1] We found that almost all the variance (96·8 per cent) was related to the average number of hours spent on active duty (i.e. non-abstractions). There was a

___

[1] This was done for the following variables: Annual leave as a percentage of all leave; Average total working time per head (this consisted literally of all working time and excluded only sport, sickness, leave and refreshment breaks); Average hours spent on non-abstractions,

very high negative correlation ($r = -0.9838$) between hours of
active duty and the proportion of abstractions in the force. As
the average hours of work (on non-abstractions) increased, so the
proportion of abstractions fell: long hours of duty left little time
for leave, sickness or training. In a sense this was only to be
expected, but it is perhaps a little surprising that the relationship
was so close. In terms of the data at our disposal this association
provides an adequate explanation of the differing proportion of
abstractions in our various forces.[1]

We can conclude, therefore, that while the amount of time
each individual spends on abstractions is undoubtedly an influence
on the percentage of abstractions in a force, the total duration of
working time is most important, particularly when the working
week starts to get really long. This can be shown clearly if, for
a moment, we anticipate our later discussion of overtime. The
four forces with the lowest proportions of abstractions were precisely those working systematic overtime in the form of extra
shifts;[2] at the other extreme, however, the forces with the highest
proportions of abstractions certainly worked relatively short hours,
but were not those working the shortest hours.

It remains to examine the relative contribution of different
types of abstraction to the total. The overall figures are given
below in Table VI.3. Before reading them it should be remembered that the totals to which these contributions were made were
by no means the same. The provincial unweighted average of
abstractions as a percentage of potential duty time was 42·2 per
cent and the Metropolitan was 33·8 per cent. These figures,

TABLE VI.3

**Percentage contribution to total abstractions (1965–66)**

|  | Training | Sports | Leave | Sick leave | Refresh- ments | Total |
|---|---|---|---|---|---|---|
| *Provincial forces* | | | | | | |
| Police officers | 13·8 | 0·8 | 70·3 | 4·6 | 10·6 | 100·1 |
| Civilians | 1·1 | 0·3 | 89·2 | 4·7 | 4·7 | 100·0 |
| *Metropolitan* 'B' and 'S' Division | | | | | | |
| Police officers | 13·2 | 0·2 | 59·0 | 6·8 | 20·7 | 99·9 |
| Civilians | — | — | 81·6 | 3·1 | 15·3 | 100·0 |

[1] This correlation was significant at the 0·1 per cent level.
[2] Essex, 'B' and 'S' Divisions of the Metropolitan police, and Bedfordshire.

however, were for police officers and civilians combined; Table VI.3 shows them separately on account of the rather different patterns they display.

The most obvious conclusion to be drawn from this table is the overwhelming importance of leave, which accounted for the bulk of abstractions in all groups. The rather low figure for Metropolitan police officers was probably an indirect result of the longer hours worked (see below p. 146). The provincial figure of 70·3 per cent is probably more typical.

Civilians have been shown separately on account of their rather different pattern: leave was even more important than with police officers, sickness very similar, and refreshments were distinctly lower.[1] The other major difference was that the amounts of time spent on training and sports were almost negligible.

For police officers it will be seen that training took second place after leave in the provincial forces. The Metropolitan proportion was very similar, but was less than the figure for refreshments. If anything this figure probably underestimated the amount of time spent on training as the Metropolitan figures did not include recruit training.[2]

We can now consider how far abstractions reduce the effective strength of the police, in terms of average day to day work, rather than the maximum that can be mustered on special occasions. If we translate the percentage figures stated in Table VI.2 into what we have termed their Manpower Equivalents we get the following results. In the provincial forces of our survey we find that the weighted figure of 42·3 per cent for abstractions is the equivalent of 2,897 out of a total of 6,849 persons. In this sense, therefore, the average effective strength of these forces in the grades covered by the survey was 3,952. If we apply the same proportion (42·3 per cent) to the total strength (78,625) of the provincial forces at 31 December 1965 we find that the Manpower Equivalent for abstractions was 33,283. If we subtract this number from the paper strength we get an average effective strength of 45,342.

We can make similar calculations for the Metropolitan police. Owing to the complicated structure of the force they are more

---

[1] This was mainly due to administrative differences. In some provincial forces meal breaks were not counted as part of working hours.

[2] In the provincial forces some of the training time was probably occupied in travelling, whereas this may have been less in the Metropolitan police.

approximate but may, nevertheless, be of some interest. The mean of 'B' and 'S' Divisions (including civilians), based on a total of 1,337 persons covered by our survey, was 33·8 per cent. Applied to the total strength as 31 December 1965 of 22,766 we find the Manpower Equivalent of the abstractions was 7,695. This made the average effective strength 15,071.

It must be emphasized that these are extremely general calculations. They combine policemen, policewomen, cadets, civilians and traffic wardens. (In due course we shall see that this may make the situation seem more favourable than if we considered police officers by themselves). They also ignore the problem of spreading the available manpower to provide a 24-hour service; the numbers reached still have to be divided between whatever shifts are necessary. Nevertheless at the very least it can be argued that figures such as these give a rather more realistic impression of the police cover normally afforded to the community than the maximum strength shown on paper.

## The work load per person

The working conditions of the police service are laid down in regulations made by the Secretary of State under the relevant Police Act.[1] Broadly speaking these specify the overall hours of work and the amounts of leave to which members of the service are entitled. They also cover overtime and the provision of time off in lieu. In the main the hours of work are reckoned on the basis of an eight-hour day; if a 44-, 46- or 48-hour week is being worked this is achieved by regulating the number of rest days so as to arrive at the desired average over a period of time.

When manpower is short, however, it may not always be possible to give the time off in lieu, and, indeed, some forces have to work systematic overtime. (Details of this are given later, see p. 149). In addition the job may at any time require officers to continue working after the nominal end of their tour of duty—for example after a road accident a patrol simply has to stay until everything necessary has been done. Likewise the detective must often keep going as long as his enquiries are profitable. It follows, then, that life in the service is such that occasional overtime, in

[1] At the time of our surveys the current regulations were the Police Regulations 1965, S.I. 1965 No. 538.

the form of longer tours of duty, is likely to occur from to time time, and the systematic working of extra shifts may have to be undertaken if manpower in an area is in short supply.

In our surveys we were interested only in recording what happened. Where leave was granted to make up for overtime this would be allowed for by our methods of calculation. If, on the other hand, the situation was such that compensating leave was not taken, our surveys would show the extra time entailed. In view of the inevitabliity of departures from the regulation norm it is of some interest to see where these were located and how extensive they were.

The best measure derived from our survey was obtained by counting all time apart from leave and sickness. We refer to this as working time.[1]

The average figures for the various types of forces were :
Provincial forces 77·5 hours working time per fortnight
Metropolitan (average of 'B' and 'S' Divisions) 91·2 hours per fortnight
Metropolitan (Central Traffic Division) 86·8 hours per fortnight

The mean for the provincial forces was, if anything, misleadingly high, being affected by two extreme values. The median was 75·6, and ten of the twelve were within the comparatively limited range 71·7 to 78·8 hours per fortnight. This is not surprising in view of the relatively standardized conditions of work. The low figures, depending on the time of year, were probably due to more leave or sickness. High figures were due to overtime.

In themselves these may not look particularly long hours, but it must be remembered that they are averages covering all ranks (including civilians) and do not show the number of shifts worked, nor the amount of week-end duty. Certain ranks and departments, indeed, may work particularly long hours of duty which are concealed within the general average.

Table VI.4 shows the average hours worked by members of each main department. These averages are based on the total hours worked and the total number of individuals. They are,

[1] Refreshment breaks are provided for in the official 8-hour day. A very small amount of the time recorded under sport has also been included. This covered not only participation in, but the administration of, sporting events. Statistically this amount was almost negligible, 0·3 per cent of potential duty time.

## TABLE VI.4

### Average hours of working time by departments per fortnight (1965–66)

| Department | Provincial forces | | | Metropolitan 'B' & 'S' Div. | Specialist departments |
| --- | --- | --- | --- | --- | --- |
| | Avge hrs worked | Min. | Max. | Avge hrs worked | Avge hrs worked |
| Traffic Wardens | 78·5 | 76·0 | 79·5 | — | — |
| Traffic | 75·1 | 62·5 | 87·8 | 92·3 | 86.8* |
| Beat Patrols | 76·8 | 70·1 | 89·5 | 85·3 | — |
| C.I.D. | 88·5 | 82·2 | 95·5 | 116·3 | 122·1† |
| Women Police Constables | 72·9 | 62·0 | 91·5 | 89·7 | — |
| Administration | 74·5 | 62·4 | 83·1 | 88·5 | — |
| Station Staff | 73·0 | 60·7 | 91·9 | 86·4 | — |
| Training Courses | 80·5 | 62·2‡ | 91·5 | 98·0 | — |
| Training Instructors | 84·4 | 61·3 | 98·0 | 94·3 | — |
| Other Duties§ | 80·3 | 65·5 | 93·0 | 104·2 | — |
| | 77·5 | | | 91·2 | |

* Central Traffic Division (excluding H.Q. staff).
† This is an average figure for the Fraud Squad, Flying Squad and Stolen Vehicles Department. It was derived from the working hours recorded in the pocket books of the officers concerned. It covers all police ranks up to Detective Chief Superintendent but no civilians.
‡ Three forces had no officers engaged in training during the survey fortnight.
§ The category of Other Duties has been used to include a rather mixed group which, in different police forces, may be included in a variety of departments. For the comparative purposes of this survey the following principal groups have been included in the category of Other Duties: Vice Squad, Firearms and Aliens, Warrant Officers, Coroner's Officer(s), Crime Prevention Squad, Gaolers, Photographic and Dog Handlers. This does not necessarily mean, however, that every force in the survey has a separate sub-department concerned with these duties.

therefore, rather weighted by the numbers in the larger departments.

It will be realized that general figures such as these must conceal quite substantial differences both between forces and between the members of any one department. Furthermore where forces had a high proportion of their strength away on sick or annual leave the hours actually worked by the remainder will have been understated as the calculation does not allow for the smaller number of officers actually on duty. Nevertheless certain conclusions may be drawn.

The first concerns the overall difference between the Metropolitan and the provincial forces. For every department the average hours worked by our two Metropolitan divisions was higher than the corresponding average for the provincial forces. Admittedly in some departments the provincial maximum over-lapped the Metropolitan average, but these were the extremes, and they were certainly balanced by minimum figures which were often well below the provincial average.

The second main observation is of the contrast between the C.I.D. and other departments. Apart from the rather special cases of training departments, the C.I.D. in most provincial forces worked longer hours than any other department. On this basis it could be said that, as a rough average, in the provincial forces they worked about ten hours a fortnight longer. If we assume their civilian staff do not work such long hours it is likely that the average detective works an hour a day more than his uniformed colleague.

In extreme cases the detective's working hours can be very much longer. Indeed the entire Metropolitan C.I.D. might be regarded as coming into this category. The average for our two divisional C.I.D.'s was nearly 20 hours a fortnight more than the provincial average, while that of the three specialist squads (about whose work we were given information) was even higher. However the absence of civilians may have exaggerated this contrast. A further complication was that a murder took place in 'B' Division near the beginning of the survey period, so that the crime investigation figures for the division were probably higher than they might otherwise have been.

Nevertheless it seems quite justifiable to say that C.I.D. officers in general regularly work longer hours than most uniformed officers, and that in the Metropolitan area this is particularly so. Among the special squads the highest figures were for the Flying Squad whose average working hours were 130·5 in a fortnight. If, as one must assume, the provincial forces are working reason-able hours then the Metropolitan, particularly its C.I.D., must be significantly overworked.

The next group of departments having high average hours of work were 'Training' and 'Other Duties'. The most likely explana-tion of the training figures is the amount of study and preparation required. 'Other Duties', as shown in the note to Table VI.4, comprised a somewhat heterogeneous group of specialists, often concerned with criminal investigation work, for example photographers and vice squads, whose hours of work may have approached those of the C.I.D.

The figures for traffic wardens deserve comment as an example of the possible working performance of a specialized group with strictly limited functions. The hours worked were moderately high, and there was very little variation between forces. The low figure for abstractions, averaging 34·4 per cent, meant that their effective strength was particularly high.

*Overtime*

Closely linked with the question of hours of work is the problem of overtime. In themselves the figures recorded in Table VI.4 may not seem excessive but, as *The Times* put it in a feature entitled 'The Lonely Beat', . . . 'easily the most common complaints are the inconvenience of shift work and the long hours. Although forces attempt to lighten the load as far as possible, the average policeman still works at least some part of most weekends and on many Bank Holidays'.[1]

Since our survey was conducted the length of the working week has been authoritatively discussed by the Working Party on Police Manpower set up by the Police Advisory Board.[2] They obtained figures of the weekly hours of work prevailing at 31 March 1966 which may be summarized in the form of Table VI.5 below.[3]

The figures given by the working party need little comment. They show, above all, that in 1966 only a third of all constables were in forces working the regulation 42-hour week, although rather more than another third worked a 44-hour week. They re-emphasize the conclusions, drawn in our preceding section, as to

[1] 'The Lonely Beat', published in *The Times* on 13, 14 and 15 Feburary 1965.
[2] 'The Police Advisory Board comprises representatives of the Home Office, the local authority associations and all ranks of the police service of England and Wales. In January 1966 the Board set up three working parties to consider problems of police manpower; equipment; and operational efficiency and management. . . . The reports of the working parties were presented to the Police Advisory Board in December (1966).' From the Home Secretary's Preface to the Reports. Home Office: *Police Manpower, Equipment and Efficiency*, London, H.M.S.O., 1967.
[3] Derived from the figures presented in Appendix 2, p. 60. We have not, however, repeated the slight arithmetical error in the published total.

the difference between the Metropolitan and other forces. They also indicate a quite noticeable difference between the County forces and those of Cities and Boroughs. Only 35 per cent of the county officers were working the 42-hour week, compared with 54 per cent in the boroughs, and 12 per cent of the county officers were on a 46-hour week compared with less than 4 per cent in the boroughs. The longer working hours of the counties were probably due to a mixture of manpower shortage and the greater demands liable to be made on uniformed officers in rural areas, particularly in the investigation of minor crimes.

TABLE VI.5

**Actual weekly hours of work (constables) (1966)**

|  | Metropolitan | | Cities and Boros excluding Metropolitan | | Counties | | Total | |
|---|---|---|---|---|---|---|---|---|
|  | No. | % | No. | % | No. | % | No. | % |
| 42 hours | — | — | 13,824 | (54·1) | 12,954 | (35·2) | 26,778 | (33·2) |
| 44 hours | — | — | 10,925 | (42·5) | 19,344 | (52·6) | 30,269 | (37·5) |
| 46 hours | — | — | 961 | (3·7) | 4,467 | (12·2) | 5,428 | (6·7) |
| 48 hours | 18,278 | (100) | — | — | — | — | 18,278 | (22·6) |
|  | 18,278 | (100) | 25,710 | (100) | 36,765 | (100) | 80,753 | (100) |

Our own survey results can do little more than confirm the working party's figures and indicate how the overall totals were influenced by variations between departments, and by different practices regarding the duration (as opposed to the number) of shifts worked. For technical reasons the calculation of overtime in our survey had to be done in two stages: first, counting the number of hours worked in excess of eight hours in any one shift; and second, counting the hours due to working more than the regulation number of shifts. The figure for what we call long tours of duty was obtained directly from each booklet and coded as a separate item. The number of extra shifts, however, had to be computed in a more complicated way which involved estimating overtime figures for people who, for one reason or another, worked less than the regulation number of shifts in the fortnight.[1] These figures, therefore, are somewhat more approximate than others we have used. Nevertheless they should be reasonably good

[1] See Appendix B.3 for a description of the method of estimation.

indications of the general order of magnitude of the overtime burden on a force although, being averages, they do not reflect the maximum or minimum loads falling on some individuals.

The variations between forces were so great that we present, in Table VI.6 below, the revised figures for all the forces in our survey.

TABLE VI.6

**Overtime worked by police officers (1965–66)\***

| Force | Average hours overtime per fortnight | Proportion of overtime due to extra shifts % | Proportion of police officers working extra shifts % |
|---|---|---|---|
| Plymouth | 3·8 | 30 | 11 |
| Hastings† | 2·9 | 17 | 6 |
| Pembrokeshire† | 6·2 | 7 | 5 |
| Dorset† | 4·8 | 25 | 13 |
| Bristol | 2·6 | 25 | 8 |
| Bath | 16·4 | 7 | 14 |
| Barrow-in-Furness | 1·9 | 30 | 7 |
| Birkenhead | 6·2 | 61 | 46 |
| Leicestershire and Rutland | 9·5 | 54 | 53 |
| Northumberland | 8·6 | 20 | 19 |
| Bedfordshire | 11·9 | 59 | 81 |
| Essex | 11·4 | 66 | 91 |
| *Metropolitan* | | | |
| 'B' Division | 17·3 | 49 | 95 |
| 'S' Division | 13·4 | 63 | 96 |
| Central Traffic Division | 12·2 | 65 | 90 |
| Fraud Squad | 26·4 | 28 | 93 |
| Flying Squad | 49·0 | 19 | 94 |
| Stolen Vehicles Branch | 37·8 | 21 | 97 |

\* For the purposes of this table cadets have been included with police officers. Civilians and traffic wardens have been excluded and it has been assumed they work no overtime. See Appendix B.3 for method of calculation.

† The figures are for the surveys conducted in the winter or very early spring. Those are compared with the hours worked in the summer in Chapter VIII.

It will be seen that in terms of the average hours of overtime worked the forces fell into fairly clearly defined groups.[1] First of all there was a group with relatively low hours of overtime (up to 4·8 per fortnight). Then there were two forces, quite different

[1] The only exception was Bath, whose figures were quite out of line. We have no explanation for this.

in character, with the intermediate figure of 6·2 hours per fortnight. After these were two more with relatively high figures (8.6 and 9·5), and finally three with over eleven hours.

These groupings were among provincial forces, and it might be said that the Metropolitan began where the others left off—'S' and the Central Traffic Division working only a little more overtime than Essex and Bedford. (The 'B' Division figure might well have been similar but for the special influence of the murder enquiry being undertaken during the survey period.) Finally we have the three special squads[1] working overtime on a scale which set them apart from all the others.

Between them these forces illustrate fairly well the main customs in the arrangement of working hours that are to be found in the police service. The other two columns in Table VI.6 allow us to make some assessment of the impact of extra shift working.

It is clear that in the group with the lowest average hours of overtime the proportion of officers working extra shifts was invariably low, with a maximum of 13 per cent. Even so the contribution of such officers to the total volume of overtime was disproportionate to their number. This is not surprising, but it is worth noting because it emphasizes that where the general level of overtime is low the working of only a few extra shifts can make a substantial difference to the total for the force.

Birkenhead and Pembrokeshire had identical overtime averages, but derived from quite different patterns of work. The Birkenhead figure resulted from a small amount of regular overtime in the form of extra shifts,[2] while the Pembrokeshire figure derived from the rather longer shifts liable to be worked in rural areas.

Northumberland and Leicestershire and Rutland had rather similar figures, but based on different patterns of work. As with Pembrokeshire the Northumberland figure was largely due to the working of longer tours of duty; the Leicestershire and Rutland

---

[1] This, of course, is a colloquial and conveniently brief title. Their official designations are:

        C.6 Metropolitan and City Police Company Fraud Branch.
        C.8 Flying Squad.
        C.10 Stolen Motor Vehicle Investigation Branch.

[2] See the Chief Constable's Report for 1964 for details. County Borough of Birkenhead, *Chief Constable's Annual Report 1964*, p.3. As only a part of the force worked the 44-hour week our overtime figure may be a slight over-estimate.

force, on the other hand, was working a 46-hour week and this was responsible for about half the overtime worked.[1]

The highest figures in the provincial group, Essex and Bedfordshire, were influenced substantially by the working of a 48- and 46-hour week respectively. Between a half and two-thirds of overtime was due to extra shifts; these proportions indeed, might have been even higher had it not been for a fair amount of working longer tours in addition. The resulting totals indicate the effects of the systematic working of extra shifts.

The figures for the three Metropolitan divisions were not so very different from the highest provincial ones. The relatively low contribution of extra shifts to the 'B' division total was undoubtedly due to the working of longer shifts in connection with the murder enquiry.

The three special squads make an interesting contrast. Virtually all members worked extra shifts, but their influence on the total was less than might have been expected; this was undoubtedly due to the working of very long hours. The Stolen Vehicles branch averaged 30 hours overtime a fortnight, while the Flying Squad average reached 39·5. If the survey fortnight was anything like typical then these squads work at a different level from any other section of the police that we have encountered.[2]

In so far as we can reach a tentative general conclusion from these figures it must surely be that for most forces it is the working of extra shifts that produces the really high figures for overtime. Moderately high figures, however, may be produced, particularly in rural areas, by the relatively widespread working of longer tours.

*The nature of the work load*

Our chief purpose in conducting the surveys was to discover how police work was spread between the numerous tasks facing the service. We have already discussed the broad classifications which we decided to use, and we can now present our results in these terms. First, more or less in terms of the sequence of events,

---

[1] The fact that the Table shows this as affecting only half the force is misleading as not all men would have been due for their extra shift during the survey period, while the incidence of annual leave was also relatively high at this time. Annual leave accounted for 27·7 per cent of all leave during the survey period.

[2] We are not in a position to compare them with Regional Crime Squads.

between Law Enforcement, the Administration of Justice, the Treatment of Offenders, and, as a residual category, Civil Duties; the overall results are summarized in Table VI.7.

As it turns out the Law Enforcement category was rather widely drawn and included so much of police work that, in this context, it has not been as informative as we should have hoped. More valuable, however, were the figures for the Administration of Justice. The provincial and Metropolitan averages were remarkably close to each other, but it will be seen that the range among the provincial forces was from 6·9 to 14·7 per cent. On the face

TABLE VI.7

**Distribution of working time according to function (1965–66)**
(Percentages)

|  | Law enforcement | Administration of justice | Treatment of offenders | Civil duties |
|---|---|---|---|---|
| *Provincial Forces* |  |  |  |  |
| Avge of survey forces* | 74·0 | 10·8 | 0·8 | 14·4 |
| Highest proportion | 80·8 | 14·7 | 1·3 | 19·2 |
| Lowest proportion | 71·6 | 6·9 | 0·3 | 9·9 |
| Weighted estimate (all provincial forces) | 74·5 | 10·4 | 0·9 | 14·3 |
| *Metropolitan* |  |  |  |  |
| Avge 'B' and 'S' Div.* | 81·5 | 10·7 | 0·4 | 7·4 |
| Central Traffic Div. | 78·1 | 9·4 | 0·2 | 12·3 |

\* These averages were based on the total number of hours contributed by all forces. They are not averages of the rates recorded by the separate forces. Where forces were surveyed twice we have used the results for the first of the two surveys only.

of it this is quite considerable, but the distribution shows that, in effect, there were two almost completely separate groups. The six below the mean were, with one exception, Borough forces, and only two had a Higher Court sitting in their area during the period. The Higher Courts concerned sat for a total of only four days. Five out of the six forces which were above average were county ones, and Higher Courts were sitting in four of the areas for a total of nine days or more.[1] We shall examine the relationship between the volume of court cases and the time spent on court work in more detail later (see Chapter VIII), but for the moment it seems fair to say that much of the variation between

[1] The precise figure for one area was inadvertently not recorded.

forces in the amount of court work was due to the demands of the Higher Courts.

The figures for civil duties were heavily influenced by the general supervision of traffic. Civil, but non-traffic, incidents played a relatively minor part. Variations between forces seem largely to have been due to differences in the volume of traffic supervision.

The Treatment of Offenders function played a negligible part. The range was so small that differences between forces were of virtually no significance in terms of the burden of work falling on the police.

Our second breakdown of police work was according to what we termed *Area of Operation*, and this proved a more fruitful. grouping of activities. The results are summarized in Table VI.8

## TABLE VI.8

**Distribution of working time according to area of operation (1965–66)**
(Percentages)

|  | *Traffic* | *Crime* | *Civil order* | *Internal organization* |
|---|---|---|---|---|
| *Provincial forces* | | | | |
| Avge of survey forces* | 22·8 | 28·6 | 39·1 | 9·5 |
| Highest proportion | 28·9 | 33·0 | 50·6 | 14·9 |
| Lowest proportion | 17·6 | 22·0 | 32·0 | 3·7 |
| Weighted estimate (all provincial forces) | 23·0 | 28·0 | 40·3 | 8·6 |
| *Metropolitan* | | | | |
| Avge 'B' and 'S' Div. | 17·7 | 31·3 | 43·1 | 7·8 |
| Central Traffic Div. | 85·2 | 3·1 | 1·0 | 10·7 |

* These averages were based on the total number of hours contributed by all forces. They are not averages of the rates recorded by separate forces. Where forces were surveyed twice we have used the results for the first of the two surveys only.

Probably the most important figures are those for the amounts of time spent on traffic and criminal work. They include all work under these heads, whether outside or inside the station or in court.

Bearing in mind the differences between police areas the range among the provincial forces was surprisingly small. Only three forces were more than 3 per cent either side of the weighted estimate of some 23 per cent for traffic work. We can, therefore, say with some confidence that in most forces in England and

Wales traffic work would account for between a fifth and a quarter of the total time of the force.

The Metropolitan figures for traffic were rather lower, and special allowance has to be made for the fact that in the 'B' Division area a proportion of traffic work was done by the Central Traffic Division. This can be done by dividing the work of the Central Traffic Division and allocating the appropriate proportions to the cover of the 'B' Division area. As a result the figure for 'B' Division traffic work goes up from 15·5 per cent of the total time to 18·7 per cent.[1] This in turn brings up the average for the two divisions to 19·3 per cent; a rather low figure, but not excessively so if seen in relation to traffic work in provincial cities. The limitations of such a comparison are, however, obvious.

Despite the claims of traffic, in most forces rather more time went on criminal work. (It will be remembered that our definition was a wide one and included petty crime.) Among the provincial forces the mean proportion was 5·8 per cent higher than the traffic figure. In the Metropolitan police the figures were rather different: 'S' Division spent only 2·7 per cent more time on crime than on traffic, but in 'B' Division the murder enquiry, plus the greater volume of crime in the area, was reflected in the crime figure of nearly 39 per cent as against a traffic figure of 19·3 per cent.[2]

The relative predominance of criminal work was by no means universal, and in three of the twelve provincial forces the traffic figures equalled or exceeded the crime ones. This number, however, was too small to allow generalization. When the proportion of time spent on traffic was correlated with that spent on criminal work the result showed no systematic relationship between the two (for the provincial forces $r = -0·1403$).[3]

Traffic and Criminal work together accounted for almost exactly 50 per cent of working time. The remaining time was

[1] This figure is based on the new total achieved by adding one twelfth of the Central Traffic Division's working hours to the 'B' Division figures. Central Traffic Division covers twelve Land Division areas.

[2] Both figures corrected to allow for work done by C.T.D. The number of crimes reported in 'B' Division area was 965, and in 'S' Division was 460.

[3] It should be mentioned that if the number of hours worked under these heads is correlated the resulting correlation for the provincial forces was high ($r = 0·8986$). This effect, however, would seem largely to be due to the size of the forces rather than to the distribution of their work.

divided between Civil Order and Internal Organization. Civil Order in practice was dominated by patrolling, which accounted for over 90 per cent of the time under this heading. The simple fact that, on average, nearly 40 per cent of the police service's time was spent on a general purpose activity is itself important. In the last resort all that can be said is that such a use of time has to be justified in terms either of the prevention of crime or by the availability of the constable to deal with a situation without actually having to be summoned to it.[1]

Correlating the proportion of time spent on Civil Order with the other two main variables showed no significant relationship with traffic work in the provincial forces ($r = -0.2999$), but a moderate negative correlation with the share of time given to criminal work ($r = -0.6863$, $t = 3.2686$; significant at the 1 per cent level). This was a fairly strong negative correlation, and we are justified in saying that there was a tendency for high figures for patrolling to be associated with low rates for work directly associated with crime. The relationship is likely to have been influenced by a number of factors, such as the strength of the C.I.D. and the extent to which it monopolized crime investigation. These will be examined more closely in the next chapter.

Our final area of operation was 'Internal Organization'. The provincial average for this was rather under 10 per cent, and the range was from 3.7 to 14.9 per cent. Although these figures are rather widely scattered we are doubtful as to how much trust should be placed in them, simply because of the difficulty, already mentioned, of defining the concept. We have a strong impression that there are significant differences between forces in the amount of effort that goes on such domestic matters, but it is doubtful whether our technique was sufficiently precise to explore them in a satisfactory way. It is, however, a topic that would merit investigation on its own.

Having described the overall pattern of police activity in the broadest possible terms we shall now consider some of the categories by themselves. Not all are of equal importance, and we shall deal with certain groups in more detail in the next

---

[1] With the development of Unit Beat Policing (see Chapter VII, p. 180) the old concept of the constable keeping his eyes open and generally getting to know people in his area has been given new life by a deliberate concentration on the gathering of what has come to be termed 'criminal intelligence'.

chapter, but it is worth stating the relative magnitude of some items commonly referred to in discussions of police work. The relevant information is summarized in Table VI.9.[1] As we have already discussed Abstractions we shall concentrate on the classifications of Active Duty.

It will be seen that the distribution was dominated by a small number of items. The two most general ones, patrolling and general duties, together accounted for almost exactly half the total active duty time both in the provincial and the Metropolitan forces. We have already discussed patrolling, itself the largest single activity, but have said little about general duties. Originally we tried to avoid such a category, but the fact remained that there were forms of duty which occupied quite lengthy periods but which did not easily fit into our more specific classifications.

Many of these general duties are associated with communications. The staff of operations rooms, radio operators and telephonists relay messages covering the whole range of police work, but with little opportunity to distinguish between different functions, or even areas of operation. Supervision was a further problem. Many sergeants and inspectors spent much of their time directly supervising the work of their men. Sometimes it could be classified, as for example in the C.I.D. under Crime Investigation, but more often it had to go under General Duties. This had the logic that, if the supervising officer could not subdivide his time, then it should be subdivided *pro rata* according to the work done by his men. Much of police work consists also of waiting for things to happen, being on standby duty, being at the police station enquiry desk, waiting to drive a senior officer to a conference, and so on. In all these situations either the individual may not know much about the purpose of what is going on or, more likely, a multitude of brief acts are undertaken, so that classification is difficult if not impossible. At this point, therefore, we can only note the high total figures for general duties which show how much police work is of this kind.

As would be expected from the figures given earlier Crime

---

[1] This is based on the total number of hours recorded, so that among the provincial forces somewhat greater weight has been given to the larger forces. Re-weighting, however, did not seem justified, both because in earlier tables (such as VI.2) it has been shown to make very little difference and because, in any case, the larger forces accounted for the majority of officers and civilians.

## TABLE VI.9

### Distribution of total work load—provincial forces and Metropolitan police (1965–66)

| | Provincial forces* | | | Metropolitan 'B' and 'S' Division | | |
| | Potential duty time | | Active duty time | Potential duty time | | Active duty time |
| | Hours | % | % | Hours | % | % |
|---|---|---|---|---|---|---|
| 1. Crime Investigation | 78,273 | 10·0 | 17·3 | 22,530 | 14·31 | 21·61 |
| 2. Foreign Enquiries | 15,179 | 1·9 | 3·4 | 1,737 | 1·10 | 1·66 |
| 3. Traffic Supervision | 34,281 | 4·4 | 7·6 | 3,443 | 2·18 | 3·30 |
| 4. Traffic Accidents (no process) | 3,747 | 0·5 | 0·8 | 628 | 0·39 | 0·60 |
| 5. Traffic Incidents (possible process) | 8,295 | 1·1 | 1·8 | 4,989 | 3·17 | 4·78 |
| 6. Civil Incidents | 7,206 | 0·9 | 1·6 | 1,647 | 1·04 | 1·57 |
| 7. Public Order | 2,152 | 0·3 | 0·5 | 1,177 | 0·74 | 1·12 |
| 8. Private Duties | 1,638 | 0·2 | 0·4 | 154 | 0·09 | 0·14 |
| 9. Criminal Courts (Magistrates') | 10,494 | 1·3 | 2·3 | 2,604 | 1·65 | 2·49 |
| 10. Criminal Courts (Higher) | 3,693 | 0·5 | 0·8 | 892 | 0·56 | 0·85 |
| 11. Traffic Courts (all types) | 14,767 | 1·9 | 3·3 | 4,115 | 2·61 | 3·94 |
| 12. Civil and Coroners' Courts | 2,417 | 0·3 | 0·5 | 468 | 0·29 | 0·44 |
| 13. Juvenile Courts (all cases) | 2,012 | 0·3 | 0·4 | 264 | 0·16 | 0·25 |
| 14. After Conviction (adults) | 1,769 | 0·2 | 0·4 | 197 | 0·12 | 0·18 |
| 15. After Conviction (juvenile) | 828 | 0·1 | 0·2 | 85 | 0·05 | 0·08 |
| 16. Patrolling | 136,569 | 17·4 | 30·2 | 35,091 | 22·29 | 33·66 |
| 17. General Duties | 96,900 | 12·4 | 21·4 | 17,543 | 11·14 | 16·82 |
| 18. Internal Organization | 32,397 | 4·1 | 7·2 | 6,678 | 4·24 | 6·40 |
| 19. Training (incl. instruction) | 42,000 | 5·4 | | 6,683 | 4·24 | |
| 20. Sports | 2,553 | 0·3 | | 122 | 0·07 | |
| 21. Leave | 236,635 | 30·2 | | 31,947 | 20·30 | |
| 22. Sickness | 15,398 | 2·0 | | 3,530 | 2·24 | |
| 23. Misc. (mainly refreshments) | 33,635 | 4·3 | | 10,844 | 6·89 | |
| | 782,937 | 100·0 | 100·0 | 157,368 | 99·87 | 99·89 |
| | Total hours = 452,716 | | | Total hours = 104,242 | | |

* Where forces were surveyed twice only the results of the first survey have been used in compiling this table.

Investigation is the largest single specific activity; indeed in the Metropolitan police it occupied slightly more time than General Duties. It is interesting to note that court work connected with criminal cases occupied between a sixth and a seventh of all time spent on criminal work. In the provincial forces the ratio of court time (Magistrates', Higher and Juvenile) to crime investigation was 1:5, and in the Metropolitan police 1:6. Whether these proportions are high or not must be a matter of opinion.

A more authoritative judgement has, however, already been passed on the figures for traffic work. The Select Committee on Estimates used our preliminary results to arrive at the overall conclusion that 14·3 per cent of the time of the provincial police was spent on traffic work. They commented—'Your Committee believe that it is now time to say that this is too high a proportion of the time of policemen, trained to preserve order and fight crime, to be acceptable in social or economic terms'.[1] In point of fact their figure of 14·3 per cent was a considerable underestimate owing to the omission of patrolling by traffic departments; our figure of 23 per cent is a much better estimate.[2] The precise terms in which the committee would have expressed itself had it realized the correct figure was substantially higher than the one it had been using can only be a matter for conjecture, but it would presumably have been even more critical.

In its report the committee went on to advocate the employment of traffic wardens 'as . . . alternative sources of manpower: and, in detail, . . . the simplification of inquiry procedures under the fixed penalty system'.[3] We shall examine this point further in Chapter IX. For the moment it must simply be said that Table VI.9 understates the amount of traffic work, though in detail it allows us to show, even on this basis, how much takes the form

---

[1] *Estimates*, Sel. Cttee. 1st Report, p. xxiv; 1966–67 (145).

[2] The discrepancy between our present figures and those calculated by the committee was probably due to the speed at which the committee had to work. The figure of 14·3 per cent was an average of the averages for each provincial force and thus treated all forces as equal regardless of size. It would have been better to have given weight to the larger forces by working on the total number of hours in all forces combined. This would have resulted in a figure of 13·6 per cent—somewhat smaller than the committee's figure. The big discrepancy, however, was due to the committee's failure to include patrolling by traffic departments.

[3] *Ibid.*, p. xxiv.

of general supervision and how little time is spent on accidents and incidents. The total proportion of time spent on accidents and incidents amounted to 2·7 per cent of all active duty in the provincial forces as against 17·2 per cent for supervision of one kind or another. This is a ratio of 1:6·4. Again it is difficult to say whether this figure is high or low, but there is evidence that supervision may lead to a reduction in accidents, so that the small proportion of time spent on accidents and incidents should not necessarily be regarded as a bad thing.

The ratio of traffic court work to non-court work is also exaggerated by Table VI.9. Adding on the patrolling of traffic departments produces a ratio of 1:6·4 which is the same as the corresponding ratio connected with criminal work.

The traffic work of the Metropolitan police as shown by Table VI.9 was rather different. The overall proportion of traffic work, as we have already seen, was lower in the Metropolitan area than in the provinces (19·3 per cent[1] as against 23 per cent), and the emphasis appears to have been rather more on what might be termed the 'law enforcement' approach to traffic than the 'supervision' approach. Thus, of the time shown in Table VI.9 the ratio of court to non-court traffic work was 1:4 (compared with 1:6·4 for the provinces), and relatively more time was spent on accidents and incidents as against supervision as such. The total time on accidents and incidents amounted to 5·4 per cent as against 13·6 per cent[1] on all other forms of supervision. This is certainly a higher proportion than was found in the provinces.

Most other forms of duty which we isolated were found to involve less time than might have been expected. Foreign Enquiries—those tasks undertaken for other forces, official and semi-official bodies—turned out to involve less than 3½ per cent of time in the provincial forces and only just over 1 per cent in the Metropolitan. The Metropolitan figure was particularly low because, on account of its size, many enquiries from outside the divisional areas with which we were concerned would still come from within the force and therefore were not counted as 'foreign' for this purpose. Even so, the provincial figure was not particularly high.

The time spent on Civil Incidents was even smaller; under

---

[1] This figure has been adjusted to take into account the contribution of the Central Traffic Division.

2 per cent in the provinces and less in the Metropolitan. It is, of course, good that Civil Incidents of any seriousness were so rare as to make small demands on police time; our figures, however, probably underestimate the time spent on answering minor queries which would not take sufficient time to be recorded under our system. It does, however, seem that under the traditional system of policing the scope of the police in acting as general social workers was distinctly limited. It may be that Unit Beat Policing with its greater emphasis on the neighbourhood will afford more possibilities in this direction.

The figures for 'public order' might be cited as evidence of the long-term success of the service, founded as it was largely to ensure the maintenance of public order. No doubt much patrolling could be seen as having such a function, but even so the figures for time spent specifically on public order could hardly have been lower—$\frac{1}{2}$ per cent in the provinces and $\frac{3}{4}$ per cent in the Metropolitan area.[1]

### Conclusions

In this chapter we have described the broad pattern of police work as revealed by our manpower surveys. Our main findings, which relate to a sample of provincial forces in 1965, and to the Metropolitan police as in April 1966, may be summarized as follows:

1. Under normal circumstances the effective strength of the police service was rather less than two-thirds of its total strength on paper. This was due to what, in police circles, are called 'Abstractions'. This slightly artificial concept is based on the assumption that the whole of an officer's time is available to the police service and abstractions are the necessary and desirable provisions for leave, refreshment breaks and training appropriate to a twentieth-century service.

2. In the provincial forces abstractions averaged 42 per cent of potential duty time, and the Metropolitan figure was 34 per cent. Differences between forces were almost entirely due to variations in the length of the working week. Regular overtime, as in the Metropolitan police, was the major influence and, naturally, reduced time available for leave.

[1] The survey period, incidentally, included the State Opening of Parliament.

3. Leave accounted for 70·3 per cent of all abstractions for police officers in the provincial forces, but only 59 per cent in the Metropolitan. The proportions for civilians were even higher, due to their lower figure for refreshment breaks and insignificant amounts of time spent on training. For police officers training accounted for about 13 per cent of abstractions. Sick leave was less than 5 per cent of abstractions except for Metropolitan officers.

4. The average hours actually worked per fortnight were:

| | |
|---|---|
| Provincial forces | 77·5 |
| Metropolitan ('B' and 'S' Divisions) | 91·2 |
| Metropolitan (Central Traffic Division) | 86·8 |

5. In all forces Criminal Investigation departments averaged longer hours than other departments. The difference was the equivalent of an hour a day in the provincial forces, and rather more than two hours a day in the Metropolitan. Three specialist squads from Scotland Yard averaged 122 hours a fortnight.

6. Our figures for overtime working confirmed those already published. They indicated that, in most cases, high figures resulted from the working of extra shifts. The Scotland Yard Squads, however, not only worked extra shifts, but long tours of duty as well.

7. Law Enforcement accounted for 74 per cent of working time in the provincial forces and 81·5 per cent in the metropolitan land divisions. The Administration of Justice occupied just over 10 per cent, and the treatment of offenders less than 1 per cent. Civil duties formed the balance of working time: 14·4 per cent in the provincial forces and 7·4 per cent in the Metropolitan divisions.

8. The general duty of maintaining Civil Order (mainly by patrolling) was the largest single area of operation—about 40 per cent in most forces. Crime was the next most important area, averaging 28 per cent in the provinces and 31 per cent in the Metropolitan divisions. Finally, traffic work accounted for 23 per cent in the provincial forces and 17·7 per cent in the Metropolitan land divisions. This pattern was based on averages and did not apply in all areas; in some, for example, traffic work took more time than crime.

9. The separate classes of work within this pattern were notable mainly for the small amounts of time spent on such activities as 'foreign enquiries', civil incidents, public order and so on. The maintenance of public order, for instance, occupied only $\frac{1}{2}$ per cent in the provinces and $\frac{3}{4}$ per cent in the Metropolitan divisions.

The general picture that has emerged from this data is of an organization still dominated by a form of operation devised more than a century ago to meet the then dominant problem of maintaining public order. In this the police have been highly successful. Their adaptation, however, to the two major problems of the mid-twentieth century—crime and traffic—has been uneven and of varying success from area to area.

The most significant fact about the broad pattern of work was that about half the total time was spent on activities of a non-specific nature. These were not directly concerned with crime, traffic or other definite incidents, but were directed either to the support of operations, e.g. in communications, or to such duties as patrolling whose precise effects are difficult to establish.

Probably the most important result of the examinations of the whole question of police manpower made by the Home Office Working Parties on Police Manpower, Equipment and Efficiency,[1] and by the Police Research and Planning Branch,[2] has been the realization that the traditional beat system is not the only possible form of organization. The Police Research and Planning Branch has introduced the concept of Unit Beat Policing[3] and this has already led to a radical reappraisal of manpower requirements. This was no doubt given some impetus by the economic difficulties of 1967 and 1968. For example, *The Times* of 23 December 1967 carried a report by its Home Affairs Correspondent which, after saying that cuts in the building programme were likely, commented:

> More surprising is that police recruitment may come under examination. There is an impression that, with increasing use of the unit beat system, establishments for some forces may be too high.

This speculation was confirmed within a few weeks when the Home Secretary, Mr. J. Callaghan, in reply to questions about the limiting of police recruitment, said:

> The increase in police strength has been unparalleled in the last three years, and we have been making up past deficiencies. We have now reached the stage when I think that the question of establishment needs to be looked at on a much more scientific basis than it was in the past, especially in view of the change in policing systems . . .

---

[1] Taverne Report, 1967.
[2] Since retitled Police Research and Development Branch.
[3] Described more fully on pp. 180 ff.

... the fact that the various establishments have been built up on an unscientific basis in the past is the reason why we are now working them out properly and are not recruiting men if they are not necessary. ...[1]

Our surveys, therefore, came at what future historians may see as the end of an era based on the concept of policing as a general purpose activity. Our earlier chapters have shown, in general terms, how the disposition of resources was increasingly influenced by local experiments and by the initiatives of the central government; our subsequent chapters will examine the more specialized aspects in greater detail and will attempt an appraisal of some of the developments of the mid-1960's.

[1] Houses of Commons Debates, 15 February 1968, Cols 1556 ff.

A.S.I.M.—12

# VII

# Criminal Investigation and Traffic Work

THIS is the first of several chapters in which we consider some more detailed aspects of police work. Our data being of a general kind it would be unwise to attempt a very close analysis, but we can produce some evidence on topics of current interest. In this chapter we shall discuss work related to crime and traffic. Chapter VIII will be concerned with court work and with comparing surveys of the same forces made in winter and summer. The next chapter will deal with the work of women police, traffic wardens and civilians, while Chapter X will cover urban and rural differences, training and aspects of mobility.

*Criminal investigation*

In Chapter VI we showed that the investigation of crime, in one form or another, tended to be the principal specific activity of the forces participating in our surveys. Patrolling occupied more time, but is a general purpose activity. In the provincial forces work directly concerned with crime occupied about 28 per cent of active duty. Our two Metropolitan divisions averaged 31·4 per cent.[1] We shall now discuss how the forces concerned used this time.

Several questions have to be considered. First, we need to make some estimate of the work load. Second, we shall consider the role of the C.I.D. in the force, and the incidence of crime related to the strength of that department. Third, we examine how criminal work is divided between the various departments. Fourth we relate the hours worked both by the whole force and by

[1] This figure may have been an underestimate of the volume of criminal work in the force as a whole. The Commissioner's Office includes the important central C.I.D. Departments with quite substantial staffs, but it also includes larger numbers in other departments. Furthermore our 'B' Division figures were probably unusually high on account of a murder enquiry. It does not seem possible to refine the figure quoted without more evidence than is available.

members of the C.I.D. to the numbers of crimes reported and arrests made. Fifth, we see how C.I.D. time was distributed between abstractions and active duty, and between functions. In particular we examine the relationship between investigation time and court work. Sixth, we see how much time is spent report writing and in the station. Finally we consider some implications for the relationship between the work of the C.I.D. and uniformed officers.

The most obvious measure of the load of criminal work is the number of crimes reported to the police. Its limitations as a unit are that it appears not to take into account the variety of crimes and the differing amounts of investigation involved, the volume of paper work and so on. Nevertheless it is probably still the best single index of the volume of criminal work, and clearly the most appropriate for a fairly general survey. The forces in our surveys kindly provided us with the number of crimes committed during the fortnight each survey was held, and also gave the number of arrests made within the same period.

Before discussing our results we should mention that our figures for the number of crimes reported, although based on a short period and so subject to chance fluctuations, were sufficiently closely correlated with the annual totals for 1965 to be regarded as representative.[1]

This descriptive information is summarized in Table VII.1, in which the actual figures have been standardized to allow for differences in population. This gives an indication of the relative volume of crime in the survey areas, but it does not necessarily imply that the burden on the C.I.D. varies in the same way; much will depend on the relative strength of the department in each force and the extent to which responsibility for criminal investigation is shared with other departments.

When the figures for reported crimes and for arrests per 100,000 of the population were correlated it became clear that they were not significantly related to each other.[2] They would appear,

---

[1] Our figures were compared with the annual number of crimes reported to the police and recorded in *Supplementary Criminal Statistics* 1965, Table 4, total a, i. The basis of comparison is described in Appendix B.4, but using the Wilcoxon test it was clear that the sample for the survey period was not significantly different from the annual data. See p.275 for further details.

[2] $r = 0.4622$, $t = 1.9350$; not significant.

therefore, to relate to rather different aspects of police work. This discrepancy is quite understandable. There may be a time lag between crimes and arrests, crimes may be prosecuted by way of summons (rather than arrest) in some areas but not others, while arrests may be made for breaches of public order, such as drunkenness and obstruction, which may involve little in the way of criminal investigation.

### TABLE VII.1

**Volume of criminal work in survey period (two weeks) (1965–66)**

| | Crimes reported per 100,000 population (1) | per C.I.D. member† (2) | Arrests per 100,000 population‡ (3) | C.I.D. as % of total force (4) |
|---|---|---|---|---|
| Plymouth | 106 | 4·4 | 39 | 11·5 |
| Hastings* | 91 | 3·9 | 24 | 10·8 |
| Pembrokeshire* | 48 | 2·9 | 15 | 7·5 |
| Dorset* | 122 | 7·6 | 18 | 8·7 |
| Bristol | 60 | 2·3 | 54 | 10·0 |
| Bath | 169 | 6·5 | 58 | 13·8 |
| Barrow-in-Furness | 210 | 9·1 | 37 | 10·3 |
| Birkenhead | 72 | 2·6 | 37 | 9·7 |
| Leic. and Rutland | 61 | 3·9 | 10 | 9·2 |
| Northumberland | 72 | 4·7 | 17 | 9·7 |
| Bedfordshire | 69 | 2·9 | 33 | 11·5 |
| Essex | 95 | 5·2 | 18 | 13·6 |
| Average (weighted) | 86 | 4·4 | 25 | 10·8 |
| Metropolitan | | | | |
| 'B' Division | 445 | 9·5 | 49 | 16·3 |
| 'S' Division | 119 | 6·3 | 31 | 10·3 |
| Average (weighted) | 237 | 8·1 | 38 | 13·1 |

\* The number of crimes has been averaged over the two survey periods for those forces which were surveyed twice.

† The term C.I.D. member includes all civilians in the department.

‡ We did not obtain figures for crimes dealt with by summons.

The rather wide variations in crime rates shown in column (1) of Table VII.1 were only to be expected as our sampling had been designed to include forces in high and low crime areas. Nevertheless the range in the provincial forces was quite considerable—from 48 to 210 per 100,000 population—and there was a large gap between the rates of the two Metropolitan divisions.

The difference between the provincial and Metropolitan averages, 86 and 237, was large and, no doubt, indicative of the vast problem of dealing with crime in the Metropolis. 'B' Division had the highest rate encountered anywhere, while even 'S' Division would have ranked fourth among the provincial forces.

Such figures have little meaning in terms of police administration until they can be related to the resources available to deal with crime. This is not an easy matter. There are no published standards of case-loads for detectives, and rather different points of view have been expressed at various times. The earliest published discussion of the subject appears to have been that of The Departmental Committee on Detective Work and Procedure (1933–38) which commented:

> We have naturally considered whether any guidance regarding the proper detective strength for a force can be obtained by reference to the statistics of local crime, on the principle that, taking one branch of detective work with another, it might be possible to determine the strength of the C.I.D. personnel required to deal with any given number of recorded crimes, but we have come to the conclusion that, having regard to the variety of local conditions, it is not possible to arrive at any certain conclusions from these figures. The only safe course, in our view, is to take careful account of the personnel, organisation and equipment of each force in relation to the actual work which should be attended to by the detective staff, and to adjust the former to the latter so that the various branches of the work can be accomplished effectively and without overstrain. In this connection it will be necessary also to take account of the strength of the uniform branch, particularly in the county forces.[1]

This view, however, was by no means universally held, for, over roughly the same period, the Metropolitan police had a committee sitting to enquire into the establishment of the C.I.D. In about 1938 this committee managed to devise a 'unit of work' for a detective. It is not known exactly how this was done, but presumably it took into account some of the variables we have just mentioned such as numbers of crimes, arrests and so on.

After the second world war this approach was maintained and an Establishments Committee produced a formula taking into

[1] Home Office, *Report of the Departmental Committee on Detective Work and Procedure*, London, H.M.S.O., 1939, Vol. I, p. 98.

account various factors 'such as the number of reported crimes, arrests, sets of correspondence and pages of typescript produced, and the type of area and travelling facilities available at each station, and recommended that the authorised establishment should be redistributed according to the number of units credited on this basis to each station'.[1]

In due course the Dixon Committee on *The Employment and Distribution of Strength in the Metropolitan police* examined the working of this formula and concluded that a distribution sufficiently similar for practical purposes could be arrived at simply by using the number of reported crimes without taking any other factors into account.

The question, however, has to be taken a further stage, to ask not merely 'where' but 'how many' detectives there should be. The committee ascertained that in 1938 the proportion of crimes to the number of C.I.D. officers in divisions had been 205:1. This was not regarded as adequate, both because the rate of crime had been rising fairly rapidly at that time, and because working conditions had since been improved.[2] The committee, indeed, enumerated all the points which are still being raised in discussions of the subject—the overtime worked by C.I.D., the limits on the amount of investigation possible for each case, and the possibilities of relief through the employment of civilian shorthand typists to save the amount of time spent on report writing.

Their conclusion was that, taking all these points into account, 'an establishment based on the number of reported crimes in the proportion of one C.I.D. officer of the rank of Inspector and below to 150 crimes would give local and aggregate establishments reasonably commensurate with the volume of work'.[3]

It would seem that, on the whole, this rule of thumb figure is as near to an agreed ratio as has yet been produced in the police service. Much of the work of the Home Office Police Research

---

[1] The quotation is from the unpublished report of the Dixon Committee (1956). We are indebted to the Commissioner of the Metropolitan police and the Home Office for permission to refer to and quote from the report.

[2] 'Since 1938 the amount of ordinary leave for all ranks has been substantially increased,* and on this account alone less work can be handled by each man in the course of a year.

    * For constables, for example, by 6 days' ordinary leave and 6 days for Bank Holidays.' (Dixon Report, Pt. III, p. 323.)

[3] *Ibid.*, p. 554.

and Planning Branch is, however, relevant and it remains to be seen whether further refinements can be achieved.[1]

Probably the major change that has taken place since the pre-war period and, indeed, even since the Dixon Committee began its deliberations, has been the steady introduction of civilian specialists into Criminal Investigation Departments. These have included not only the shorthand typists referred to, but also those with more technical qualifications in such skills as photography, examination of scenes of crime, fingerprint work and the keeping of criminal records.

The detailed effects of introducing civilians into C.I.D.s were beyond the scope of our research, but Table VII.2 affords the basis for an estimate in that we have calculated the case-load per

TABLE VII.2

### Place of civilians in criminal investigation departments (1965-66)

| | Total strength of dept. (1) | Civilians as % of dept.† (2) | Crimes reported* per C.I.D. officer (3) | per C.I.D. member (4) |
|---|---|---|---|---|
| Plymouth | 50 | 6·0 | 125 | 114 |
| Hastings | 16 | 11·7 | 112 | 101 |
| Pembrokeshire | 16 | 6·3 | 78 | 75 |
| Dorset | 51 | 15·7 | 232 | 198 |
| Bristol | 115 | 11·3 | 65 | 60 |
| Bath | 21 | 9·5 | 187 | 169 |
| Barrow-in-Furness | 15 | 13·3 | 272 | 237 |
| Birkenhead | 39 | 10·3 | 70 | 68 |
| Leic. and Rutland | 71 | 19·7 | 127 | 101 |
| Northumberland | 75 | 16·0 | 145 | 122 |
| Bedfordshire | 61 | 13·1 | 88 | 75 |
| Essex | 218 | 21·5 | 172 | 135 |
| Total/Averages | 648 | 15·4 | 135 | 114 |
| Metropolitan | | | | |
| 'B' Division | 102 | 11·8 | 278 | 247 |
| 'S' Division | 73 | 13·7 | 190 | 164 |
| Total | 175 | 12·6 | 242 | 210 |

* This is the survey figure expressed as an annual rate.
† Where forces were surveyed twice the strength of the department was taken as the mean of the two figures.

[1] *Estimates*, Sel. Cttee, 1st Report, pp. 17–18; 1966–67 (145).

police officer, and per C.I.D. member, and the difference is fairly clear.

It will be seen that the lowest proportion of civilians was 6·0 per cent and the highest 21·5 per cent, with a mean of 15·4 per cent. There appears to have been no universal explanation. Shortage of manpower may have been an influence in areas where regular overtime was worked, but this only affected a few areas. Operational influences do not seem to have been important. Neither the crime rate in the area nor the case-load per C.I.D. officer was significantly correlated with the proportion of civilians in the department.[1] The most likely explanation was a structural one, namely that the employment of civilians in C.I.D.s was related to the size of the department. There was a fairly pronounced tendency for the proportion of civilians to be highest in the larger departments.[2] This was not invariably the case, but it applied sufficiently to suggest that the police service is no exception to the tendency for specialization to flourish in large organizations, and civilians in C.I.D.s are invariably specialists of one kind or another.

Table VII.2 provides a basis for considering two of the issues mentioned earlier—the contribution of civilians and the case-load per officer. It will be seen from column (3) that, even when the contribution of civilians was discounted, the provincial average of crimes per C.I.D. officer (135) was comfortably below the 150 mark, and only four forces exceeded it. When civilians were included in the calculation the average went down by about 20 cases, but even then the same four forces exceeded the average case-load of 150. The two Metropolitan divisions, as might be expected, were both well above the 150 mark.

It seems likely, however, that this method of calculation somewhat understates the burden on the individual officers in charge of cases. Some C.I.D. members (e.g. those concerned with criminal record work, or with crime prevention), might do little in the way of investigation, while even the other specialists would not have

---

[1] Correlating proportion of civilians in C.I.D. with case-load per C.I.D. officer gave $r = 0·3449$ (not significant). Correlating civilians in C.I.D. with reported crimes per 100,000 of population gave $r = -0·0320$ (not significant).

[2] Correlating total strength of department with civilians as percentage of department gave $r = 0·6195$, $t = 2·9523$. At the 2 per cent level with 12 d.f, $t$ is significant.

to conduct enquiries and maintain the continuity of the investigation. We have, unfortunately, no means of estimating the case-load on investigating officers.

So far as the employment of civilians was concerned it may be that the change in the average case-load of some 20 cases referred to above (according to whether or not civilians were included) represents a rough guide to their contribution in the C.I.D. On this basis their maximum contribution might be as much as 25 cases per detective a year (in a force where a fifth of the department are civilians) down to an almost negligible minimum. Much, however, would depend on the size of working units in a force.

Broadly speaking there was a fair degree of association between the crime rate of an area and the strength of its C.I.D. Thus in the provincial forces the total strength of the C.I.D. (including civilians) was highly correlated with the number of crimes reported during the survey period ($r = 0.9248$, $t = 8.4186$; significant at $0.1$ per cent level). When the same calculation was made but including the two Metropolitan divisions the resulting correlation was still high but not quite so high ($0.8550$).

On the other hand there was also a high correlation between the criminality of the area (expressed in crimes per 100,000 of the population during the survey period) and the number of crimes reported per C.I.D. member. In this case $r = 0.8100$, which was significant at the $0.1$ per cent level. These two sets of facts suggest that while there may be a rather general association between the strength of the C.I.D. and the intensity of the crime problem with which it has to deal, this association breaks down when the level of criminality gets above a certain point, and the police organization is no longer able to adapt to the increasing scale of problems by deploying more of its resources in the appropriate specialist department. This point had clearly been reached in some of the forces in our surveys.

While in some ways it might seem inefficient for the police service not to adapt by increasing the C.I.D. element, there may be quite good reasons for not doing so. In most cases the C.I.D. strength was adequate in terms of the Dixon formula, while there are other legitimate claims on the strength of the force. It should be remembered that a policy of always increasing the C.I.D. to match the crime rate would rapidly lead to an impossible situation in which forces would become dominated by their Criminal

Investigation Departments. This would be not only to overlook the many other necessary duties that uniformed officers have to perform, but to reject the commonly accepted theory that a substantial uniformed branch is needed for crime prevention purposes. This aspect was emphasized by the Dixon committee, for one of its main recommendations was that when an increase in the strength of the Metropolitan police could be achieved first priority should be given to augmenting the number of uniformed men on patrol and beat duties.

This leads naturally to the question of how crime investigation work was distributed between departments. The details are shown in Appendix D, Table 5. As would be expected, the C.I.D. was responsible for the bulk of the work both in the provincial forces (56·5 per cent) and in our two Metropolitan divisions (59·2 per cent). Next came Beat Patrols, whose large numbers of men in total contributed 24·5 per cent in the provincial forces and 26·9 per cent in the Metropolitan divisions. All other departments added rather small proportions to the total, with 'Other Duties' and 'Station Staff' accounting for most of the remainder. It was noteworthy that traffic departments averaged only 2·7 per cent in the provinces and even less in the Metropolitan area.

These averages conceal quite large variations, among which something of a pattern may be discerned. The forces in which work was spread so that the C.I.D. proportion was below average tended to be counties, while the policy of treating crime investigation as a relatively specialized function largely confined to the C.I.D. seems to have prevailed in some of the more densely populated urban areas. (This means that in such areas the work of beat patrols tended to be unrelieved by specific activities, with very large amounts of time being described simply as 'patrolling'). The range, in fact, was fairly considerable. Concentration of crime investigation in the hands of the C.I.D. was at its maximum in Barrow-in-Furness, with a figure of 79·4 per cent, while its lowest was 31·2 per cent (Pembrokeshire). The contribution of beat patrols ranged from 44·3 per cent in Pembrokeshire to only 6·5 per cent in Birkenhead. Traffic Departments also showed some variation, from 0·9 per cent to 9·1 per cent; the characteristics of the forces concerned do not suggest any particular reasons for this. The 'Other Duties' group had the widest range of all. This can probably be explained by the different emphasis they placed on such sub-departments as Dog Handlers, Vice-Squad and so on. In the larger forces these were apt to be separate entities and so included 'Other Duties' in our survey, whereas in the smaller they might all be included within other departments.

In the previous chapter we summarized the data on the average hours worked in the various departments and showed that the C.I.D. normally worked longer hours than other departments. We can now examine this point a little further by comparing the hours worked with the crime rate and also with the number of arrests made. These relationships are summarized in Table VII.3 below.

These results should be interpreted with considerable caution. Obviously the time spent on investigation did not necessarily

TABLE VII.3

**Time spent on crime investigation related to crimes and arrests (hours) (1965–66)**

|  | Average per crime reported | | Average per arrest | |
|  | Whole force | C.I.D. | Whole force | C.I.D. |
|---|---|---|---|---|
| Plymouth | 26·1 | 14·4 | 70·6 | 39·1 |
| Hastings* | 23·4 | 13·9 | 106·6 | 63·6 |
| Pembroke* | 58·5 | 18·3 | 179·7 | 56·1 |
| Dorset* | 18·5 | 7·7 | 117·8 | 48·9 |
| Bristol | 43·3 | 24·3 | 48·9 | 26·9 |
| Bath | 13·6 | 8·8 | 39·7 | 25·5 |
| Barrow-in-Furness | 8·9 | 7·1 | 50·7 | 40·3 |
| Birkenhead | 33·8 | 24·4 | 65·4 | 47·4 |
| Leic. and Rutland | 27·2 | 15·0 | 161·1 | 88·9 |
| Northumberland | 21·6 | 13·0 | 93·5 | 56·3 |
| Bedford | 37·4 | 19·0 | 78·1 | 40·2 |
| Essex | 19·4 | 11·9 | 100·7 | 61·7 |
| Average† | 23·9 | 13·5 | 81·9 | 46·3 |
| Metropolitan | | | | |
| 'B' Division | 15·4 | 9·0 | 138·5 | 81·2 |
| 'S' Division | 16·8 | 10·1 | 63·7 | 38·4 |
| Average† | 15·8 | 9·4 | 98·8 | 58·5 |

* These figures are based on the first survey held in each area.
† These averages are based on the aggregate of crimes and hours in all areas.

relate to the crimes committed within the survey period, and on which the above figures are based. In particular the 'B' Division figures of investigation time were inflated by the enquiry into a murder committed a few days before the survey began.

The first point concerns the difference between the two sets of averages of investigation time per crime reported, and per arrest. Both sets of figures are necessarily artificial as we did not know how time was divided between successful and unsuccessful investigations. These averages are based on the assumptions first, that *all* time went on crimes reported, and, alternatively, that all time went on investigations which led to arrests. Obviously the averages shown in our Table understate the differences which might arise in real life. Probably all we can say is that it might be profitable to analyse crime investigations into those that were fruitful and those that were not, and to see at what point it was possible to tell that success would not be achieved.

Secondly, the average time spent by whole forces, both per crime and per arrest, was subject to much more variation than the corresponding averages for the C.I.D. only. It is, of course, difficult to know how much significance (in a real as opposed to a statistical sense) should be seen in such variance. The average number of hours per arrest ranged from 25·5 to 88·9.

One other possible use of our data is to produce some guidelines for manpower planning. The results no doubt have their imperfections, but may provide stimulus for thought. For example Table V.4 shows that the average number of hours worked by members of C.I.D. in the provincial forces was 88·5 per fortnight or, in round terms, 44 per week. The corresponding Metropolitan figures were 116·3 and 58. If these figures are then related to the average number of hours per arrest it would appear that the average provincial C.I.D. might expect to make one arrest per member per week. If we exclude civilians the figure per police officer in the C.I.D. would be slightly higher, about 1·1 per week. Making a similar calculation for the Metropolitan police the expectation would also be one arrest per week. In this case the longer average time spent per arrest is balanced by the longer working hours of the force.

On this basis it would seem that the rule of thumb figure of 150 cases a year might be on the high side although, of course, there is no means of knowing how much effort would be needed to increase the present clear-up rates of 40·2 per cent for England and Wales and 22·3 per cent for the Metropolitan police district.[1]

Lastly, in this connection, we can examine the relationship between the number of arrests and the hours worked on criminal investigation. To do this we correlated the number of arrests made with the total number of hours spent on crime investigation, first by the force as a whole and secondly by the C.I.D. The results were closely similar in each case: quite high positive correlations, significant at the 0·1 per cent level.[2] This would seem to justify the conclusion that arrests are made as a result of putting in enough hours of work. In itself this is a rather old-fashioned conclusion—that there are no short cuts in detection—but the fact that the correlation was as high on an all-force basis as when C.I.D. work only was counted, suggests that concentration on the C.I.D. alone might not be the most rewarding way of tackling the crime problem.

We can now turn to look a little more closely at the use of C.I.D. time. Although total working hours were longer than in most other departments, and the proportion of abstractions was correspondingly lower, the frequency of the different types of abstraction was much the same as for all departments combined. Examination of the figures for the different ranks, however, revealed the interesting fact that detective sergeants and constables enjoyed lower rates of sickness[3] than their uniformed colleagues. In most cases the amount of sick leave among the uniformed ranks in the provincial forces was two to three times as high.[4] Indeed, during the survey period seven out of the twelve forces lost no time at all due to sickness among detective sergeants and constables, while the overall contribution of sick leave to abstractions was only 2·1 per cent. This did not, however, apply in the Metropolitan divisions where the sickness rates for detectives and uniformed men were virtually the same.

We gained no direct evidence on the explanation for these

---

[1] SOURCES: *Criminal Statistics, England and Wales, 1966; 1966–67* Cmd. 3332. *Commissioner of Police of the Metropolis, 1966.*

[2] Arrests correlated with hours investigation by whole force gave $r = 0.8252$,
$$t = 5.4656.$$
Arrests correlated with hours investigation by whole force gave $r = 0.8195$,
$$t = 5.3495.$$

[3] This included both certificated and uncertificated sickness.

[4] Detailed figures are given in Appendix D, Table 8.

differences, but likely factors of importance might be the higher proportion of indoor work and, perhaps, a greater involvement in the job.

We can now subdivide the active duty time of the C.I.D. according to function. The results are shown in Table VII.4 below.

TABLE VII.4

**Allocation of active duty by function—C.I.D.** (1965–66)
(Percentages in each category)*

|  | Law enforcement | Admin. of justice | Treatment of offenders | Civil duties |
|---|---|---|---|---|
| *Provincial forces* | 85·7 | 12·8 | 0·8 | 0·8 |
| *Metropolitan* |  |  |  |  |
| 'B' and 'S' Divisions | 90·0 | 9·1 | 0·6 | 0·3 |
| Special Squads | 95·0 | 5·0 | — | — |

\* These figures are averages based on the total hours worked under these headings by all forces combined.

It will be seen that only two functions involve significantly large amounts of time: law enforcement and the administration of justice. These are nearly synonymous with crime investigation and court work and raise the interesting question of the relationship between the two. Law enforcement as defined, however, is rather broader than crime investigation, and we have therefore calculated a set of ratios based on crime investigation alone related to criminal court work.

For the provincial criminal investigation departments the ratio of Court: Investigation time averaged 1:6·5. The variance was fairly large with a range from 1:4·2 to 1:12·4. As was said in Chapter VI the most likely explanation for this variation was the occasion or absence of higher court sittings during the survey period. The Metropolitan ratio ('B' and 'S' Divisions) was 1:9·6, while for the special squads it was 1:19. These ratios were rather higher than the corresponding ones for whole forces stated in Chapter VI, particularly that for the Metropolitan divisions. They are consistent with the possibility that detective work of a more elaborate kind takes far longer in relation to court time than the simpler crime work of uniformed men. This information is, perhaps, just one more indication of the degree of difference between the work of the two branches.

It is very difficult to judge whether these ratios are reasonable. Perhaps it is best simply to indicate what they imply in days out of the working week which have to be spent in court or doing work related to it (in our rather narrow sense). For example in the provinces the ratio implies that in a working fortnight of 11 or 12 days, the greater part of two days is spent on court work in this sense. Allowing roughly for the fact that some members are civilian typists it seems for the police officers that two days a fortnight would be a reasonable estimate.

Two days may not seem a great deal, but the total is likely to be spread over more than that number and, in addition, a significant amount of time is likely to be spent on relevant paper work. At the request of the Chief Constables we included a section on time spent report writing, again in a narrow sense, and we should mention here that not only did C.I.D.s contribute the bulk of all report writing in almost all forces, but that on average this activity accounted for 17·4 per cent of their working time in the provincial forces, and 19·7 per cent in the Metropolitan divisions. In the special squads it averaged 27·9 per cent, with the fraud squad reaching 49·2 per cent.

Although our definition of court work recognized the fact that some activities undertaken beforehand are essentially for the benefit of the court and are not part of the investigation, it did not include much of the groundwork for prosecutions that would occupy C.I.D. time, for example the preparation of exhibits, consultations with the Director of Public Prosecutions and so on. From a C.I.D. point of view, therefore, our definition might be regarded as rather narrow. It was, then, all the more significant that for most criminal investigation departments court work and report writing together would involve nearly a third of working time.[1] Under these circumstances it would not be surprising if C.I.D. officers felt frustrated by the volume of paper and court work. Indeed the fact that these figures are averages implies that in some weeks such activities may occupy the bulk of working time.

Finally we should mention what we have termed 'Station Time'. This again was recorded at the request of the Chief Constables as

[1] This involves only a minimum of double counting. The preparation of antecedents, which is unlikely to be a large proportion of court work, would also rank as report writing.

an attempt to get a measure of its opposite, namely the amount of time officers were out and about, available to deal with the public. This may not be quite so important in the case of the C.I.D., but it gives some impression of the location of work which may be of some interest. The overall average for the provincial forces showed that almost exactly half C.I.D. working time was spent in the station (49·8 per cent). The figure for the two Metropolitan divisions was slightly higher at 53·4 per cent.

No suggestion is being made that time in the station is not well spent. From a supervisory point of view, however, it might be worth knowing that the possibilities of getting out and about are as limited as they appear to be. They underline the importance of such experiments as the various beat systems described by the Working Party on Operational Efficiency and Management in Appendices I and II to their report. It would seem that what is termed Unit Beat Policing is particularly concerned with the flow of information, and may prove an effective means of overcoming some of the problems of the volume of office work.

Unit beat policing was conceived by the Police Research and Planning Branch of the Home Office and, with the co-operation of the Lancashire police, was first tried in Accrington. The basis of the scheme is that each sub-division is divided into a number of areas, whose size is determined by local conditions but is likely to be in the region of seven or eight thousand population. 'Two areas comprise one motor car beat, and the car is on patrol for 24 hours; it is manned by one constable, equipped with personal radio, and controlled from the sub-divisional station. Superimposed on each of the car beats are two constables, one for each area. These men are known as the area constables and, as far as possible, live within their area. They have overall responsibility for their particular areas and when off duty are not replaced, cover being provided by car. . . . The car beat men and the area constables are assisted by a detective constable for each car beat. This gives a maximum of 4 men on duty at any one time on each of the four car beats, i.e. 2 area constables, 1 man on the car beat and 1 detective constable. A flow of information concerning the beat passes between members of the team. Apprehensions and other good police work are considered as the work of the team and not of any individual. This encourages team working and cuts out the 'lone wolf' attitude. The team is equipped with personal radio and is supervised by the sergeants and inspectors in the normal manner.

It is anticipated that the flow of information will become voluminous, and to ensure that this information is made available to the whole team, and indexed for its future members, some form of collating is necessary. The team must remain on their beat as much as possible, since any time spent away from it is non-productive and should be avoided. A detective constable has therefore been appointed as collator; he works in the sub-divisional office, keeping a record of all the information fed into him by members of the various teams and ensuring that each man is kept up to date with the latest developments on his beat.

Like the rest of his team, he is equipped with personal radio, and can be approached for information about any of the beats; he forwards information about known criminals to the force criminal intelligence bureau. The crime prevention officer in the division has been brought into the scheme and is supplied with information in regard to vulnerable premises and other aspects in his particular field. He also contributes to the flow of information.'[1]

It remains to be seen how far such a deliberate division of function both between members of the C.I.D. and between the C.I.D. and the uniformed branch results in greater efficiency. In general terms it is likely to be of great importance in making better use of manpower, but the means by which it does so are particularly interesting in the context of our results.

Broadly speaking we have described what might be termed the traditional system of crime investigation which involved, to a greater or lesser extent, a separation between the C.I.D. and the uniformed branches. The merits of specialized criminal investigation work in developing technical skill and, indeed, *esprit de corps*, are obvious. Its demerits are also important, not least in the context of rising crime rates. We found quite a high correlation (see p. 173) between the criminality of an area and the number of crimes reported per C.I.D. member. This suggested that above a certain level of crime no force could deploy a sufficiently high proportion of its strength directly in the C.I.D. to keep case-loads at a reasonable level. Once above such a level the only solution, other than simply ignoring minor crimes, must be to make better

[1] Taverne Report, p. 140.

use of uniformed officers. This is likely to be the first technical advantage of unit beat policing.

The second advantage may be the explicit emphasis on the use of information. The statistical part of our surveys barely covered this aspect, but from the amount of report writing involved it seemed that the sheer volume of paper work might inhibit the collation and interpretation even of such information as was already in the department's possession. Unit beat policing appears to offer a solution to this problem, partly by the very fact of identifying it as a problem, and partly by the introduction of the collator with his specific role as assembler, analyst and disseminator of information.

No one would claim that unit beat policing offers a solution to all problems, but its importance as the first major reappraisal of the long-established beat system can hardly be underestimated. Considered from a manpower angle its greatest virtue is that it should introduce specific aims to patrolling—the activity which traditionally has occupied the maximum possible amount of time, and whose achievements have proved so difficult to demonstrate in tangible form.

## Traffic

The second major branch of police work is the supervision of traffic. In total, as we have shown, traffic work accounted for 23 per cent of time in the provincial forces and 19·3 per cent in the Metropolitan police district. The problems, however, differ in several ways from those in the crime field, and the organization created to solve them also has its special characteristics. A brief discussion of these differences is necessary before considering the work load.

All police work can be divided into one or other of two main classes: dealing with incidents which are reported or in some other way become inescapably obvious, and the remainder in which the initiative to act or not is in the hands of the police. All branches of a force have their unavoidable tasks; crimes are reported and serious road accidents must be dealt with. They cannot be ignored and the only possibility of reducing their contribution to the total work load lies in varying the effort put into each case. One can contrast, for example, the amount of effort put into a murder enquiry as against a larceny from a parked vehicle. Some such selection of this kind is an inevitable and necessary means of adjusting the load to work capacity.

While traffic work has its unavoidable major incidents it is, perhaps, to a large extent subject to policy decisions about how much work is to be done. The most important of these is the formation of a specialist traffic department, to be found in all forces, and sometimes even amounting to an entire division as with the Metropolitan central traffic division. The equipping of such units involves considerable capital expenditure in the form of vehicles, garages, maintenance facilities and so on, with the result that this investment tends to tie a given proportion of the force to traffic work. As they do little work of other kinds this means that the load of traffic work undertaken by that part of the force is relatively fixed. Even more specific examples may be cited; the formation of a unit for towing illegally parked vehicles away will mean that the group of officers concerned does very little else. The employment of traffic wardens also has a similar effect. Their functions are highly specialized and they cannot be used for anything but traffic work. Greater flexibility is possible with beat patrols, but even with them such traffic work as they do tends to be dominated by relatively fixed forms of supervision such as point duty and attendance at school crossings.

These considerations imply that too much attention should not be paid to assessing the load of traffic work as, to some extent, it is a reflection of the way the strength of the force is deployed. Nevertheless Table VII.5 gives a broad indication of the work load in terms of offences and accidents in relation to the strength of the force as a whole, and of the traffic department in particular.

The first point to note is that the number of traffic offences and the number of traffic accidents reported were quite highly correlated $(r = 0.8125)$'[1] This is not to suggest there was a causal relationship, although the story of the South-West traffic experiment would seem to support the view that levels of patrolling by traffic departments do affect the accident rate,[2] but there was at least a strong positive association. This means also that we are justified in combining the two sets of figures to give a rate of

---

[1] When $r = 0.8125$, $t = 5.2142$, significant at 0.1 per cent level.
[2] *Estimates*, Sel. Cttee. 1st Report, pp. 141–2; 1966–67 (145).

## TABLE VII.5

### Volume of traffic work during survey fortnight (1965–66)

| | Traffic offences reported | Road accidents reported | Total (1) + (2) | Total(3) per force member | Total(3) per member of traffic department | Accidents per member of traffic department |
|---|---|---|---|---|---|---|
| | (1) | (2) | (3) | (4) | (5) | (6) |
| Plymouth | 557 | 102 | 659 | 1·52 | 14·64 | 2·67 |
| Hastings* | 207 | 42 | 249 | 1·59 | 9·96 | 1·68 |
| Pembrokeshire | 129 | 66 | 195 | 0·97 | 9·75 | 3·33 |
| Dorset* | 1,186 | 298 | 1,484 | 2·79 | 21·82 | 4·38 |
| Bristol | 763 | 329 | 1,092 | 0·95 | 12·27 | 3·70 |
| Bath | 162 | 63 | 225 | 1·48 | 14·06 | 3·94 |
| Barrow-in-Furness | 78 | 33 | 111 | 0·76 | 5·55 | 1·62 |
| Birkenhead | 213 | 81 | 294 | 0·73 | 5·55 | 1·53 |
| Leic. and Rutland | 534 | 262 | 796 | 1·03 | 5·94 | 1·96 |
| Northumberland | 224 | 221 | 445 | 0·58 | 8·09 | 4·02 |
| Bedfordshire | 434 | 180 | 614 | 1·16 | 10·59 | 3·10 |
| Essex | 1,328 | 611 | 1,939 | 1·21 | 13·75 | 4·33 |
| Total | 5,815 | 2,288 | 8,103 | 1·18 | 11·19 | 3·16 |
| Metropolitan | | | | | | |
| 'B' Division | 1,017† | 236† | 1,253 | 2·00 | 24·1 | 4·54 |
| 'S' Division | 609 | 415 | 1,024 | 1·44 | 18·6 | 7·55 |
| Total | 1,626 | 651 | 2,277 | 1·70 | 21·3 | 6·08 |
| C.T.D.‡ | 1,405 | 438 | 1,843 | | 4·6 | 1·10 |

    * These figures relate to the surveys held during the summer.
    † These numbers have been adjusted by adding one-twelfth of the cases reported by C.T.D., and the number in columns 5 and 6 has been similarly adjusted by adding one-twelfth of the strength of the C.T.D. to the Divisional Traffic Department.
    ‡ Central Traffic Division.

total traffic offences and accidents combined, as a reasonable index of the total work load due to specific incidents.

Secondly, there was a high correlation $(r = 0·8179)$[1] between the total volume of traffic offences and incidents and the total strength of the force. There was, however, a rather less close relationship with the strength of the traffic department $(r = 0·7325)$[2] which tends to confirm our general observation at the beginning of this section that traffic work is more likely to affect the whole

    [1] When $r = 0·8179$, $t = 5·3181$, significant at 0·1 per cent level.
    [2] When $r = 0·7325$, $t = 4·0255$, significant at 0·2 per cent level.

force than criminal work which is more concentrated in the hands of the C.I.D. While the strength of the traffic department was fairly highly correlated with the number of accidents *and* incidents reported, the correlation with the number of offences as such was somewhat lower $(r = 0.6661)$.[1]

It will be seen that the average number of traffic offences and accidents reported per force member was 1.18 for the provincial forces, and 1.70 for the Metropolitan. The range was from 0.58 to 2.79. The rank order does not suggest any particular explanation for the variation between forces. The two highest figures were for a largely rural county and a seaside resort with no through traffic, but both in the holiday season. The lowest figure was contributed by an equally rural county and was followed by a heavily built up area which was also a port. Column 5 relates the total to the strength of the traffic department. For most forces this makes only a moderate difference to their position in rank order, though obviously those with large traffic departments such as Hastings and Leicestershire and Rutland show lower rates, while 'S' and 'B' Divisions with fairly small traffic departments show higher ones.

Columns 5 and 6 of Table VII.5 undoubtedly overstate the work load of traffic departments in so far as it consists of dealing with reported offences and accidents. This is because other departments are likely to have dealt with some of them. Nevertheless, bearing in mind that these figures relate to a fortnight, it will be seen that in only three out of the fourteen areas (including the Metropolitan divisions) did the average number of incidents per traffic department member exceed one per day by a significant margin. The number of accidents, indeed, averaged just over three per fortnight per member in the provinces, and six in the Metropolitan divisions.

As our figures have not shown a particularly clear relationship between the indices of the volume of traffic work and the strength of the traffic department it will be necessary to examine the nature of traffic work more closely, and to see how it was distributed between departments.

Table VII.6 shows how traffic work was divided between its four main aspects—supervision, dealing with accidents unlikely to result in 'process', dealing with incidents likely to result in

[1] When $r = 0.6661$, $t = 3.3409$, significant at 1.0 per cent level.

process, and court work. Supervision was defined in a positive way, which involved definite activities such as directing traffic on point duty, dealing with traffic jams, supervising pedestrian or school crossings, escorting wide loads and so on. Patrolling by members of traffic departments, in the sense of being out and about driving along roads was not treated as supervision unless the officer concerned had to deal with a specific situation. Patrolling, however, was recorded separately so that its contribution to the total can be seen.

### TABLE VII.6

#### Frequency of main types of traffic work (1965–66)*

|  | Provincial forces | | Metropolitan 'B' & 'S' Div.† | | Central Traffic Division | |
|---|---|---|---|---|---|---|
|  | Hours | % | Hours | % | Hours | % |
| Supervision | 31,569 | 40·6 | 3,605 | 21·5 | 1,945 | 9·5 |
| Patrolling (traffic depts.) | 19,402 | 24·9 | 2,905 | 17·4 | 12,404 | 60·9 |
| Accidents (no process) | 3,747 | 4·8 | 677 | 4·0 | 583 | 2·9 |
| Incidents (possible process) | 8,295 | 10·7 | 5,308 | 31·7 | 3,838‡ | 18·8 |
| Court work | 14,768 | 19·0 | 4,248 | 25·4 | 1,599 | 7·9 |
|  | 77,781 | 100·0 | 16,743 | 100·0 | 20,369 | 100·0 |

* This table is based on the results of the first round surveys only.
† Includes allowances for contribution of C.T.D. to traffic work in 'B' Division area.
‡ Removal of vehicles causing obstruction accounted for 1,243 hours (32·4 per cent.)

As far as the provincial forces were concerned the dominant activity was clearly supervision of one kind or another. If we treat the patrolling of traffic departments as supervision the total amounted to approximately two-thirds (65·5 per cent). Accidents and incidents accounted for about a sixth (15·5 per cent); of these about two-thirds were regarded as likely to result in proceedings being taken.

The remaining fifth (19·0 per cent) was occupied by Court work. It is interesting to note that although the overall proportion of court work was not so very different from that relating to criminal investigation, the ratio between 'process' incidents and court work was quite unlike any other. The amount of time spent on court work was nearly double the time spent on the incidents as such. Without too much exaggeration we could say that each hour of dealing with incidents, including of course minor ones, generated about two hours of court work. In comparative terms these averages mean that whereas a detective would have to spend about six and a half hours on investigation before he spent an hour in court, the traffic work needed to generate an hour's attendance at court would take no more than half an hour.

The Metropolitan patterns, as presented by 'B' and 'S' Divisions and by the Central Traffic Division, were very different from that of the provincial forces and, indeed, from each other. All three divisions did far less direct supervision. The 'B' and 'S' Division rate was approximately half the provincial one, and the central Traffic Division's was only a quarter. The low figure for C.T.D. was probably due to their highly mechanized state which makes it impossible to compare their work with that of ordinary land divisions. The relatively low figure for supervision in 'B' and 'S' Divisions may have been due to the facts that neither employed traffic wardens at the time of the survey, and that the volume of London traffic led to a much higher proportion of time being occupied with incidents likely to end in 'process'.

The figures for patrolling by the traffic departments of 'B' and 'S' Divisions did not differ very much from the provincial average, and indeed the traffic department of the largest provincial city (Bristol) had a figure (20·3 per cent) which can be regarded as closely similar. There is, however, some internal evidence that the traffic departments of some forces recorded their patrolling as supervision and, although we have adjusted their figures as far as possible,[1] it seems wise to consider the two sets of figures together. If this is done it seems that the provincial forces and the Central Traffic Division devoted rather similar proportions of time (66–71 per cent) to patrolling/supervision, while 'B' and 'S' Divisions averaged considerably less (40 per cent).

The figures for 'no-process' accidents were even lower in the Metropolitan area than in the provinces, while the process figures were substantially higher. In the Central Traffic Division the difference was principally due to the time spent towing away

---

[1] The adjustment was made by summing the time entered under supervision and patrolling, and dividing this by the crude average ratio in which these classifications were divided in the remaining forces.

vehicles regarded as obstructing traffic. If the time spent on this was excluded the amount of 'process work' would have been only slightly higher than the provincial average. In 'B' and 'S' Divisions, however, the proportion of time occupied by work on incidents involving possible process was nearly three times as high as in the provinces. We have no evidence to account for this.

On the other hand, the Metropolitan area showed a considerable saving in terms of court work. The C.T.D. figure was less than half the provincial proportion, while the 'B' and 'S' Division figure, although higher in absolute terms was much more favourably related to the time spent on incidents likely to involve process. It would seem that in the Metropolitan area the procedure for handling court work in traffic cases has resulted in less time being spent on court work than on the incidents themselves. This was particularly marked in the case of the Central Traffic Division. The ratios of 'process incident time' to 'court time' summarize the differences rather neatly; they are best shown in terms of the incident time which generated one hour of court time: provincial 34 minutes, 'B' and 'S' Division 73 minutes, C.T.D. 143 minutes.

The question of how work is distributed between departments is possibly of more importance in relation to traffic than to crime. This is because the introduction of traffic wardens may alter the volume and nature of traffic work quite considerably, and because there is some scope for variety in administration, particularly in the handling of court work. We have already indicated the volume of patrolling by the traffic department (approximately 25 per cent of all traffic work in the provincial forces) and we shall not discuss this any further.

Supervision was the largest single category of traffic work in the provincial forces (40·6 per cent), and was quite important in 'B' and 'S' Divisions in the Metropolitan police (21·4 per cent). The main departmental responsibilities are shown below in Table VII.7.

The first point that can be made about these figures is that, although traffic wardens were employed in only three of the provincial forces (admittedly among the larger ones) and not in all areas even in these three, they nevertheless contributed a substantial proportion of the total. When it is remembered that there were only 83 all told, out of a total of 6,849,[1] we can see that

[1] These figures are of persons completing booklets in the survey.

17·2 per cent of all traffic supervision was done by 1·2 per cent of the total strength. It would seem clear, therefore, that the addition of only small numbers of wardens can make a disproportionate contribution to the volume of traffic supervision.[1] This is all the more true now that wardens have power to deal with moving vehicles which, at the time of our surveys, they did not.

It is not surprising that, relative to their numbers, members of traffic departments also made an above average contribution to traffic supervision. In their case 10·6 per cent of the provincial

TABLE VII.7

**Distribution of traffic supervision by departments (per cent)**
**(1965–66)**

| Department | Provincial | | | 'B' & 'S' Divisions |
|---|---|---|---|---|
| | Average | Max. | Min. | Average* |
| Traffic Wardens | 17·2 | 44·6 | 18·6† | — |
| Road Traffic | 24·2 | 49·9 | 11·7 | 22·6 |
| Beat Patrols | 49·3 | 77·5 | 35·6 | 74·3 |
| Administration | 2·1 | 8·2 | — | 0·6 |
| Station Staff | 5·4 | 15·7 | 0·6 | 1·5 |
| Others | 1·7 | | | 1·0 |
| | | | | |
| Total hours | 99·9 | | | 100·0 |
| | 31,596 | | | 3,605 |

\* These figures have been adjusted by adding one-twelfth of the relevant C.T.D. figures to those for 'B' Division.

† Only three forces employed traffic wardens at the time of the surveys, and then only in parts of the force areas. The minimum figure related to Essex which only employed wardens in two out of a total of nine divisional areas.

strength did nearly a quarter of the total work. This, of course, was an average, and in some forces the proportion was as high as a half, while in the lowest it was less than 12 per cent. The principal factor affecting this variation would appear simply to be the relative strength of the traffic department in the force, but it is difficult to establish this precisely owing to the distortion of the figures resulting from the employment of traffic wardens in three of the forces. The long hours worked on traffic supervision by wardens inevitably reduced the proportion worked by other departments. As a result the correlation between the contribution

[1] This point is examined in more detail on p. 217 where we discuss the impact of traffic wardens in relation to local conditions.

of the traffic department to supervision and the strength of that department in the force was only 0·6344.[1]

If the figures are recalculated excluding traffic wardens and the work done by them we find that traffic departments were then responsible for 29·3 per cent of traffic supervision, and the correlation with the strength of the department was 0·6902 for provincial forces. This was slightly higher than when wardens were included, and was significant at the 1 per cent level.[2]

Somewhat surprisingly there was virtually no difference between Borough and County forces in the contribution of traffic departments to total supervision. Indeed the average for Boroughs, at 29·8 per cent was slightly higher than the average for counties (28·9 per cent). Traffic supervision by beat patrols was almost exactly proportionate to their number. All other departments combined contributed only about 11 per cent to the total.

The two types of accident or incident—those expected to result in 'process' and those not—amounted to 10·7 and 4·8 per cent respectively of all traffic work in the provincial forces. The two were closely correlated ($r = 0·9136$)[3] so that there were in general no grounds for concluding that some forces were consistently more or less prosecution minded than others. Obviously there was some deviation, but the major factor seems to have been the volume of incidents. In addition the work created by both types of incidents was distributed between departments in an almost identical way, so that for practical purposes we can discuss the two together. The figures are summarized in Table VII.8.

It will be seen that the distribution of what was presumably mainly the outdoor part of the work was, in the provincial forces, not very dissimilar from that of traffic supervision. Beat patrols were, on average, more important and, curiously, traffic departments seem to have played a slightly lesser role. It is not clear why this should have been, but on examining the contribution of the traffic departments of the provincial forces it seems that there was a fairly high correlation[4] between the strength of such depart-

[1] Expressed in terms of police officers in the department as a proportion of police officers in the force. When $r = 0·6344$, $t = 2·8425$; at the 2 per cent level with 10 d.f. this value of $t$ is significant.

[2] When $r = 0·6902$, $t = 3·036$; at the 2 per cent level with 10 d.f. this value of $t$ is significant.

[3] When $r = 0·9136$, $t = 7·7814$, significant at 0·1 per cent level.

[4] $r = 0·8320$, $t = 5·1948$, significant at 0·1 per cent level,

ments in the force and the proportion of incidents they dealt with. This tends to suggest the simple conclusion that accidents have to be dealt with when and where they occur, and that if the traffic department is relatively large it will handle bigger proportions— the highest figure was 34·4 per cent; while if it is smaller it will handle correspondingly less—the lowest figure was 8·1 per cent. The differences between urban and rural areas do not appear to have been at all relevant in this connection: the two highest and the two lowest figures were all found in urban areas. This may be somewhat surprising, but it adds support to the view expressed at the beginning of this section, that the nature of traffic work is quite considerably influenced by the structure and policy of the force.

TABLE VII.8

### Percentage distribution of traffic incident work between departments (1965–66)

|  | Provincial | | Metropolitan 'B' & 'S' Divisions | |
|---|---|---|---|---|
|  | Possible Process | Non-Process | Possible Process | Non-Process |
| Traffic | 21·0 | 23·7 | 25·1 | 26·6 |
| Beat Patrols | 58·4 | 56·3 | 40·2 | 66·6 |
| Administration | 7·4 | 5·8 | 16·7 | 1·9 |
| Station Staff | 10·0 | 10·4 | 9·1 | 3·8 |
| Others | 3·2 | 3·8 | 9·1 | 1·0 |
|  | 100·0 | 100·0 | 100·2 | 99·9 |
| Total hours | 8,295 | 3,747 | 5,308 | 677 |

The Metropolitan divisions showed a far larger proportion of time spent on incidents likely to result in process. Two differences from the provincial forces can be seen. First, that the 'non-process' accidents virtually stopped with the incident itself: follow-up within the station appears to have been minimal. Second, in the process incidents the contribution of traffic departments was similar to the provincial proportion, but beat patrols did less and administration and station staff did far more. This probably resulted from the greater specialization in the Metropolitan police where enquiries connected with traffic incidents tend to be made by specialist officers rather than whoever dealt with the incident when it occurred.

On these figures it would seem that it might be possible to reduce the work of the beat officer by anything up to a third if the later stages are undertaken by specialists. We have no evidence of the significance of this as far as the beat officer is concerned, but it may well be connected with the remarkably favourable ratio of 'incident time' to 'court time' discussed above (see p. 188).

This brings us to the court aspect of traffic work. This accounted for 19·0 per cent of all traffic work in the provincial forces, and 25·4 per cent in the Metropolitan. These averages were based on quite a wide range of figures which, in the provinces, went from 10·8 per cent to 24·7 per cent. The Metropolitan figures were 19·2 per cent for 'B' Division and 31·4 per cent for 'S' Division. The Central Traffic Division, which operated by handing the administration of its cases over to land divisions for the process work, showed the very low rate of 7·9 per cent. In this respect it was quite similar to the traffic departments of provincial forces.

The distribution of court work between departments in traffic cases is shown in Table VII.9. To a large extent the figures are self-explanatory, but some points deserve mentioning. First, it is clear that, compared with the time spent dealing with incidents likely to result in process, traffic and beat patrols were far less involved at the court stage. In total their contribution accounted for about 79 per cent of the time spent in dealing with the incidents and ensuing enquiries, but only for about 44 per cent of time spent on court work. This was clearly the result of the second feature, the handling of much court work by administration departments, process departments or other specialized units. The nomenclature varied from force to force, but the essential point

TABLE VII.9

Percentage distribution of traffic court work between departments

| Department | Mean | Provincial Max. | Min. | Metropolitan 'B' & 'S' Divisions |
|---|---|---|---|---|
| Traffic | 12·1 | 22·8 | 2·6 | 15·8 |
| Beat Patrols | 32·2 | 42·0 | 6·3 | 40·6 |
| Administration | 31·5 | 72·9 | 1·9 | 20·6 |
| Station Staff | 10·7 | 36·7 | 0·4 | 13·5 |
| Other | 13·5 | 63·3 | 1·4 | 9·6 |
| Total | 100·0 | | | 100·0 |
| Total hours | 14,767 | | | 4,248 |

is that rather more than half (55 per cent) of traffic court work was handled by people who were, in this capacity, essentially administrators.

It is interesting to contrast the way in which it has become possible to streamline the handling of traffic cases administratively, with the burden of criminal court work still falling on the C.I.D. Criminal Investigation Departments accounted for only 10·8 per cent of the strength of the provincial forces, but were responsible for 41·7 per cent and 36·2 per cent respectively of all time spent on criminal court work in the Magistrates' and Higher courts. This difference between the ways of handling traffic and criminal court work is presumably due largely to the formal way in which many traffic cases are dealt with. It seems unlikely that criminal cases will ever be handled in this way, but it remains to be seen how far the streamlining of committal proceedings introduced by the Criminal Justice Act 1967 will affect the amount of court work expected of the C.I.D. On the face of it some reduction of time spent in magistrates' courts might be achieved, but much will depend on whether the volume of relevant paper work goes up or down.

*Conclusions*

1. During the survey fortnight an average of 86 crimes were reported per 100,000 population in the provincial forces, with a range from 48 to 210. In the Metropolitan area 'S' Division had a rate of 119 and 'B' Division of 445 crimes per 100,000 population.

2. Reported crimes averaged 4·4 per C.I.D. member in the provincial forces, and 8·1 per member in the Metropolitan divisions. These implied annual case-loads which, in the provincial forces were clearly below the conventional upper limit of 150 per C.I.D. officer but which, in the Metropolitan divisions were well above.

3. In general criminal investigation departments included a fairly substantial proportion of civilians. The average was 15·4 per cent in the provincial forces, with a range from 6·0 per cent to 21·5 per cent. The Metropolitan figures were a little below the average.

4. C.I.D. strengths were fairly highly correlated with the criminality of the areas concerned, but it also seemed there was

a point above which this correlation no longer held good. Where this happened the case-load per officer became notably higher and it appeared that the force was no longer able to adapt to increasing criminality by deploying more of its resources in the C.I.D.

5. On average nearly 60 per cent of crime investigation work was done by the C.I.D. but there was a wide range of practice. Some urban forces gave the C.I.D. a near monopoly, but in counties the work was more evenly divided between C.I.D. and uniformed departments. In general, beat patrols did about a quarter of all crime investigation work. Traffic departments averaged 2·7 per cent in the provincial forces.

6. C.I.D. members in the provincial forces worked an average of 13·5 hours for each crime reported; the corresponding Metropolitan figure was 9·4 hours. The range, however, was considerable —from 7·1 to 24·4. The average number of hours worked per arrest was 46·3 in the provincial forces and 58·5 in the Metropolitan divisions. There were high positive correlations between the number of hours spent on criminal investigation work and the number of arrests. The correlations were equally high whether they related to investigation undertaken by the C.I.D. or by the whole force.

7. Sickness rates among C.I.D. members were, in the main, less than those of their uniformed colleagues.

8. The claims of court work—defined in a fairly narrow sense— meant that it would occupy two days a fortnight of the average C.I.D. officer's time.

9. Report writing was another activity which involved a substantial amount of C.I.D. time—17·4 per cent in the provincial forces and 19·7 per cent in the Metropolitan. In the special squads the proportion was even higher (27·9 per cent).

10. The average number of traffic offences and accidents reported per force member was 1·18 for the provincial forces and 1·70 for the Metropolitan. There was no obvious explanation for the variation between forces.

11. The number of 'no process' accidents reported was closely correlated with the number reported for 'process'.

12. Patrolling by traffic patrols accounted for a quarter of all traffic work in the provincial forces, but only 17 per cent in the Metropolitan divisions.

13. Supervision comprised 40·6 per cent of traffic work in the provincial forces but only 21·5 per cent in the Metropolitan divisions.

14. Accidents which did not involve proceedings were unimportant in terms of time—only about 4 per cent of all traffic work.

15. 'Possible process' incidents, however, were more common —10·7 per cent in the provinces and 31·7 per cent in the Metropolitan divisions.

16. Traffic court work took a fifth of all traffic work in the provinces and a quarter in London. Nevertheless the handling of traffic cases was more expeditious in London.

17. In spite of the fact that few forces employed them at the time of our survey, traffic wardens were clearly capable of contributing substantially to traffic supervision. They comprised only 1·2 per cent of total strength but did 17·2 per cent of all traffic supervision.

18. Although traffic departments were responsible for nearly a third of all supervision (if the contribution of wardens is discounted) their relatively small size meant that the bulk of traffic work was done by departments, particularly by Beat Patrols.

19. The extent to which court work has been streamlined in traffic cases can be shown by the fact that more than half the time under this heading was contributed by people who were essentially administrators.

20. As compared with the criminal side, traffic work can more clearly be seen as divided into different levels. First is the irreducible minimum of outdoor work created by the more serious accidents, conspicuous offences and particularly important traffic control points. The next level consists of traffic supervision done *inter alia* by beat patrols. Thirdly, there is patrolling by road traffic departments. Fourth, is what could almost be described as the new dimension of supervision by traffic wardens. Finally there is court work which falls into two separate branches—the administration of process work and actual attendance at court. Apart from the first, the effort put in at the various levels is probably more influenced by policy than in some branches of police work.

# VIII

# Court Work and the Policing of Holiday Areas

WE have already referred to Court work at various points in our discussions of the total work load and of crime and traffic. We must now draw these observations together, and add one or two of a different kind.

We began by showing that, although it looms large and figures high on many policemen's lists of complaints, the average proportion of working time spent on court work was not as large as perhaps might have been expected. Even with our definition of court work, which included the preparation of antecedents, though not of the case for the prosecution, the overall average for the provincial forces was 10·4 per cent, for the Metropolitan land divisions 10·6 per cent and for the Central Traffic Division 9·4 per cent. It seems, therefore, quite safe to say that, in broad terms, the administration of Justice involves at least 10 per cent of total police time.

We say 'at least' because our definition of court work was a moderate compromise. It is easy to argue that some work done outside the court should, nevertheless, be included under this heading for it is done exclusively for the benefit of the court. The problem, however, is where to draw the line. Between the arrest of the criminal and his appearance in court the C.I.D. may be heavily involved in documenting the case, getting all the necessary statements, preparing exhibits, checking alibis, having meetings with the prosecution, and so on.[1] It is a matter of interpretation whether or not this is regarded as being the completion of the investigation or the first stages of the trial. We treated it as part of the investigation and only included the preparation of ante-

[1] Particularly since the passing of the Criminal Justice Act 1967 Section 11 of which requires notice to be given of the particulars of any alibi (so that its validity may be checked by the police).

cedents under court work. If our figure for the administration of Justice seems low in police eyes at least it can hardly be challenged as depending on a definition which is too widely drawn.

We distinguished five types of court work—criminal (divided into magistrates' and higher), traffic (of all kinds), civil and coroners', and juvenile.[1] Their relative contribution to the total load of court work is shown below.

### TABLE VIII.1

### Distribution of types of court work (1965–66)

| Type of court | Provincial forces | | Metropolitan 'B' & 'S' Division | | Metropolitan C.T.D. | | C.I.D. squads | |
|---|---|---|---|---|---|---|---|---|
| | Hrs | % | Hrs | % | Hrs | % | Hrs | % |
| Criminal (Magistrates') | 10,432 | 31·0 | 2,604 | 31·2 | 135 | 6·8 | 635 | 60·2 |
| Criminal (Higher) | 3,848 | 11·4 | 892 | 10·7 | 119 | 6·0 | 420 | 39·8 |
| Traffic | 14,186 | 42·1 | 4,115* | 49·3 | 1,599 | 80·1 | — | |
| Civil and Coroners' | 3,211 | 9·5 | 468 | 5·6 | 74 | 3·7 | — | |
| Juvenile | 2,025 | 6·0 | 264 | 3·2 | 70 | 3·5 | — | |
| Total | 33,702 | 100·0 | 8,343 | 100·0 | 1,997 | 100·1 | 1,055 | |
| Court work as % of active duty time | 10·4% | | 10·6% | | 9·4% | | 5·0% | |

* This figure has *not* been adjusted to allow for traffic work done by C.T.D. to do so it would be necessary to add 133 hours.

It will be seen that, although the proportion of time occupied by court work was closely similar for the provincial forces and for our Metropolitan divisions, the distributions of types of work were not quite so alike. Nevertheless the most significant point revealed by the table is clearly the contribution of traffic cases. In the provinces they were almost exactly of equal importance to criminal court work, while in the Metropolitan divisions they accounted for virtually half the total, taking 7½ per cent more of all court time than in the provinces.

The chief difference between the provinces and the metropolis was probably the higher figure for traffic courts in the Metro-

[1] Further subdivision was impossible for lack of space.

A.S.I.M.—14

politian divisions, in spite of the fact that they spent less total time on traffic work (19·3 per cent as against 23·0 per cent). The obvious explanation would seem to be that, as we have shown, traffic work in the Metropolitan divisions was far more a matter of dealing with incidents which might result in court proceedings than was the case in the provincial forces.

As far as the criminal courts were concerned almost exactly three-quarters of the work was connected with magistrates' courts, and a quarter with the higher courts. The significance of this mainly lies in the fact that the Higher Court figures are due to a relatively small number of cases which have a great potential for generating work. The system of the administration of justice is, therefore, particularly sensitive to changes in the number of cases for trial in the Higher Courts. An increase in either aspect might have a quite disproportionate effect on the system and make considerable demands on police manpower. It is commonly said that the proportion of persons pleading Not Guilty has risen steeply in recent years; if this is the case even the streamlining of procedure introduced by the Criminal Justice Act 1967 may be unable to prevent the system becoming clogged, with consequently far greater delays before trial.

This is borne out by the fact that, in 1965, the Higher Courts of England and Wales dealt with approximately 27,000 people, while Magistrates' Courts convicted approximately 507,000 people (excluding motoring offenders).[1] Any shift in this somewhat precarious balance would clearly involve a drastic increase of the burden of court work on the police.

It is not possible to comment much on the two remaining categories—Civil and Coroners' Courts and Juvenile Courts. The time involved in each was quite a small proportion of the total and it is difficult to know how the figures should be regarded. It is perhaps worth commenting that the Civil and Coroners' figure in the provincial forces seems to have been higher than we expected, amounting to nearly a third of the figure for criminal work for magistrates' courts. This may partly result from the fact that Coroners' Officers often work full time and undertake a

[1] The Higher Courts figure refers to the total number of persons for trial. The Magistrates' Courts figure is for persons convicted.

SOURCE: *Criminal Statistics for England and Wales 1965*, Tables IIa, IVa, IVb; 1966–67 Cmnd. 3037.

certain amount of enquiry work, together with relevant administration, all of which would have been recorded under this heading.

The spread of Juvenile Court work between departments was rather different from that of criminal work for magistrates' courts. The C.I.D. proportion was less (30·7 per cent), women police officers accounted for considerably more (10·7 per cent), and administration departments were also responsible for rather more. This probably reflects both the youth of the offenders concerned and the mixture of criminal and traffic cases that are heard in juvenile courts.

It is also informative to consider court work in terms of the average amount of police time involved per case. The forces supplied us with the numbers of cases tried at the various courts during the survey period and we were able to relate these to the hours recorded under the various types of court work. Obviously such measures have their limitations, many cases would be only partially dealt with during the period, different definitions of a case may have been used by different forces, and so on. Nevertheless our figures provide a basis for discussion, and may even lead to further research. The information is summarized in Table VIII.2.

## TABLE VIII.2

**Average time spent on court work—hours per case (1965–66)**

|  | Traffic cases (all courts) | Criminal cases Mag. courts | Higher courts | Coroners'* inquests |
|---|---|---|---|---|
| Provincial forces | 3·2 | 7·8 | 33·9 | 27·5 |
| Metropolitan 'B' & 'S' Divisions | 3·4 | 5·1 | 18·2 | 66·9 |

\* This figure may exaggerate the true figure as it assumes that all time recorded under the heading Civil and Coroners' Courts was in fact occupied on Coroners' work.

To a large extent the figures speak for themselves. Our earlier analysis would have led one to expect the increase in length per case, with traffic as the shortest and higher court criminal cases as the longest. Perhaps the most interesting point is simply the magnitude of the time involved, particularly in the criminal cases in the provinces. Even in the magistrates' courts the average criminal case involved a total almost as long as the official working day, while the higher court figure represents rather more than four full days. The range, too, was quite considerable in the magistrates' court figures, from 2·9 hours to 11·8. As would be expected the higher court figures varied even more, but as the number of cases was smaller and proceedings are apt to be spread over longer periods of time and to involve cases tried outside the force area, they may be less reliable.

A second point to note is the fact that the Metropolitan figures for criminal cases produced distinctly lower averages than the corresponding provincial ones. We have no evidence to explain this except, perhaps, to suggest the possibility that the sheer volume of work in the London area may have led to a somewhat more expeditious handling of court work.

The figures for Civil Cases and Coroners' Inquests have been included for the sake of completeness, but they may involve a large margin of error. This is because we have assumed that all work under this heading was for coroners' inquests, whose numbers we were given, but we had no information concerning any civil cases with which police officers might have been concerned.

Our general conclusion about court work must be that it occupies at least 10 per cent of police time, with traffic providing at least as much work as crime, and sometimes more. This is in spite of the considerably greater speed with which traffic cases are handled. Criminal cases, incidentally, appear to involve somewhat less police time in London than in the provinces, particularly those in the higher courts. It remains to be seen whether, and for how long, the procedural changes introduced by the Criminal Justice Act of 1967 reduce the police contribution to the administration of justice.

### The policing of holiday areas

Although much police work goes on more or less unchanged throughout the year it is well known that crime and traffic show seasonal patterns. We could not hope to demonstrate these, although we hoped by spreading our surveys to take some of the variation into account. We were told, however, that in areas popular for seaside holidays the influx of summer population led to greatly increased work so that, to get a true picture, we ought to survey them both in and out of season.

Our sample included three such areas, and their Chief Constables agreed to let us hold the survey relatively early in the year and to repeat it during the holiday season. The areas concerned were the borough of Hastings, and the counties of Dorset and Pembrokeshire. Hastings is a holiday resort on the south coast having, in 1965, a population of 66,000. Booklets were completed by 157 members of its police force in both surveys.[1] Dorset is a county on the south coast combining seaside resorts, agricultural land and the Borough of Poole, which is an industrial town and small port. At the time of the surveys the population of the county was 312,000 and booklets were completed by 531 and 532 members of the force respectively.[2] Pembrokeshire is a county on the south-west coast of Wales with little industry except for the tanker town at Milford Haven. In 1965 its population was 95,000 and the numbers of the police force taking part in the surveys were 201 and 202 respectively.[3]

These three were the only areas for which we could make direct seasonal comparisons. Our other surveys were spread over some six months or so but the stratification of the sample meant that it would be quite invalid to use them to compare work at different periods.

Seasonal comparisons face the problem that policemen, like other people, tend to take their holidays in the summer. When we come to consider the total work load we shall have to distinguish between the total number of hours worked and the average load per available person. In other words policemen in such areas may face a genuine increase in the volume of work in absolute terms, or they may suffer a relative increase due to the absence of their colleagues on leave, or both. Our first task, therefore, must be to compare the main indices of work over the two periods.

---

[1] In all surveys the number completing booklets was slightly less than the full strength of the force. Senior officers did not take part, and neither did civilians employed on non-police duties (mainly domestic). Our figures, therefore, are usually 3 or 4 per cent less than the total employed by the force. The surveys in Hastings were held over the following dates: 1–14 February, and 12–25 July 1965. Population figures have been taken from the Police Almanac 1965, and rounded to the nearest thousand.

[2] The Dorset surveys were conducted from 8–22 March and from 19 July–1 August 1965.

[3] The surveys covered the periods 29 March–12 April and 26 July—8 August 1965.

TABLE VIII.3

**Main items of work load in and out of season**
**(numbers during survey periods) (1965–66)**

|  | Hastings | | Pembrokeshire | | Dorset | |
|---|---|---|---|---|---|---|
|  | Winter | Summer | Spring | Summer | Spring | Summer |
| Crimes reported | 73 | 47 | 43 | 47 | 363 | 401 |
| Traffic offences | 190 | 207 | 86 | 129 | 738 | 1,186 |
| Road accidents | 22 | 42 | 61 | 66 | 172 | 298 |
| Criminal cases |  |  |  |  |  |  |
| Magistrates' courts | 37 | 41 | 47 | 66 | 137 | 162 |
| Higher courts | — | — | 1 | 3 | 4 | 20 |
| Traffic cases | 101 | 113 | 58 | 105 | 370 | 497 |

It will be seen that the impact of the summer season differed considerably between the three areas. Hastings had a substantial decrease in crime (by about a third), an increase of about 10 per cent in traffic offences, but a near doubling of road accidents. Court work increased by about 10 per cent.

In Pembrokeshire there was little change in the volume of crime or road accidents, but traffic offences increased by 50 per cent. Court work also showed substantial increases (40 per cent for criminal and 81 per cent for traffic) but it is not possible to tell when the relevant offences were committed.

Dorset had a 10 per cent increase in crime and a 60 per cent increase in traffic offences. Road accidents increased even more steeply (73 per cent). The volume of criminal and traffic court work was also higher, by 18 per cent and 34 per cent respectively. Higher court work was also substantially more, twenty compared with four cases.

The most consistent phenomenon, therefore, would seem to have been an increase in the volume of traffic work in the form of offences or accidents or both. Somewhat surprisingly there was also more of most kinds of court work. Crime increased slightly in two areas but decreased in the other. The increases in themselves might not have been much greater than the chance fluctuations which might be expected anyway from time to time, and their impact may have resulted quite as much from the depletion of strength due to annual and other leave. We must, then, turn to consider changes in the effective strengths of the forces.

Forces kept a special record of the amount of annual leave

taken during the survey periods, and this can be used to make an estimate of the effective depletion of strength.

Table VIII.4 shows quite clearly that the forces managed to spread their annual leave to a considerable extent. Even in out of season periods the numbers taking annual leave averaged about half (and in Dorset considerably more than half) of those taking it in the summer period. The effective reduction in strength was thereby lessened, so that the differences between in and out of season were equivalent to 7·6 per cent, 14·9 per cent and 4·3 per cent in the three forces.

## TABLE VIII.4

### Depletion of effective strength due to annual leave (1965–66)

|  | Hastings | | Pembrokeshire | | Dorset | |
|---|---|---|---|---|---|---|
|  | Winter | Summer | Spring | Summer | Spring | Summer |
| Annual leave (hrs) | 560 | 1,030 | 1,116 | 2,393 | 3,995 | 4,929 |
| Manpower equivalent (at 42 hrs per wk) | 13 | 25 | 27 | 57 | 95 | 118 |
| Difference between seasons |  | 12 |  | 30 |  | 23 |
| Difference between seasons as % of strength |  | 7·6 |  | 14·9 |  | 4·3* |

* This figure is based on the strength of the force at the time of the first survey. By the second it had increased by 21, thus on paper nullifying the effect of the extra annual leave. However, some of the new recruits would still have been undergoing initial training. We have, in effect, discounted them for the purpose of this calculation.

If we try to compare these figures with those for the increased work load several points should be borne in mind. First, it is clear that the most widespread increase was in traffic work, and we do not know how annual leave affected different departments. Second, our indices referred only to major items of work. It is quite possible that work of a more trivial nature increases more steeply, and the officer on the beat is likely to be affected simply by having more people around even if, in fact, they cause no serious trouble. This intangible aspect is one which, obviously, our figures cannot measure. We shall, however, see whether the proportion of work on specific incidents, especially perhaps those of a civil kind, increased. Third, it will be important to examine the figures for overtime and extra shifts as those not on leave are particularly likely to have to finish their jobs at the expense of working late or on their days off. Most of the relevant information is summarized in Table VIII.5.

The first point to note is that in only one of the three areas was the proportion of abstractions higher in the summer than in the winter. It seems that increased figures for leave may be compensated for by decreases in sickness and in training. For example, in

TABLE VIII.5

**Seasonal changes in overtime and hours of work (1965–66)**

|  | Hastings | | Pembrokeshire | | Dorset | |
|---|---|---|---|---|---|---|
|  | Winter | Summer | Spring | Summer | Spring | Summer |
| Total hrs potential duty time | 17,575 | 17,876 | 23,174 | 23,496 | 60,406 | 63,315 |
| Total hrs active duty | 9,409 | 9,779 | 13,581 | 13,108 | 34,755 | 36,811 |
| Percentage abstractions | 46·5 | 45·3 | 41·4 | 44·2 | 42·5 | 41·9 |
| Average hrs active duty per head | 59·9 | 62·3 | 67·6 | 64·9 | 65·5 | 66·7 |
| Active duty per head (corrected to allow for annual leave)* |  | 67·4 |  | 76·2 |  | 69·6 |
| Overtime—hrs per head (corrected)* | 2·2 | 3·8 | 5·2 | 6·6 | 3·2 | 3·5 |
| Average number of shifts | 9·4 | 9·1 | 9·4 | 8·9 | 9·4 | 9·0 |
| Average number of shifts per head (corrected)* |  | 9·9 |  | 10·4 |  | 9·2 |

* These corrections have been made by substracting the difference in manpower between the seasons (as calculated in Table VIII.4) and dividing the hours worked by these reduced strengths. In order to keep the out of season figures in line with those published elsewhere in this book we have not attempted to correct the averaging of overtime for the first round surveys. Both figures, therefore, are slight understatements, but they express the difference between the two periods correctly.

Hastings during the winter survey 697 hours were lost through sickness, 1,313 were spent on training; together they amounted to 2,010 hours, an average of nearly 13 hours for each member of the force. In the summer, on the other hand, sickness only involved a loss of 246 hours, and training occupied 970. Hence the increase of 470 hours annual leave was more than counterbalanced by the reduction of nearly 800 hours due to sickness and training. The Dorset pattern was rather similar, although the reduction in training was much greater. Pembrokeshire, on the other hand, showed only a small reduction in training time and virtually none in sickness;[1] so the extra leave in the summer meant a net increase in abstraction time.

The fourth row in the table shows that the increase in what we have called Active Duty,[2] when averaged over the whole force, was slight in two forces, while in Pembrokeshire there was a decrease. However, when allowance was made for extra annual leave the hours worked by those not on leave increased to the amounts shown in the fifth row of the table. The increases on this basis averaged 7·5 hours per fortnight for Hastings, 8·6 for Pembrokeshire and 4·1 for Dorset. Although these increases were real enough it should be remembered that they were spread over a working fortnight and so averaged less than an hour a day. Unfortunately we had no information as to the length of season during which these hours prevailed.

The remaining rows of Table VIII.5 relate to overtime and the numbers of shifts worked. It will be seen that the amount of overtime, in the sense of lengthening the working day, was hardly affected, the increases between out and in season ranging from 0·3 to 1·6 hours per fortnight. On the other hand the numbers of shifts worked increased by 0·5 and 1·0 in Hastings and Pembrokeshire respectively, but actually decreased in Dorset (due to the growth of the force).

In general, therefore, it would seem that the holiday season does bring the expected increase in work for those not on holiday, but that the increase in terms of hours may not be so very marked; its most common form being the working of one extra shift in a fortnight. Before dismissing this as trivial the non-policeman should reflect, however, that such extra work is undertaken under relatively irritating and frustrating conditions. The policeman is not on holiday while those around him are; the extra work is particularly likely to be at week-ends—thus depriving him of taking his family out in the way that others do; and the work, though not much more serious (apart from traffic accidents) is probably more full of trying incidents, with crowds of people around and, no doubt at the back of the policeman's mind, the chance of real trouble in the form of drunken violence or even

---

[1] In contrast to Hastings the force was a rather youthful one with a very low figure for sickness during the first survey.

[2] I.e. all forms of duty other than those included under abstractions.

battles between teenagers—not likely, but possible and un-predictable.[1]

The pattern of active duty does not show as many changes as might have been expected. Undoubtedly the most significant increase was in traffic work, particularly in the two county forces. The Dorset proportion increased from 20·6 per cent to 24·5 per cent and the Pembrokeshire one from 21·5 per cent to 28·2 per cent. In Hastings the increase was less, from 25·2 per cent to 25·8 per cent, but here the winter figure was unusually high. These increases covered all types of traffic work, but were mostly concentrated in the specific forms of traffic work, rather than patrolling by traffic departments. Indeed the aggregate of all patrolling by the traffic departments was slightly less at the height of the season than out of it.[2] This was presumably because the work capacity of traffic departments was more or less fixed, and the extra time spent on incidents reduced the remainder available for patrolling.

Somewhat unexpectedly the seasonal comparisons lend force to our earlier remarks about the effect of tying staff down in specialized departments, and it seems that, in these three forces, the whole of the increase in traffic work was borne by the more general departments. Indeed, as is shown in Table VIII.6 the total traffic work done by traffic departments was slightly less at the height of the season than out of it. Seen in percentage terms the contribution of traffic departments to traffic work, even including all time spent patrolling, was quite substantially lower in season than out —38·8 per cent compared with 52·5 per cent. When a similar comparison was made, but excluding patrolling, the contribution of traffic departments to the more specific forms of traffic work fell from 28·2 per cent to 17·2 per cent.

It remains to note that the extra traffic work during the summer season was principally undertaken by Beat Patrols. This was particularly true as far as general supervision was concerned, especially in the two county forces. It was also true of all other

---

[1] One of our areas, Hastings, was the scene of riots between what were then known as 'mods and rockers' over the August Bank Holiday in 1964. Reinforcements from the Metropolitan police were flown in to assist the local force.

The lessons of this experience are referred to in the *Inspector of Constabulary*, *1964*, p. 5; 1964–65 (251).

[2] Summer aggregate 3,155 hours. Winter/Spring 3,140.

forms of traffic work in the three forces, with the single exception of dealing with incidents likely to result in process in Pembrokeshire.

Other forms of work can be dealt with more briefly, mainly because changes were only slight, and not as unexpected. The proportion of time spent on crime investigation was scarcely changed; two forces showed slight upward movements and one down—none of more than one per cent of active duty time.

TABLE VIII.6

**Seasonal distribution of traffic work***
**between departments (per cent) (1965–66)**

| Department | Hastings | | Pembrokeshire | | Dorset | | Total Winter/ | |
|---|---|---|---|---|---|---|---|---|
| | Winter | Summer | Spring | Summer | Spring | Summer | Spring | Summer |
| Traffic | 52·0 | 44·8 | 45·8 | 34·8 | 55·7 | 38·6 | 52·5 | 38·8 |
| Beat patrols | 33·4 | 36·6 | 33·3 | 46·0 | 25·5 | 38·8 | 29·1 | 40·2 |
| W.P.Cs. | 0·1 | 1·3 | 2·0 | 6·0 | 0·2 | 0·6 | 0·6 | 2·1 |
| Others | 14·6 | 17·3 | 18·9 | 13·1 | 18·6 | 22·0 | 17·8 | 18·9 |
| Total | 100·1 | 100·0 | 100·0 | 99·9 | 100·0 | 100·0 | 100·0 | 100·0 |

* Including patrolling by traffic departments

Foreign enquiries showed similar slight fluctuations. Civil incidents showed a slight tendency to rise, but again only to a slight extent. It should, however, be remembered that even the slight increase of one per cent of the whole force's active duty time may mean that the volume of such cases has gone up by a third or even a half, so that to some members of the force, often W.P.Cs., this increase will be quite conspicuous.

Public order work showed only insignificant changes around figures which were all less than 2 per cent—a salutary reminder to those whose impressions of policing in seaside towns is dominated by ideas of the 'mods and rockers', and similar well publicized riots, that the British are a singularly orderly people. It is also an interesting indication of the direction of social changes since the founding of the first modern police forces primarily to maintain public order (see Chapter II).

The only remaining fact to be mentioned is that the increase in specific activities, whether dealing with traffic or civil incidents, such as re-uniting lost children with their parents, was achieved by reducing time spent on general patrolling, the figures for which were mostly lower in season than out.

Our seasonal comparisons seem to justify two main conclusions. First, that the most definite increase in work is that done with traffic, involving both general supervision and dealing with accidents. This increase largely falls upon non-traffic specialists. Unfortunately we do not know whether this is due to more traffic men taking leave, or simply to the fact that it is the size of the department which controls the amount of work it can do, so that any increase in load beyond a certain point has to be borne by others. Either way it is something of a paradox.

The second general conclusion is that although the work load of those not on leave does not increase very markedly in terms of hours, the timing of the increase is likely to be all important. The chances are that the extra shift, when it is worked, will be at a week-end, so that the policeman's sense of deprivation is heightened.

## Conclusions

1. Court work, which in our surveys included attendance, travelling time and the preparation of antecedents, accounted for just over 10 per cent of police time both in the provinces and the Metropolitan area.

2. Traffic cases accounted for 42 per cent of court work in the provinces and 49 per cent in the Metropolitan divisions.

3. In the provincial forces criminal cases occupied virtually the same total time as traffic cases. A quarter of the time spent on criminal court work was concerned with cases in the Higher Courts and three-quarters in magistrates' courts.

4. Juvenile courts took little time: 6 per cent of court work in the provinces and only 3·2 per cent in the Metropolitan area.

5. Civil and Coroners' courts took 9·5 and 5·6 per cent of court time respectively, but this may give a slightly exaggerated impression as some enquiries on behalf of coroners may also have been included.

6. The average time spent per traffic case was between three and three and a half hours.

7. Criminal cases in the magistrates' courts averaged 5·1 hours

in the Metropolitan area, and more than half as much again in the provincial forces.

8. Criminal cases for the higher courts demanded most time of all. In the provincial forces this amounted to 33·9 hours per case, or rather more than four eight-hour shifts. The Metropolitan figure was barely half as much, but even so was three and a half times the magistrates' court average.

9. The aspect of police work which appeared to be most affected by holiday periods was traffic. Each of the three areas where comparisons were made showed increases in offences, accidents or both.

10. Increased traffic work was also accompanied by more traffic court work and, indeed, for a tendency for court work generally to increase.

11. Most forces managed to spread leave and training so that the proportion of abstractions either fell or, at least, rose only fractionally during the holiday season.

12. The work falling on officers not on leave seems to have increased by about one shift a fortnight, but the length of the working day itself was hardly affected.

13. The extra burden of traffic work was shouldered by beat patrols. The contribution of traffic departments to traffic work fell from 52·5 per cent to 38·8 per cent.

14. There was a slight tendency for civil incident work to increase, but its amount was still small.

15. There was a tendency for tours of duty to be rather more occupied with special incidents and less with uneventful patrolling.

# IX

# Policewomen, Traffic Wardens and Civilians

In this chapter we consider the contribution of three groups whose roles in the police service have been apt to evoke ambivalent attitudes. These are women police officers, civilians and traffic wardens. None of these groups was introduced into the service without controversy, and although now they are far more widely accepted it is common to find some policemen having reservations about their value. This is entirely understandable, for they represent a departure from the early conception of the service as a body of men each one of whom was physically able to undertake the whole range of tasks that might confront him.

This conception has been abandoned, with some reluctance, as a result of the shortage of suitable men, the realization that there are some virtues in specialization and the recognition that for some purposes it may be distinctly cheaper to employ civilians. The force of these arguments has been irrefutable. The only point left for discussion is the degree to which such groups should be employed in the service.

To such questions no survey can give a final answer, for it is essentially a product of its time and can only reflect the range of current practice. The figures in Table IV.10 provide ample illustration. For example in 1950 civilians employed by Lancashire amounted to only 5 per cent, but by 1965 the proportion had more than tripled (to 16 per cent). Yorkshire West Riding similarly increased from 8 per cent to 21 per cent. Obviously, therefore, we cannot claim that today's maximum is the extreme that could be justified, nor that any current practice is necessarily efficient. What we can do, however, is to show how large these groups are, what they do and how this relates to the overall pattern of work. We may also be able to dispose of some misconceptions.

Before discussing the groups in turn we must see how large they are in relation to the remainder of their forces. The relevant figures are presented in Table IX.1.

TABLE IX.1a

### Employment of women police officers, civilians and traffic wardens (1965–66)

| Force | Police officers* | | | | Civilians† | | Total police and civilians‡ = 100% | Traffic wardens |
|---|---|---|---|---|---|---|---|---|
| | Women | | Men | | No. | % | | No. |
| | No. | % | No. | % | | | | |
| Plymouth | 17 | 3·9 | 395 | 91·0 | 22 | 5·1 | 434 | — |
| Hastings§ | 4 | 2·6 | 135 | 86·5 | 17 | 10·9 | 156 | — |
| Pembrokeshire§ | 11 | 5·6 | 167 | 85·6 | 17 | 8·7 | 195 | — |
| Dorset§ | 10 | 1·9 | 452 | 87·1 | 57 | 11·0 | 519 | — |
| Bristol | 40 | 3·8 | 939 | 88·4 | 83 | 7·8 | 1,062 | 47 |
| Bath | 5 | 3·3 | 134 | 88·1 | 13 | 8·6 | 152 | — |
| Barrow-in-Furness | 4 | 2·8 | 131 | 91·6 | 8 | 5·6 | 143 | — |
| Birkenhead | 12 | 3·1 | 356 | 92·0 | 19 | 4·9 | 387 | — |
| Leics. & Rutland | 17 | 2·3 | 649 | 87·5 | 76 | 10·2 | 742 | — |
| Northumberland | 22 | 2·9 | 658 | 88·2 | 66 | 8·8 | 746 | — |
| Bedfordshire | 15 | 3·1 | 424 | 86·4 | 52 | 10·6 | 491 | 8 |
| Essex | 33 | 2·2 | 1,296 | 86·1 | 177 | 11·8 | 1,506 | 20 |
| Total | 190 | | 5,736 | | 607 | | 6,533 | 75 |
| Average | | 2·9 | | 87·8 | | 9·3 | | |
| Metropolitan | | | | | | | | |
| 'B' Division | 20 | 3·2 | 579 | 92·3 | 28 | 4·5 | 627 | — |
| 'S' Division | 11 | 1·6 | 656 | 92·5 | 42 | 5·9 | 709 | — |

* All ranks combined.

† The principles governing inclusion of civilians in the surveys are described in Chapter V, p. 134 and Appendix C.

‡ Excluding cadets.

§ These figures average the results of the first and second surveys of these forces.

The strengths of the various groups have been expressed as percentages of the total number of police officers and civilians in the service. It will be seen that the average proportion of women police officers was 2·9 per cent or, expressed another way, for every policewoman in the service there were 30 policemen. The highest and lowest figures were respectively 5·6 and 1·9 per cent in the provincial forces, while the lowest figure of all was 1·6 per cent in 'S' Division of the Metropolitan police. No explanation of the pattern of variation suggests itself.[1]

In the provincial forces the civilian strengths averaged 9·3 per

[1] One possible factor might be the experience of forces concerning the wastage rate for women officers. There is no comprehensive information on this, but the reports of the Commissioner of Police of the Metropolis indicate that wastage is a serious problem.

cent. This average, however, was composed of three almost distinct groups—three forces having very low figures, five being above the average, and the remainder forming an intermediate group. Four out of five forces with above average proportions of civilians were relatively large county forces, some of whose Chief Constables seemed to us to be particularly interested in the possibilities of saving manpower.[1] At the other extreme were three Borough forces which seemed on the whole to have been organized on rather traditional lines. The intermediate group had no particular characteristics in common.

The table also shows a slight negative relationship between the proportion of women police officers and of civilians in the provincial forces. The correlation $(r = -0.4018)$[2] was certainly not significant. It may have been due to the tendency for more civilians to be employed in county forces, whereas there is more scope for police women in urban areas.

The Metropolitan figures are misleading because they do not allow for the fact that large numbers of civilians are employed at the Commissioner's Office and also in the Receiver's Office. In any other force most of such civilians would be included in the Headquarters strength, including Central Traffic Division, and thus in our survey. We have, therefore, to estimate, on a *pro-rata* basis, the number of these civilians and police officers who should be treated as performing services for 'B' and 'S' Divisions.

The making of such estimates is bound to involve a margin of error, but even so it would appear that, taking the Commissioner's Office into account, the Metropolitan force as a whole employed the highest proportion of civilians found in our surveys.[3]

It is difficult to demonstrate precisely the reasons for the variations in the proportion of civilians employed in the various forces. Taken as a whole the number of civilians was closely correlated

[1] This was the impression gained by members of the research team.

[2] $t = 1.5197$; at the 5 per cent level with 10 d.f. this value of $t$ is not significant.

[3] These allowances were made in the following way. The Research and Planning Branch of the Metropolitan police kindly supplied us with the numbers of police officers and civilians employed in the Commissioner's Office. From them we excluded those which did not usually have parallels in provincial forces (Central Traffic Division, Forensic Science Laboratory, Regional Crime Squad, Special Branch, Solicitors). This gave us totals of 1,516 police officers, and 1,461 civil staff. Dividing these equally between the 23 land divisions gave figures of 66 and 64 respectively, and these were added to

with the number of male police officers ($r = 0.9490$). Statistically this is highly significant (at the 0.1 per cent level), but in common-sense terms it is not very surprising to say, in effect, that the number of civilians goes up as the size of the force goes up. The correlation was, perhaps, so high because of the heavy weight given to the practice of the largest forces which happened to employ relatively high proportions of civilians.

### TABLE IX.1b

**Employment of civilians in the Metropolitan police (1965–66)**

| Adjusted totals | Police officers and cadets | | Civilians | | Total |
|---|---|---|---|---|---|
| | *No.* | % | *No.* | % | = *100%* |
| 'B' Division | 698 | 88.1 | 94 | 11.9 | 792 |
| 'S' Division | 735 | 87.4 | 106 | 12.6 | 841 |

If, however, we correlate the proportion of civilians with the number of male police officers the resulting correlation, though positive ($r = 0.4121$) does not reach the 5 per cent level of significance.[1] Even if, as might have been expected, size was of some relevance it was by no means a sufficient explanation. The other obvious possibility was that the employment of civilians would be related to the shortage of manpower. Once again, however, a positive, but not significant, correlation was found.[2] Our data were not collected with a view to exploring this point, and for the time being we can only suggest that another important factor must be the Chief Constable's attitude to specialization in police work.

At the time of our surveys the employment of traffic wardens was still fairly rare, and this is shown by the table. No general comment about employment policy is possible.

---

the divisional strengths. It was assumed that the proportion of W.P.C.'s was the same as that which obtained in the relevant division. We also added one twelfth of the strength of Central Traffic Division (police and civilians) to 'B' Division. We did not include the staff of the Receiver's Office; some of the work done by this staff may in other areas be done by officials of the local authority, and it was difficult to know how to allow for this. It means, however, that our figures are rather on the conservative side.

[1] When $r = 0.4121$, $t = 1.6921$, not significant.

[2] The correlation between the number of vacancies for men and the percentage of civilians employed in the provincial forces was $r = 0.4520$. When $r = 12$, $t = 1.7552$, not significant. The numbers of vacancies were taken from *Inspector of Constabulary. 1965*, Appendix I; 1966–67 (90).

A.S.I.M.—15

*Women police officers*

For the purposes of this section we have combined the figures relating to the different ranks. This means that a direct comparison with male officers is not possible; the number of women officers, however, was small and it did not seem worth separating the supervisory ranks.[1]

The hours worked by women police officers were likely to be fairly similar to those for male officers, but Police Regulations provide for the normal 8-hour day to be shortened, and for the refreshment break to be extended, where a woman's duty 'is wholly or mainly patrol duty'. This, however, is at the discretion of the police authority.[2] Our results showed that the average hours worked by women officers in the provincial forces, calculated on the same basis as those in Table VI.4 (that is all forms of active duty plus training and refreshment breaks), were 73·25 per fortnight. This was rather less than the average for all members, but was close to the average for constables in the provincial forces working in urban areas (74·5 hours), though less than the corresponding figures for mixed areas (80·3) and for rural areas (81·7).

In the Metropolitan divisions, however, just as male officers worked longer hours than in the provinces so did women officers. The average for 'B' and 'S' Divisions was 86·0 hours per fortnight, while the correponding figure for male constables in the urban parts of 'B' and 'S' Divisions was 88·3. On the whole, therefore, women officers worked only slightly fewer hours than their male colleagues in comparable areas:[3] in most cases the difference did not exceed an hour a week on average. This suggests that the discretionary power to prescribe shorter working hours for women was not much used. We shall show below that this was probably due to the relatively small amount of patrolling which they did.

|  | No. | % |
|---|---|---|
| [1] For the record the numbers were: inspectors/chief inspectors | 6 | 3·2 |
| sergeants | 21 | 11·1 |
| constables | 163 | 85·8 |
| Total | 190 | 100·1 |

[2] The Police Regulations 1965 (S.I. No. 538/1965) Section 21 (2), (3).
[3] Generally speaking women officers work in the more urban areas.

The proportion of time spent on abstractions (46·3 per cent) was only slightly higher than the average for male constables in the provincial forces (45·3 per cent). This time was divided in a very similar way to that of all police officers, and the higher overall total probably resulted from the slightly shorter week worked by women officers. In the Metropolitan divisions the proportion of abstractions (46·3 per cent) was far higher than for men (34·8 per cent). It seems that the explanation for this was the large amount of time spent on training. This amounted to almost a third of the time counted under abstractions. Each woman officer averaged 17 hours' training in the fortnight, whereas the figure for men was only just over 5 hours. This was probably due to the relatively high proportion of women probationers. Other differences were slight.

Women officers undertake most of the types of work done by men, but with a rather different emphasis. Some of the main ones are summarized in Table IX.2. The largest single difference found in our surveys was the much smaller amount of patrolling. The proportion of active duty spent on patrolling by male constables in urban or mixed areas (including the Metropolitan) ranged from averages of 43·9 per cent to 52·4 per cent, but for women

TABLE IX.2

**Average percentages of active duty time spent on various classifications (1965–66)**

| | Women officers | | Male Constables | | | |
| | | | Urban areas | | Mixed areas | |
| | Provinces | Metropolitan | Provinces | Met. | Provinces | Met. |
|---|---|---|---|---|---|---|
| Crime investigation | 25·6 | 19·2 | 10·3 | 13·1 | 8·5 | 5·6 |
| Traffic work (all types) | 5·2 | 2·0 | 10·7 | 11·0 | 16·0 | 12·7 |
| Civil incidents | 6·7 | 7·6 | 2·0 | 1·5 | 1·6 | 1·9 |
| Magis. court (criminal) | 4·3 | 3·9 | 1·5 | 2·0 | 1·2 | 0·8 |
| Higher court (criminal) | 1·6 | 0·6 | 0·6 | 0·4 | 0·5 | 0·4 |
| Juvenile courts | 2·1 | 4·5 | 0·3 | 0·1 | 0·2 | 0·1 |
| Patrolling | 21·4 | 17·8 | 44·2 | 43·9 | 48·0 | 52·4 |
| General duties | 23·7 | 20·0 | 18·6 | 15·0 | 14·3 | 14·8 |
| Internal organization | 4·2 | 15·0 | 4·3 | 5·1 | 2·4 | 2·5 |
| Others (combined) | 5·2 | 9·4 | 7·5 | 7·9 | 7·3 | 8·8 |
| Total | 100·0 | 100·0 | 100·0 | 100·0 | 100·0 | 100·0 |

officers the averages were 21·4 per cent in the provinces, and 17·8 per cent in the Metropolitan.

Women officers also spent less time on traffic work of all types, particularly in the Metropolitan area where it accounted for only 2 per cent of active duty compared with 11·0 per cent for constables in the urban parts of the Metropolitan police district. No doubt this resulted from the lower figures for patrolling.

The time gained by women officers through not having to patrol so much was used most of all in connection with crime. In the provinces 25·6 per cent of women officers' time was spent under the heading of crime investigation, and in the Metropolitan divisions the proportion was 19·2 per cent. The nearest figures for men were for constables in urban areas: provinces 10·3 per cent and Metropolitan 13·1 per cent. We do not know what forms of criminal work were involved, but the contrast with male officers was greater than we had expected. One possible influence may have been the number of women shoplifters.

The emphasis on Civil Incidents was not surprising. We have already commented, in Chapter VI, on the rather low overall figure under this heading, but the figure for women officers clearly indicates quite a significant amount of time. Even so it was very much less than the time spent on crime investigation.

Women officers spent a relatively high proportion of their time on all forms of court work, except traffic courts. To some extent the high figure might be accounted for by a policy of always having at least one woman officer in attendance when a court is sitting. It might, on the other hand, be associated with the amount of criminal work.

The figures for general duties were higher, but only by about 5 per cent, than those for men. This difference was somewhat less than we should have expected from the greater amount of time that women officers spend in the station. The Metropolitan figure for internal organization seems remarkably high. It may possibly have reflected the difficulty of obtaining civilian clerical staff in the London area.

We can summarize this discussion by saying that, on the whole, the woman officer's job seems to have been somewhat more concerned with specific activities than that of her male colleagues. With its high proportion of crime investigation and civil incident work, it may also be more interesting.

*Traffic wardens*

When our surveys were held traffic wardens were still relatively uncommon, and only three out of the forces in our surveys employed any at all. Even in these they were only employed in a few localities. It was, therefore, difficult to assess their contribution.

The theory behind the employment of traffic wardens, and other civilians for that matter, is that they relieve police officers of duties which can be undertaken by persons who could not fulfil the physical requirements of attested constables and who, because of their specialized roles, need only a minimum of training. At the time of our surveys wardens were only concerned with the supervision of parked vehicles, so that in classifying their work as traffic supervision we have rather exaggerated its scope. Subsequently, however, their powers have been extended to include the direction of moving vehicles so that it is now more realistic to refer to their work as traffic supervision, and to equate it with that done by police officers.

The crucial question is whether the employment of wardens sets police officers free for other work, or whether it merely allows the amount of traffic supervision to be increased. Both consequences might be desirable, but for policy making it is clearly necessary to know which result is likely to be achieved. While our data do not describe the type of work done, which at that period was rather limited in scope, they do indicate how much time can be made available for traffic supervision when wardens are employed.

Detailed figures for the three forces are given in Appendix E, but the main ones are summarized below.

The figures in Table IX.3 relating to traffic wardens' hours

## TABLE IX.3

### Traffic supervision and traffic wardens (1965–66)

| | Average hours spent on traffic supervision per fortnight | |
| --- | --- | --- |
| | All members of division doing any supervision | Traffic wardens |
| Bristol—'A' Division | 8·2 | 70·6 |
| Essex—Chelmsford Division | 8·2 | 76·0 |
| Essex—Colchester Division | 8·0 | 67·3 |
| Bedfordshire—'B' Division | 5·0 | 75·8 |

show more variation than might be expected, but this was due to the small size of the groups, which were particularly sensitive to changes in effective strength due to leave and sickness. The general inference, however, is clear, that on average, one traffic warden did as much supervision as would be done by some 8–10 police officers in the course of normal patrolling. (The Bedfordshire figure exaggerates this point as the division included some rural and suburban areas which would create little traffic work anyway. The wardens operated in the centre of Bedford itself.)

The second point, clear from Appendix E, is that the time spent on traffic supervision by police officers seemed to be largely un-affected by the presence (or absence) of wardens. The general nature of the divisional area was far more important. This is not altogether surprising if we consider the work of the constable patrolling his beat. In an urban area it is quite likely that he will spend some time directing traffic or keeping an eye on parking in crowded streets, and so on; this would be done in the course of his ordinary patrolling as the opportunity arose. If, as a result of the presence of wardens on his beat, he did less traffic supervision himself the time saved would most likely be added to his total for patrolling rather than be transferred to something specific such as crime investigation.

If, however, a warden can replace a policeman on a fixed point then it becomes possible to assign him to work elsewhere, and not simply spend slightly more time on undifferentiated patrolling.[1]

Our general conclusions, therefore, are that if wardens are employed in areas patrolled by beat officers their contribution will be added to that of the regular police officers, but they will not free them for other duties unless they take over the direction of traffic at fixed points. This is not to say that the employment of wardens is only justified in the latter case—extra supervision of parking may be highly desirable—but it should not be argued on grounds of *saving* manpower unless men on fixed points are relieved.

Whatever the reason for employing wardens it is clear that they

---

[1] Traffic wardens were introduced under Section 2 (1) of the Road Traffic and Roads Improvement Act 1960. The functions they may perform have been laid down in Functions of Traffic Wardens Orders, of which two have been made: 1960 (S.I. No. 1582) and 1965 (S.I. No. 1151). The second of these contained provisions empowering wardens to control and regulate road traffic.

can devote a great deal more time to supervision than the beat officer (something like eight times as much) and, now that they can take over fixed points, they can in some respects be regarded as cheaper substitutes for regular police officers. It is doubtful how far this argument should be pursued because in many cases the appointment of wardens is not a substitute for the appointment of police officers, but a supplement in a time of manpower shortage. We cannot, therefore, say either how many of the wardens appointed by 1965[1] actually released police officers for other duties or how many were employed in areas whose establishments of police officers were completely filled. Furthermore, wardens are sometimes paid (in whole or part) out of funds derived from parking fees and may, therefore, be partly self-financing. In the three forces which had them during our surveys it seems that wardens mainly constituted an extra expense. They would, however, have been cheaper than employing the same number of extra policemen (who, in practice, might have done much less traffic supervision).

*Civilians*

We have already traced the increase in the number of civilians employed in the police service, and it is clear that they can make a major contribution. However, the Home Office Memorandum to the Select Committee on Estimates in 1966 commented:

> It is not possible to say how far the regular establishment has been kept down by the employment of civilians; but clearly, if the 15,771 civilians now employed in police services were withdrawn, a very substantial number of additional police officers would be required and the efficiency of the service much reduced.[2]

Any estimate we might attempt to make can only be based on the contribution made by civilians to the work of the forces in

---

[1] In October 1965 the total number of traffic wardens employed in England and Wales was 1,513. The Report of H.M. Chief Inspector of Constabulary for 1964 stated that in 1964 the Inspectors had recommended the appointment of 20 traffic wardens specifically 'to release police officers for other duties'. In that year the net increase in the number of wardens was 217.

SOURCE: *Estimates*, Sel. Cttee. 1st Report. Memorandum submitted on behalf of the Secretary of State for the Home Department. App. F. & G. pp. 15–16; 1966–67 (145).

[2] *Ibid.*, p. 17

our survey. We can only discuss this in relation to the provincial forces as the structure of the Metropolitan police is too complicated to justify the drawing of conclusions from information about work at divisional level.

During our first surveys the provincial forces employed 606 civilians. Their average time spent on active duty was 65·0 hours per fortnight, compared with a figure of 65·8 hours for all members of these forces (including civilians). The average figures for working time were, in an interesting way, rather different. The average for working time (obtained by adding time spent on training, sport and refreshment periods) was 67·4 hours for civilians, but 78·5 for police officers. In other words civilian work included in the 'abstractions' category averaged only 2·4 hours a fortnight, whereas for police officers the corresponding figure was 12·7.

It is clear, therefore, that although police officers put in more hours of what we have called working time, the difference between them and the civilians was almost entirely accounted for by time spent on training and on refreshment breaks. The time available for active duty was virtually the same. It follows that any discussion of the advantages or disadvantages of employing civilians can only be about the nature of the work they are capable of doing, and the extent to which they can work overtime or at week-ends.

We have no information on the extent to which civilians worked at week-ends, but we have overtime figures comparable to those for police officers (not corrected to allow for extra shifts). They refer basically to the amount of time worked after the end of the official tour of duty. The results are quite clear. In the provincial forces the average overtime of this kind worked by civilians was 0·84 hours per fortnight, whereas for police officers it was 3·83 hours—a ratio of about 1:4·6. In the Metropolitan divisions with their longer hours of overtime the average for civilians was 2·2 hours and for police officers was 6·7—a ratio of 1:3. These figures, however, understate the disparity in areas where extra shifts were being worked as a matter of routine.

We can, therefore, say that the case that police officers work overtime while civilians do not, is broadly made out. At the very least even when civilians do work overtime, police officers work substantially more. On the other hand, the much greater figures of abstractions for police officers virtually cancel out the difference, so that the hours on active duty are closely similar.

The range of work on which civilians may be employed in the police service is large. The memorandum of evidence submitted to the Select Committee on Estimates by the Association of Municipal Corporations listed 50 'purposes for which "civilians" other than traffic wardens are employed'.[1] Some of these are of a strictly domestic character, such as 'boilerman', 'cook', 'groundsman' and so on, but no doubt others could be added. In our surveys we confined ourselves to those non-domestic activities which might equally be performed by police officers or civilians according to who was available. The contribution of civilians is summarized in the table below. More detailed figures, but without the totals, were published by the Select Committee as Table 5 of Appendix G to its report.[2]

The first question to answer on the basis of the data in Table IX.4 concerns how civilian time was distributed between the various activities. The second is how much of the work in each classification was done by civilians. Thirdly, we can consider the range of such civilian contributions with a view to seeing how much scope, if any, there might be for increasing civilianization.

Not surprisingly the two largest claims on civilian time were those of Internal Organization and General Duties. Next on the list, however, was Crime Investigation, reflecting the need for typing assistance and also the scope for civilian specialists of the kinds referred to already in Chapter VII (see p. 171). The remaining activities involving much civilian time were all connected with court work or traffic or both. They clearly follow from the amount of documentation required, particularly in connection with traffic incidents.

The question of how much work of various types can be done by civilians can be answered, on an average basis, from the figures in column three of Table IX.4. In doing so we should bear in mind that civilians formed 8·9 per cent of our provincial sample. The figures confirm the importance of administration, in a general sense, as the obvious field for civilian employment. It was to be expected that the highest figures would be those for traffic court work and for internal organization.

---

[1] *Estimates*, Sel. Cttee. *op. cit.*, p. 199.
[2] *Estimates*, Sel. Cttee. *op. cit.*, p. 316.

The traffic court figure (27·5 per cent) reflects the extent to which such work has moved towards an operation conducted largely on paper. The maximum among our forces was 48 per cent and three others had as much as 30 per cent of the work done by civilians. It may be that this is approaching the limit of civilian participation, as there must inevitably be a police component in the form of officers attending to give evidence in court.

## TABLE IX.4

**Contribution of Civilians to police work in the provincial forces\***
**(1965–66)**

| Classification | Total hours spent on classification† | | Percentage of work done by civilians | | |
|---|---|---|---|---|---|
| | Civilians | Police | Avge | Max. | Min. |
| 1. Crime Investigation | 7,293 | 71,045 | 9·3 | 13·0 | 1·7 |
| 2. Foreign Enquiries | 3,019 | 12,160 | 19·9 | 34·4 | 8·0 |
| 3. Traffic Supervision | 1,657 | 28,002 | 5·6 | 12·7 | 0·2 |
| 4. Traffic Accidents (no process) | 194 | 3,552 | 5·2 | 18·0 | — |
| 5. Traffic Accidents (possible process) | 1,136 | 6,910 | 14·1 | 26·9 | — |
| 6. Civil Incidents | 221 | 6,986 | 3·1 | 17·8 | — |
| 7. Public Order | 54 | 2,097 | 2·5 | 16·9 | — |
| 8. Private Duties | 28 | 1,610 | 1·7 | 6·9 | — |
| 9. Criminal Courts: (Magistrates) | 1,488 | 8,833 | 14·4 | 36·9 | 4·2 |
| 10. (Higher) | 254 | 3,439 | 6·9 | 53·8 | 0·2 |
| 11. Traffic Courts | 4,049 | 10,694 | 27·5 | 48·0 | 4·9 |
| 12. Civil and Coroners' Courts | 344 | 2,074 | 14·2 | 24·1 | 0·7 |
| 13. Juvenile Courts | 404 | 1,610 | 20·1 | 41·6 | 2·6 |
| 14. After Conviction (Adults) | 243 | 1,527 | 13·8 | 23·2 | — |
| 15. After Conviction (Juveniles) | 42 | 787 | 5·1 | 12·4 | — |
| 16. Patrolling | 11 | 135,881 | — | 0·1 | — |
| 17. General Duties | 10,563 | 84,647 | 11·1 | 15·1 | 2·5 |
| 18. Internal Organization | 8,409 | 23,970 | 26·0 | 52·2 | 3·1 |

\* The figures relate to the first round surveys in those forces surveyed twice.
† These columns include the work of cadets, but not traffic wardens.

The activities in which civilians participated to a lesser extent were those associated with the outdoor aspects of police work. Crime investigation occupied a middle position, about the average for the proportion of civilians in the force.

Our third question, concerned with the range of civilian contributions to particular activities is, in some ways, the most significant. We must, however, avoid the error of assuming that very high figures are invariably best. By definition a police force is an operational organization designed to provide the maximum possible amount of policing with the minimum of non-operational support consistent with efficiency. It could, therefore, be that a very high civilian component might mean excessive administration. This need not necessarily be so, but the possibility exists.

The largest average civilian contribution was to traffic court work. Not only was the average high, but only three forces had figures lower than 20 per cent. These, it so happened, were forces with a very low rate of employment of civilians in general. It would, on the whole, seem quite reasonable for a figure of 25 per cent to be achieved in all forces.

The classification with the next highest civilian contribution was what we termed Internal Organization. This, however, was a restricted application of the term administration,[1] and the figures suggest that some forces used it in a wider sense than we intended. It might, therefore, be unwise to attach too much importance to extreme figures, either low or high. Perhaps the most surprising fact was that no less than five of the twelve forces recorded figures of less than 20 per cent. Some of these, moreover, had fairly high average figures for civilian participation.

While moderately high averages for court work would certainly be expected it is, at first sight, surprising that some figures were so low. The range for criminal work connected with magistrates' courts, for example, was from 36·9 per cent to 4·2 per cent, and four areas had figures of less than 10 per cent. Low figures for the Higher Courts are less surprising owing to the fluctuation in the volume of such work. Civil and Coroners' Courts have some very low figures: this may be due to the fact that in some Borough forces one coroners' officer does all the necessary work himself. Juvenile court work had, at first sight, a rather high proportion of civilian participation; this may result from the volume of report writing needed in some cases and from the fact that such courts hear minor traffic offences and there would be a fair amount of administration in the form of issuing summonses.

---

[1] 'Administration' was printed as a heading on the recording booklet for the provincial surveys although the sense in which we used it was also explained. The booklet was revised for the Metropolitan surveys.

Foreign Enquiries involved quite a high proportion of civilian work. This is largely an administrative activity, but may involve C.I.D. enquiries, and it seems unlikely that the maximum will be pushed much higher.

The crime investigation figures are slightly surprising in that they are all rather on the small side when considered in relation to the numbers of civilians employed in criminal investigation departments. This may, however, have resulted from some of the work of these civilians being recorded under the various forms of court work.

The main conclusion to be drawn from examining the variation in the contribution of civilians to the different aspects of police work is that, although the actual figures varied according to the activity, the relative position of the forces was fairly stable. Certain forces were almost invariably in the bottom half of the list whatever the activity might be. Not surprisingly these forces were ones with relatively low proportions of civilians on their strengths. It would seem, therefore, that the size of the civilian contribution to an activity in a force was related not merely to the nature of that activity, but also to the general policy of the force regarding the employment of civilians.

We have to come back to the points made earlier in this chapter, that employing civilians as a policy is a response to a number of influences, no one of which is of dominant importance. Size, clearly is one factor and, even more than size, being a borough. All but one of our borough forces employed relatively fewer civilians than any of the county forces. The bigger county forces, with their greater problems of filling their establishments also seemed more alive to the possibilities of using civilians. Behind all this, however, may be a further factor, to be inferred from the style of policing in different areas, namely an attitude towards specialization in police work.

Finally we might attempt an estimate of how much further civilianization might be contemplated. On the whole it would seem that a fairly modest increase might be justified. A conservative, but reasonable, basis would be to estimate the numbers of additional civilians required to bring the proportion of civilians (shown in Table IX.1a) up to the prevailing average for our provincial forces. This would produce the following increases:

| Plymouth | from | 22 | to | 42 | i.e. | 91% |
|---|---|---|---|---|---|---|
| Pembroke | | 17 | | 18 | i.e. | 6% |
| Bristol | | 83 | | 100 | i.e. | 21% |
| Bath | | 13 | | 14 | i.e. | 8% |
| Barrow-in-Furness | | 8 | | 14 | i.e. | 63% |
| Birkenhead | | 19 | | 38 | i.e. | 94% |
| Northumberland | | 66 | | 70 | i.e. | 9% |
| | | 228 | | 296 | i.e. | 29·8% |

Although the overall increase for the sample as a whole, calculated on this basis, would be only 11·2 per cent (68 on a total of 607), for the forces then below average the increase would be much greater, about 30 per cent. It is doubtful whether such a figure could be applied without qualification, as our sample happened to contain a below-average proportion of civilians, but it gives an indication of what might be considered.

The broad issues of policy relating to the employment of civilians have been fully discussed in Part III of the Report of the Working Party on Manpower,[1] and it is unnecessary to repeat more than their general conclusions. Basing their conclusions on figures relating to Numbers 2 and 8 Districts they remarked that

> . . . a substantial degree of civilianisation has already been achieved in some parts of the country, but that progress has been uneven. Moreover, even among the more extensively civilianised forces, there is considerable variation in the way in which civilians are employed: with a few exceptions . . . the decision to employ a policeman or a civilian on any given task seems to depend largely on local conditions and preferences. Generally speaking, we think that it ought to be possible not only to raise the less highly civilianised forces to the level of those in which more progress has been made, but also to increase civilianisation in all forces.[2]

Our results certainly confirm this conclusion and, on this basis, our estimates of the possible scope for civilianization have been conservative. The Select Committee on Estimates, commenting on our results concluded, 'The main task now is to remedy the large discrepancies between forces . . .'[3] Not even the Select Committee, however, was able to estimate how much money

[1] Taverne Report.
[2] Ibid., p. 29.
[3] Estimates, Sel. Cttee. 1st Report, p. xxiv; 1966–67 (145).

would be saved by more civilianization. Neither our data nor any published information can be of much assistance on this point. The arguments which applied to the employment of traffic wardens apply even more strongly, namely that it is almost impossible to tell when the employment of additional civilians is merely enabling existing services to be maintained, or is actually releasing more officers for police duties, thus raising the standard of police cover. In the last resort, therefore, it is not so much a matter of comparing pay scales (which would usually show that civilians are cheaper, particularly when police allowances are taken into account) as of matching total local resources of police and civilians both to the finances available and to the requirements of policing the area.

In some cases the appointment of extra civilians might help to remedy a manpower shortage, but in others it might mean an increase in the number of officers available for active duty to a point above that assumed by the existing establishment. Apart, therefore, from the generalizations we have already made it seems impossible to make a financial assessment without considering the details of the employment market in each locality, and of the organization of each force.

*Conclusions*

1. Women police officers constituted 2·9 per cent of the strength of their forces (including civilians) in the provinces. One Metropolitan division was above, and the other below, this average.

2. Civilians (excluding traffic wardens) averaged 9·3 per cent of strength in provincial forces, and the proportion ranged from 4·9 to 11·8 per cent. The Metropolitan figures needed adjustment to allow for the large proportion of civilians in the Commissioner's Office who performed tasks which, in the provincial force, would have been covered by our surveys. When an adjustment was made the Metropolitan force as a whole appeared to employ the highest proportion of civilians found in our surveys ('B' Division 11·9 per cent, 'S' Division 12·6 per cent).

3. The variations between forces in the proportion of civilians which they employed could not be explained in terms of manpower shortage, and our data tended to suggest that size and the Chief Constable's attitude to specialization in police work were major influences.

4. Women police officers worked only fractionally shorter hours than male officers in urban areas; in most cases the difference was less than an hour a week.

5. Women officers spend much less time patrolling than do male officers, but a little more on general duties. Most of the extra time used on specific activities went on crime investigation, of which they tended to do about twice as much as beat patrol officers.

6. As might be expected they were the only group of police officers who spent significant amounts of time on civil incidents, averaging about 7 per cent of Active Duty Time.

7. Court work seemed to fall much more heavily on women officers than on policemen. On average they spent between three and four times as much of their active duty in court.

8. On the whole the woman police officer's job seems to have been more concerned with specific activities than those of her male colleagues. As a result it may well be more interesting.

9. Traffic wardens make it possible for the amount of traffic supervision to be substantially increased. There was no evidence that, in areas where wardens were employed, police officers did any less traffic supervision.

10. On average each warden spent as much time on supervision as the total contributed by 8–10 officers in the course of normal patrolling.

11. Although, at first sight, civilians appear to work shorter hours than police officers, our surveys showed that on those activities classified as active duty they worked almost exactly the same number of hours as police officers.

12. Civilians, however, worked far less overtime than police officers, and it may be that their hours were less flexible.

13. As would be expected their work was mainly administrative and clerical, with their largest contributions being made to Traffic Court work and Internal Organization.

14. In the absence of criteria for assessing the maximum desirable proportion of civilians in a force it was clear that some forces could increase their civilian strength by nearly a hundred per cent and still only bring themselves up to the previous average for our provincial forces. On the other hand our sample happened to contain a relatively low proportion of civilians, 8·9 per cent as against 13·3 per cent for all provincial forces, so that other forces might not be capable of quite so much expansion.

# X

# Aspects of Operational Organization

WE conclude the analysis of our data by considering some rather more technical aspects of the organization of operations. First we shall deal with shift working, the question of 24-hour responsibility and such differences as there may have been between work in urban and rural areas. We shall make a brief reference to training, and shall finish by discussing mobility and the claims of report writing.

## Shift working and 24-hour responsibility

It is widely agreed that shift working is one of the major disadvantages of the policeman's job. It is not unique in this respect but, combined with week-end duties and quite strict discipline, the contrast with the 5-day week common in many occupations is notable and unfavourable.

This was not an aspect of major importance in our survey, but our data may help to show the problem in perspective. We have only concerned ourselves with the numbers of shifts worked at different times and not with week-end duties as such. The extent of week-end working is, however, quite vividly implied by the proposal for *improved* working conditions, made by the Police Federation and quoted in the Report of the Working Party on Manpower,[1] which aimed at 'a frequency of week-end leave of one week-end in four'.

Table X.1 shows the distribution of shifts worked by all those taking part in the surveys. It involves a degree of over simplification because in fact shift systems vary in minor ways both between and within forces. Our instructions were that offset shifts should be treated as being equivalent to the standard shift to which they most closely corresponded. The system was, therefore, more flexible than we can portray it; nevertheless our data give some

[1] Taverne Report, p. 23.

indication of the extent to which inconvenient hours were being worked.

We grouped shifts as follows:

Early —usually 6 a.m. to 2 p.m. but also including 8 a.m. to 4 p.m. and 10 a.m. to 6 p.m.

Late —usually 2 p.m. to 10 p.m. but also including 4 p.m. to midnight and 6 p.m. to 2 a.m.

Night —usually 10 p.m. to 6 a.m.

Split —usually involving a morning and an afternoon or evening period with a gap of at least an hour between the two main parts.

Office hours—regular working of hours corresponding to those worked in offices generally.

### TABLE X.1

**Distribution of types of shifts worked in survey period (1965–66)**

|  | Provincial forces | | | Metropolitan divisions | |
|  | Average | Max. | Min. | 'B'&'S' | Central traffic |
|  | % | % | % | % | % |
| Early | 28·6 | 35·3 | 17·6 | 31·9 | 50·2 |
| Late | 19·9 | 30·2 | 15·9 | 25·1 | 37·4 |
| Night | 16·2 | 24·9 | 12·5 | 17·2 | 3·9 |
| Split | 19·6 | 37·8 | 2·0 | 3·4 | 0·2 |
| Office hours | 15·7 | 29·6 | 10·7 | 22·4 | 8·3 |
| Total no. of shifts | 63,715 | | | 14,640 | 4,285 |

It can be seen from Table X.1 that the problem of inconvenient hours has, at least in part, been met by the practice of minimizing the number of officers working night shifts. Approximately one out of every six shifts worked was a night shift in the provincial forces, and the Metropolitan figure was only fractionally higher. Almost as many shifts were worked on an 'office hours' basis in the provincial forces, while in the Metropolitan divisions office hours were distinctly more frequent than night shifts.

At first sight we might expect the explanation for the high proportion of 'office hours' shifts to be that they were related to the proportion of civilians employed. This was not so.[1] It would seem, therefore, that the volume of office working was dependent on the

---

[1] The correlation between the proportion of civilians in a force and the percentage of shifts worked as office hours was $r = 0.3607$. With 10 d.f. $t = 1.3396$ which was not significant at the 5 per cent level.

A.S.I.M.—16

administrative arrangements of the force in a general sense and not on the employment of a certain proportion of civilians.

The early shifts formed the largest single group. The average proportion was 28·5 per cent and the highest was 35·3 per cent. The lowest was 17·6 per cent, but this was in a county in which 37·8 per cent of shifts were split shifts. It would seem that the emphasis on early shifts is related to the general level of public activity during the day, and also perhaps to the claims of the courts. The dominant concerns therefore might be traffic supervision in the rush hours, crime in the form of walk-in thefts and larcenies from and of vehicles, and perhaps a general belief that the number of police on duty should be roughly correlated with the number of people out and about. It is not clear how far these dispositions were based on a systematic analysis of the timing of incidents of various kinds.

The late and night shifts, which might be most important from a crime prevention point of view, averaged 19·9 per cent and 16·2 per cent respectively in the provincial forces, but rather higher proportions prevailed in the Metropolitan divisions (25·1 per cent and 17·2 per cent).

One difficulty in interpreting these figures is to allow for the split shifts worked by many members of county forces. When talking about police coverage at different times it is necessary to make some allowance, and we have done this on the assumption that such time should be divided equally between the early and late shifts. If we make this adjustment the modified figures show that 38·5 per cent of shifts covered the early period and 29·7 the late. This, of course, is an estimate and we recognize that some split shifts may cover more of one period than the other; nevertheless on average these figures constitute the best estimate, and they confirm the emphasis on the early period.

Split shifts as such amounted to 19·6 per cent of the total. As would be expected they were far more frequently worked in county forces—where the proportions usually exceeded 20 per cent, and sometimes even 30 per cent. In the boroughs much lower figures prevailed, usually below 10 per cent. Such shifts were most frequently worked in the counties by officers with rural beats, and by members of the C.I.D.; in boroughs almost entirely by the C.I.D.

The Metropolitan figures were notable for the very low proportion of split shifts, and for the fairly high 'office hours' figure for 'B' and 'S' Divisions. The Central Traffic Division worked a two-shift system with, again, an emphasis on the early rather than the late shift.

One of the major influences on police operations is the fact that the service has to provide cover for all 24 hours of the day. Where the number of officers in a locality is large enough this is achieved through the shift system. In rural areas, however, this may not be possible as villages may have no more than one or two officers covering a large area. Naturally they have to have time off, so it happens that officers regularly have to take sole responsibility for the policing of their area throughout the 24 hours. Sometimes a variant of this scheme is operated whereby a pair of officers have 12 hours responsibility each. Whatever the system, however, the result is likely to be that such officers have to work longer hours than would be the case if they were part of a shift system. Most officers having such responsibility work in rural areas, but some specialists such as dog handlers, scenes of crime experts and so on, also have to arrange to be on call when required.

We shall not consider the work of those with 24-hour responsibility in detail, but it is of some importance to see what claims were made on their time. It should not be assumed that, under these circumstances, working longer hours is entirely a disadvantage. The greater responsibility, relative independence, and perhaps increased variety may be sufficient compensation.

Table X.2 first summarizes the differences in terms of the total number of hours' active duty worked during the survey fortnight; this excludes abstractions and may, therefore, somewhat exaggerate the difference as the officer with 24-hour responsibility is less likely to be spending time on training than the officer who forms part of a large unit. Table X.2 therefore also states the difference in terms of working time.

The first point shown by Table X.2 is that 956, or 14 per cent of our sample claimed to have 24-hour responsibility in their jobs. We did not attempt to verify these claims, although presumably the sergeants and liaison officers would have noticed any that were obviously inappropriate. It would seem, therefore, that at least one member in seven of the service must as a matter of routine expect to be on call for work at more or less any time.

The numbers also confirm the generalization that 24-hour

responsibility is only really common in the county forces. The overall average of 14 per cent resulted from a combination of two quite distinct groups: the six county forces with proportions ranging from 14·5 per cent to 25·4 per cent, and the borough forces ranging from 1·9 per cent to 8·6 per cent.

TABLE X.2

**Average hours worked by persons with and without 24-hour responsibility during survey fortnight (1965–66)**

|  | Numbers* with 24-hr resp. | Active duty | | | Working time | | |
|---|---|---|---|---|---|---|---|
|  |  | 24-hr resp. | Others | Differ- ence | 24-hr resp. | Others | Differ- ence |
| Plymouth | 12 | 68·5 | 64·3 | 4·2 | 79·8 | 73·2 | 6·6 |
| Hastings | 3 | 88·3 | 59·4 | 28·9 | 99·0 | 73·8 | 25·2 |
| Pembrokeshire | 41 | 81·9 | 63·9 | 18·0 | 85·7 | 77·1 | 8·6 |
| Dorset | 77 | 75·5 | 63·7 | 11·8 | 83·0 | 76·3 | 6·7 |
| Bristol | 36 | 80·4 | 61·3 | 19·1 | 86·4 | 73·9 | 12·5 |
| Bath | 13 | 65·2 | 60·8 | 4·4 | 91·0 | 75·3 | 15·7 |
| Barrow-in-Furness | 3 | 68·3 | 63·6 | 4·7 | 70·0 | 71·8 | −1·8 |
| Birkenhead | 8 | 77·8 | 66·9 | 10·9 | 86·1 | 74·4 | 11·7 |
| Leic. & Rutland | 156 | 77·6 | 72·8 | 4·8 | 81·9 | 87·4 | −5·5 |
| Northumberland | 196 | 85·9 | 59·8 | 26·1 | 91·8 | 73·7 | 18·1 |
| Bedfordshire | 106 | 83·7 | 70·8 | 12·9 | 90·4 | 86·2 | 4·2 |
| Essex | 305 | 85·5 | 65·0 | 20·5 | 89·3 | 78·1 | 11·2 |
| Total | 956 | 82·4 | 66·9 | 15·5 | 87·8 | 75·8 | 12·0 |

* We did not attempt to check an officer's claim to have 24-hour responsibility.

The amount of work actually done by such members appears to have been significantly more than the average for those without 24-hour responsibility. This was particularly so when calculated on the basis of active duty time, as those with 24-hour responsibility tended to spend little time on training (being relatively experienced) or on refreshment breaks (as they often worked split shifts). The average difference in hours worked on active duty was 15½ per fortnight. Allowing for days off this would represent between an hour and a quarter and an hour and a half extra per working day.

Calculated on the basis of working time, i.e. including training, sport and refreshment breaks, the average difference was 12 hours; this was less, but not much less than figures based on active duty time. It confirms the distinctly longer hours worked by the 24-hour responsibility groups.

The average differences varied greatly from force to force, as was only to be expected from the fluctuating demands made on those in such positions. The maximum excess in terms of active duty amounted to nearly 30 hours a fortnight, while the minimum was 4·2. Computed on a basis of working time the maximum fell to 25·2 hours, and in two forces the 24-hour responsibility members actually worked fewer hours than those without such responsibility.

The only general conclusion on shift-working and 24-hour responsibility that seems justifiable is that all shifts (except the office hours one) involve a degree of inconvenience in that they differ to a greater or lesser extent from the more conventional hours worked by the majority of the population. In this, however, the police are not unique and, as a cause of discontent, the importance of shift working as such might be exaggerated unless related to other disadvantages. We have already alluded to some, while the whole question is fully discussed by Banton in *The Policeman in the Community*.[1] At this stage it is sufficient to remark that perhaps what may be needed are positive incentives to make the job seem worth while, whether they be pay, interest or achievement.

*Police work in urban and rural areas*

The discussion of 24-hour responsibility inevitably raised the question of the differing patterns of police work that may prevail in rural areas. We can go on to examine such differences as there may be by contrasting the work of constables in the different types of area. For practical purposes we restricted ourselves to three— urban, mixed and rural. We asked officers to indicate, for each day the type of area in which they were mainly working. We defined the three types as follows:

1. Urban—Predominantly built-up areas: towns or cities.
2. Rural —Areas sparsely populated but including villages and/or the outskirts of towns not completely built up.

[1] Michael Banton: *The Policeman in the Community*, London, Tavistock Publications, 1964, particularly Chaps. 6–9.

3. Mixed—Areas which include parts of 1 and 2 above, also
large villages or small towns of rural character.

The comparative information is summarized in Table X.3. If
we consider the overall totals it is clear that the major differences
were between the Metropolitan men and the provincial, irrespec-
tive of the type of area in which they worked. Nevertheless there
was also a clear progression in hours of active duty (and of the

TABLE X.3

**Percentage distribution of constables' potential duty time
in urban, mixed and rural areas (1965–66)**

| Classification | Provincial forces | | | Metropolitan 'B' & 'S' Divisions | | |
|---|---|---|---|---|---|---|
| | Urban | Mixed | Rural | Urban | Mixed | Rural |
| Crime Investigation | 5·6 | 5·0 | 7·3 | 8·5 | 3·7 | 3·0 |
| Foreign Enquiries | 1·3 | 1·7 | 2·6 | 1·0 | 0·9 | 0·7 |
| Traffic Supervision | 4·4 | 7·3 | 3·0 | 3·2 | 3·1 | 1·1 |
| Traffic Accidents (no process) | 0·5 | 0·6 | 0·6 | 0·3 | 1·1 | 0·7 |
| Traffic Incidents (possible process) | 1·0 | 1·5 | 1·5 | 3·7 | 4·3 | 1·0 |
| Civil Incidents | 1·1 | 0·9 | 0·9 | 1·0 | 1·3 | 1·6 |
| Public Order | 0·3 | 0·2 | 0·6 | 1·0 | 0·6 | 0·8 |
| Private Duties | 0·3 | 0·2 | 0·3 | 0·1 | 0·1 | — |
| Criminal Courts (Magistrates') | 0·8 | 0·7 | 0·7 | 1·3 | 0·5 | 0·1 |
| Criminal Courts (Higher) | 0·3 | 0·3 | 0·4 | 0·2 | 0·2 | 0·3 |
| Traffic Courts (all types) | 1·5 | 1·7 | 1·3 | 2·5 | 4·1 | 0·7 |
| Civil and Coroners' Courts | 0·3 | 0·3 | 0·3 | 0·4 | 0·2 | — |
| Juvenile Courts (all cases) | 0·2 | 0·1 | 0·2 | 0·1 | 0·1 | 0·4 |
| After Conviction (adults) | 0·3 | 0·2 | 0·1 | 0·1 | 0·1 | — |
| After Conviction (juveniles) | 0·1 | 0·1 | 0·3 | — | — | — |
| Patrolling | 24·1 | 28·4 | 32·4 | 28·7 | 35·1 | 42·0 |
| General Duties | 10·1 | 8·5 | 8·3 | 9·8 | 9·9 | 18·9 |
| Internal Organization | 2·3 | 1·4 | 1·6 | 3·3 | 1·7 | — |
| Training (inc. instruction) | 5·7 | 5·1 | 5·6 | 4·4 | 2·0 | — |
| Sports | 0·3 | 0·2 | 0·2 | 0·1 | — | — |
| Leave | 31·4 | 29·4 | 27·5 | 20·8 | 22·2 | 20·7 |
| Sick Leave | 2·6 | 0·7 | 1·9 | 2·5 | 2·0 | 1·2 |
| Misc. (mainly refreshments) | 5·3 | 5·4 | 2·3 | 7·0 | 6·8 | 6·8 |
| | 99·8 | 99·9 | 99·9 | 100·0 | 100·0 | 100·0 |
| Avge hours potential duty time (= 100%) | 114·5 | 115·0 | 116·0 | 115·0 | 115·3 | 113·6 |
| Avge hours work time | 74·5 | 80·2 | 81·7 | 88·3 | 87·5 | 88·8 |
| Avge hours active duty | 62·0 | 68·1 | 72·4 | 75·2 | 77·3 | 81·0 |
| Abstractions as % of total | 54·3 | 40·8 | 37·6 | 34·8 | 33·0 | 28·7 |
| Number of officers | 2,884 | 811 | 453 | 745 | 126 | 12 |

corresponding proportions of abstractions) to the effect that the hours increased from the urban to the rural. This applied in the provinces and, to a lesser extent, in the Metropolitan area. In the provinces the hours of working time also went up in a similar way, but this did not apply in the Metropolitan divisions.

The extent of these differences was that in the provinces the rural constable spent approximately ten hours a fortnight more on active duty than his urban counterpart. The difference in terms of working time was in the same direction but rather less.

The overall pattern of work was broadly similar but for some differences of emphasis. In the provinces rural men did rather more crime investigation and foreign enquiry work. In the Metropolitan area, however, they did considerably less of both.

In the provinces traffic work occupied much the same proportion of time in urban and in rural areas, but at least half as much again in mixed areas. This was due mainly to differences in the time spent on supervision. In the urban and mixed parts of the Metropolitan divisions the volume of traffic work was not so very different from the corresponding provincial areas, though with the expected Metropolitan emphasis on incidents likely to involve process. The few rural men did very little traffic work—even in comparison with rural men in the provincial forces.

So far as court work was concerned there was invariably no difference between the three types of area in the provincial forces. In the Metropolitan divisions the only big difference was that the men in rural areas did very much less.

The biggest single difference between the types of area was in patrolling. Both the provincial forces and the Metropolitan showed a considerably higher proportion in the rural areas. This difference amounted to about 8 per cent of potential duty time in the provinces, and over 13 per cent in the Metropolitan. The very high figure for general duties in the rural part of the Metropolitan was probably accounted for by work in the station.

In the Metropolitan divisions the amount of time spent on training was highest in the urban parts and decreased to nil in the rural area. In the provincial forces there was no such trend.

Rural constables in the provincial forces enjoyed slightly less leave than their urban colleagues and, due to split shifts, less in the way of refreshment breaks. Sick leave figures varied slightly, but the healthiest group were provincial constables in mixed areas,

In conclusion it would seem that while constables in rural areas worked longer hours than their more urban colleagues much of the difference was accounted for by increased patrolling. There were fairly big differences between the Metropolitan and the provincial forces, but on the whole the contrasts between urban and rural areas in terms of specific activities were not as great as might have been expected.


*Training*

Our remarks on training will relate only to that of police officers in the provincial forces. We have already shown that the training of civilians amounted to less than 1 per cent of all time recorded under that heading, and it would be unprofitable to discuss them any further. The elaborate structure and training arrangements of the Metropolitan police cannot be analysed adequately on the basis of our surveys made at divisional level, although we have already referred to the pioneering work of the force in introducing many of the forms of training which are now widespread in the service (see Chapters III and IV).

During our first round surveys training accounted for 5·9 per cent of potential duty time.[1] As a proportion of working time, however, it was distinctly more, some 8·7 per cent. This is equivalent to about a twelfth or, roughly, one full working day a fortnight. These figures, of course, are averages based on the quite large variations between areas shown in Table X.4. The range, in fact, was from 1·4 per cent to 12·6 per cent, and this raises the question of how this variation might be explained.

One obvious possibility would be that the amount of training was related to the proportion of probationers in the force as, clearly, the need for training is likely to be at its maximum during this period. Indeed Appendix 3 of the Report of the Working Party on Operational Efficiency and Management begins with the assertion 'Every probationer must be regarded as *in training* for the whole of the term of his two years probation. This is the guiding principle behind the whole scheme for the training of probationers.'[2]

[1] 41,727 out of a total of 709,211 hours.
[2] Taverne Report, pp. 143–8.

## TABLE X.4

### Police officers' training and working time

| | Total hours (1) | No. of police officers* (2) | Avge hours per head (3) | Total working time (4) | Training as % (1) ÷ (4) (5) | % of probationers in force† (6) |
|---|---|---|---|---|---|---|
| Plymouth | 1,216 | 412 | 3·0 | 30,461 | 4·0 | 13·1 |
| Hastings | 1,307 | 139 | 9·4 | 10,381 | 12·6 | 10·1 |
| Pembrokeshire | 1,450 | 178 | 8·1 | 14,582 | 9·9 | 12·4 |
| Dorset | 4,037 | 462 | 8·7 | 35,598 | 11·3 | 14·1 |
| Bristol | 6,448 | 979 | 6·6 | 76,125 | 8·5 | 15·5 |
| Bath | 1,001 | 139 | 7·2 | 10,629 | 9·4 | 15·2 |
| Barrow-in-Furness | 447 | 135 | 3·3 | 9,977 | 4·5 | 19·1 |
| Birkenhead | 398 | 368 | 1·1 | 28,674 | 1·4 | 10·0 |
| Leic. & Rutland | 5,046 | 666 | 7·6 | 52,831 | 9·6 | 21·2 |
| Northumberland | 5,057 | 680 | 7·4 | 55,965 | 9·0 | 13·3 |
| Bedfordshire | 4,745 | 439 | 10·8 | 41,723 | 11·4 | 18·6 |
| Essex | 10,575 | 1,329 | 8·0 | 115,119 | 9·2 | 22·8 |
| | 41,727 | 5,926 | 7·0 | 482,065 | 8·7 | 16·9 |

\* This number includes police women but excludes cadets.

† This is the number of constables (including women) who had been serving less than 2 years as a percentage of all constables and W.P.Cs. in each force.

With this possibility in mind we calculated the correlation co-efficient between the proportion of working time spent on training, and the proportion of probationers among constables (including W.P.C.s). The correlation, however, turned out to be completely non-significant,[1] so that the proportion of probationers was clearly irrelevant. The only other fact that may have been important was the tendency for the low training figures to be shown by borough rather than county forces. All the forces with figures below the average for the sample were boroughs, and three of these were quite considerably below the average. County forces, however, might be expected to show higher figures as more travelling time would be involved.

Finally we should mention that the average amount of time spent on training was seven hours per fortnight. The range was from 1·1 to 10·8 hours. As would be expected this distribution was similar to that of the percentage of working time occupied by training.

[1] $r = 0·1560$, $t = 0·5466$ with 10 d.f. this is not significant.

*Station time, mobility and report writing*

These topics form a natural group relating to slightly different aspects of what we can call the general problem of mobility in the police. It can be taken as axiomatic that the preventive side of police work depends on officers being available to deal quickly with incidents whenever and wherever they occur and, though this is more difficult to plan on a scientific basis, to be conspicuously 'out and about' in such a way as to prevent the commission of as many offences as possible.

Differing views have been expressed in the service as to how much transport, and of what types, is desirable for efficient policing. Unit Beat Policing requires one vehicle for every pair of beats, that is for a group of four officers,[1] so that the total vehicle requirement may be quite large. The late Commissioner of the Metropolitan police on the other hand reaffirmed the potentialities of the man 'on foot or slow moving cycle'.[2] It would seem there might be scope for operational research to compare results achieved with different types and degrees of mobility. Our research had the more limited aim of discovering the basic facts of how much time officers spent in the station (for any reason), and what forms of transport they used when working outdoors. It is not implied that time spent in police stations is wasted, but it is obvious that the officer is not then available for preventive work outdoors.

Table X.5 summarizes the data according to departments. The average in the provincial forces for all departments and forces combined was 40·6 per cent, with a range from 32·1 per cent to 48·3 per cent. Naturally the Administration Departments and Station Staff had high average figures (90·9 per cent and 85·5 per cent respectively) and most interest attaches to the operational departments. The C.I.D. was well above average, nearly half its working time being spent in the station. W.P.Cs. were very slightly above the average, which was consistent with the varied nature of their work and the relatively low amount of patrolling which they did. The Traffic Department averaged 30·3 per cent and Beat Patrols spent just over a quarter of their time in the station

[1] 'Two area constables, one man on the car beat and one detective constable.' Taverne Report, p. 140.
[2] *Commissioner of Police of the Metropolis, 1964,* p. 10; 1964–65 Cmnd. 2710.

(26·3 per cent). This means that the average patrol officer would be out of the station for 6 hours of each 8-hour shift.

The corresponding figures for the two Metropolitan divisions followed a somewhat similar pattern, but the proportion of time spent in the station was rather higher than the provincial average (though by no means as high as in some county forces). There was not much overall difference between the two divisions ('B' = 41·1 per cent, 'S' = 42·1 per cent), but there were variations between departments which need not concern us here. The major difference was that on average Beat Patrols in the Metropolitan divisions spent about 5 per cent more of their time in the station than

TABLE X.5

**Percentage of working time spent in station or report writing**
(1965–66)

| Department | Station time Provincial forces | | | Metro-politan Avge* | Report time Provincial forces | | | Metro-politan Avge* |
|---|---|---|---|---|---|---|---|---|
| | Avge | Max. | Min. | | Avge | Max. | Min. | |
| Traffic wardens | 10·1 | 28·5 | 6·5 | N.A. | 3·4 | 7·2 | 0·5 | N.A. |
| Traffic | 30·3 | 37·9 | 17·9 | 34·4 | 7·3 | 11·4 | 5·3 | 9·9 |
| Beat patrols | 26·3 | 35·3 | 19·6 | 31·6 | 8·3 | 11·2 | 2·4 | 6·4 |
| C.I.D. | 49·8 | 58·9 | 31·7 | 53·4 | 17·4 | 26·7 | 13·0 | 19·7 |
| W.P.Cs. | 41·8 | 64·3 | 18·6 | 50·0 | 9·9 | 15·5 | 4·6 | 13·0 |
| Administration | 90·9 | 97·3 | 79·8 | 90·7 | 8·4 | 25·8 | 1·4 | 25·7 |
| Station staff | 85·5 | 99·3 | 62·4 | 84·3 | 5·8 | 9·7 | 2·3 | 12·1 |
| Training—courses | 32·8 | 100·0 | — | 16·2 | — | — | — | — |
| Training—instructors | 52·4 | 97·4 | — | 21·2 | 4·9 | 18·2 | — | 4·6 |
| Other duties | 43·9 | 69·6 | 10·9 | 27·4 | 7·6 | 15·0 | 1·3 | 14·9 |
| Total | 40·6 | 48·3 | 32·1 | 41·6 | 8·7 | 11·7 | 3·8 | 10·6 |

\* This is the average of the figure for 'B' and 'S' Divisions.

the provincial average (31·6 per cent as against 26·3 per cent). Their figures, however, were below the provincial maximum and, in general, this was true of all departments in the two divisions.

Although the averages imply that the effective patrolling strength of beat departments, in terms of hours spent out of the station, was only about three-quarters of the number theoretically possible, the average does not seem unreasonable in view of the claims of report writing, refreshment breaks and duties for which men had to remain in the station.

In view of the importance which Chief Constables attach to

having a high proportion of men out on patrol it is worth examining the variations between forces and departments. The obvious point to consider is the relationship between station time and the organization of the force. The first correlation calculated was with the proportion of civilians employed, using the figures of Table IX.1a, and this proved to be positive and significant at the 1 per cent level.[1] However, it was clearly not just a matter of the proportion of civilians as correlations almost as high were found to exist with the strength of the Administration department, and with the combined strengths of the station staff and the administration department.[2] It seems therefore that the relevant influence, in general terms, was the proportion of the force involved in administration, whether in departments called by that name or as station staffs.[3]

Something may also be learned by a rather closer examination of the detailed figures (summarized in Table 7 of Appendix D). Seven forces were below the mean for the proportion of station time and these included five out of the six boroughs. The only borough with a high figure also had the highest proportion of civilians among borough forces. It would, however, be an over-simplification to treat this just as a matter of the difference between boroughs and counties. It seems likely that it is also a matter of the size of the organization, the degree of specialization, and the number of police stations. All these combined may constitute what one might call a force's general style of policing. The Metropolitan figures, for example, suggest a somewhat different emphasis in its operations which may explain its rather high figures for station time.[4]

The other general influence was the amount of report writing.

[1] $r = 0.6844$, $t = 3.2516$ with 10 d.f. at the 10 per cent level this value of $t$ was significant.

[2] Both were expressed as percentages of the total strength of the force. For the provincial forces the correlation with the percentage in the Administration department was 0.6692; when $n = 12$, $t = 3.119$, significant at 2 per cent level. For the provincial and Metropolitan combined, the correlation with the percentage of station staff plus administration department was 0.6593. When $n = 14$, $t = 3.2804$, significant at 1 per cent level.

[3] There was in fact a negative correlation with the percentage of the force employed as station staffs ($r = 0.2432$, not significant).

[4] This is because of the higher proportion of station time recorded by all its operational departments, and also its higher general rate for report writing.

This, as can be seen from Table X.5 occupied, on average, 8·7 per cent of working time in the provincial forces, and 10·6 per cent in the Metropolitan divisions. In the provincial forces this was exactly the same proportion as was spent on training, and was equivalent to approximately one whole working day out of every twelve. Although this would average less than an hour a day it would be bound to have a considerable effect on the figures for station time. We have already shown that, for beat patrols, station time averaged 2 hours a shift. The statutory refreshment break takes 45 minutes and, on our figures, report writing would account for another 40 minutes so that there would only be 35 minutes left for any other duties. The Metropolitan figure being rather higher this argument applies *a fortiori*. These figures are, of course, averages, and within the total would have to include such longer periods as might have to be spent on occasional duty in the station.

The importance of the report writing of beat officers as an influence on the total amount of time spent in the station is confirmed by the correlation between the two variables. For the provincial forces the correlation between the force averages for report writing and station time was 0·6392, which was significant at the 2 per cent level.[1]

The section of Table X.5 dealing with report writing shows, above all, the burden that fell on the criminal investigation departments. Their average was 17·4 per cent, and the lowest figure was 11·0 per cent. Three forces had figures in excess of 20 per cent. No explanation for the pattern of variation suggests itself.

We have already discussed the figures for beat patrols. Most other departments had fairly similar averages, although local variations were quite large. The low figure for traffic wardens is perhaps another indication of the efficiency of such a specialized group. Their effective working hours were long, and they spent relatively little time in the station or on report writing.

We turn finally to the mobility of officers when at work. The overall totals in terms of forces are shown in Table X.6 below. Nearly 40 per cent of all shifts, i.e. 60 per cent of all those outdoors, were worked on foot or pedal cycle. As would be expected the highest figures in this category were found in borough forces,

---

[1] When $r = 0.6392$, $t = 2.8787$, with 10 d.f.

the maximum being 56·3 per cent in Barrow in Furness (this was equivalent to 78 per cent of all outdoor shifts). The lowest proportions were in country forces where mechanical transport is indispensable for mobility. In Bedfordshire, for example, almost as many shifts were worked in cars as on foot or pedal cycles.

TABLE X.6

**Shifts worked using different methods of transport (1965–66)**
(Percentages)

| Force | Foot or cycle | Motor cycle or scooter | Car | In court | Indoors | Total = 100% |
|---|---|---|---|---|---|---|
| Plymouth | 41·8 | 11·1 | 15·0 | 0·3 | 31·8 | 3,935 |
| Hastings* | 43·0 | 5·5 | 16·2 | 0·4 | 34·9 | 1,474 |
| Pembrokeshire* | 44·5 | 9·2 | 11·6 | 0·3 | 34·5 | 1,899 |
| Dorset* | 37·2 | 8·5 | 21·8 | 0·2 | 32·3 | 4,993 |
| Bristol | 48·8 | 3·1 | 11·8 | 0·1 | 36·2 | 10,338 |
| Bath | 43·0 | 1·9 | 19·5 | 0·7 | 34·9 | 1,399 |
| Barrow-in-Furness | 56·3 | 2·8 | 13·0 | 0·1 | 27·8 | 1,340 |
| Birkenhead | 54·8 | 3·7 | 12·6 | 0·3 | 28·6 | 3,686 |
| Leic. & Rutland | 31·2 | 8·2 | 24·0 | 0·4 | 36·2 | 6,707 |
| Northumberland | 42·0 | 5·8 | 16·9 | 0·1 | 35·2 | 7·20 |
| Bedfordshire | 24·8 | 3·5 | 24·3 | 0·8 | 46·6 | 5,467 |
| Essex | 30·0 | 6·7 | 23·4 | 0·6 | 39·3 | 15,357 |
| Total | 24,449 | 3,811 | 12,001 | 239 | 23,215 | 63,715 |
| Average | 38·4 | 6·0 | 18·8 | 0·4 | 36·4 | |
| Metropolitan 'B' Division | 44·8 | 1·7 | 15·8 | 0·1 | 37·6 | 6,885 |
| 'S' Division | 27·9 | 10·6 | 24·3 | 0·5 | 36·7 | 7,755 |
| Central Traffic Division | 0·4 | 29·3 | 47·3 | 0·4 | 22·6 | 4,285 |

* First survey only.

Motor cycles and scooters have obvious attractions as means of mobility in urban areas, for certain traffic work, and as vehicles that do not isolate the officer from his surroundings in the way that being in a car can do. Capital and running costs are also lower, but such vehicles have the immense drawback that they cannot be used for carrying passengers, or more than a minimum of equipment, while their use can present an endurance test in bad weather. It was not surprising, therefore, that they were distinctly less widely used than motor cars, averaging 6 per cent in the provincial forces, with a range from 1·9 to 11·1 per cent.

There is an indication that, in some forces, motor cycles or scooters have been regarded as alternatives to cars, rather than as additions to total mobility. This, however, was not a general phenomenon and the correlation between the use of the two types of transport was non-significant ($r = 0.0966$). On the other hand they were clearly the method of choice for traffic work in crowded urban areas as, for example, central London. They accounted for approximately 38 per cent of the outdoor shifts worked by the Central Traffic Division and, on the assumption that all cars had a crew of two, probably constituted a majority of vehicles on traffic patrol. None of the provincial forces, however, made as much use of motor cycles.

Undoubtedly the motor car is the most important method of transport. Nearly one in four of all shifts in the provincial forces were worked in cars, and this proportion was exceeded in four out of the six county forces. On average three out of four shifts involving mechanical transport were worked in cars. This does not mean, however, that the number of vehicles was correspondingly greater owing to the likelihood of many cars being crewed by two men. We have no evidence on the proportion of cars carrying more than one man, but the number of vehicles in use was probably less than might at first seem to be implied by the figures in Table X.6.

The remaining figures, for shifts spent in court and indoors are included to show how the table is made up. The low figure for shifts spent mainly in court confirms our earlier comments that the burden of court work is apt to be exaggerated in relation to the time actually spent, although it may so be chopped up into short periods as to be particularly irritating.

We can conclude this discussion by considering the degree of mobility achieved by different main departments, and the relevant information is summarized in Table X.7. This refers to the provincial forces.

The traffic department averages confirm our earlier comment on the difference between the methods of transport employed in London and those of the provincial forces. The use of motor cycles in the provinces was less than a third of that in London, and there was a correspondingly higher figure for cars. In both about a quarter of all shifts were worked indoors (these figures included office staff but not mechanics).

TABLE X.7

**Departmental use of different methods of transport (1965–66)**
(Percentages)
**Provincial forces only\***

| Department | Foot or cycle | Motor cycle or scooter | Car | In court | Indoors | Total = 100% |
|---|---|---|---|---|---|---|
| Traffic | 3·5 | 8·2 | 63·9 | 0·1 | 24·3 | 6,770 |
| Beat patrols | 62·9 | 9·7 | 12·2 | 0·4 | 14·8 | 31,808 |
| C.I.D. | 16·8 | 0·1 | 33·7 | 0·7 | 48·7 | 7,288 |
| W.P.C. | 60·5 | — | 5·9 | 0·4 | 33·1 | 1,442 |
| Remainder | 12·6 | 1·0 | 7·8 | 0·3 | 78·3 | 16,407 |
| Average | 38·3 | 6·0 | 18·9 | 0·4 | 36·5 | |

\* This table uses only the results of the first survey of those forces surveyed twice.

Beat patrols were largely unmechanized except in some of the larger counties. On average about one shift in seven was spent indoors or in court and, of the remainder, three-quarters were worked on foot or using a pedal cycle. Of the mechanized quarter about 44 per cent used motor cycles or scooters and the remaining 56 per cent used cars. The overall proportion using cars was just under 15 per cent of all outdoor shifts. This proportion varied considerably according to the type of force. Almost all the borough forces had very small proportions of beat patrols in cars, the lowest being Barrow-in-Furness with less than 1½ per cent. Most counties were far more mechanized, though it seems to have been a matter of policy whether the emphasis was on two or four-wheeled transport. Pembrokeshire, for example, made far greater use of motor cycles and scooters than of cars (11·4 per cent of all shifts as against 3·6 per cent). Some boroughs, such as Plymouth, followed a similar policy. Counties varied in their emphasis from the 'two-wheel' policy of Pembrokeshire, through the approximate equality of Dorset or Leicestershire and Rutland, to the strongly 'four-wheel' policy of Bedfordshire. We, of course, are not in a position to say what results were achieved by the various policies.

Criminal Investigation Departments spent nearly half their shifts in their offices or court, but two-thirds of their outdoor work was done by car, and the remainder on foot. In view of the need to be able to transport people to and from the station for questioning, or after arrest, passenger-carrying vehicles were essential.

Women police officers worked indoors much more than beat

patrols, but when out they fared badly for mechanical transport. This, however, may have been due to the fact that they tend to work in the central parts of urban areas, whereas the mechanized beats worked by men are usually further out.

We can summarize this description in the following terms. On average, not much more than 60 per cent of the working time of the service was spent outside police stations. The main reason for this was the volume of administration, in the broad sense of that term, which tied anything up to, and sometimes over, 20 per cent of a force to full-time indoor duty. Those nominally working outdoors could only do so for about three-quarters of their working time on account of refreshment breaks, report writing and a variety of occasional station duties.

When on outdoor work the majority of beat patrol officers relied on themselves for mobility, being restricted to patrolling on foot or pedal cycle. In most rural areas, and some urban ones, however, greater mobility was achieved by the use of motor cycles or scooters and cars. The choice between two and four wheels was a matter of local policy.

In itself there is nothing necessarily wrong with patrolling on foot or a bicycle. Everything is dependent on the size of the area and the object of the patrol. The greatest disadvantage, not directly related to the means of transport, is the vulnerability of the officer if he cannot summon assistance when needed; this is a matter of communications rather than mobility. Very few of the forces in our surveys had had experience of personal radios, which were only introduced on any scale in 1965,[1] and our results therefore exemplify some of the major disadvantages of a system of policing which was only beginning to adapt to a rapidly changing society.

It seems quite clear from this account of policing in 1965 that it could only be made more flexible at the price of increased capital expenditure in the form of a communication system linking all officers on duty, and sufficient mechanization of transport to deal rapidly with situations as they arose. The system of operations

---

[1] See 'Note' by the Head of the Police Division of the Home Office in *Estimates*, Sel. Cttee. 1st Report, p. 263; 1966–67 (145). It appears that in 1965 there were at least 1,250 pocket radios in use, and on 13 June 1966 the number was 1,590. 'By the spring of 1968, forces supplied centrally should have some 9,200 pocket sets.' A further 1,100 portable sets of other types were also in use.

recorded in our surveys was one which, in some respects, had been adapted to technological change but also in large measure derived from the patrol system evolved by our Victorian forefathers to create and preserve public order. After twenty years of a so-called manpower shortage and a decade of rapidly increasing crime the service was about to undergo the largest convulsion it has experienced since the creation of the modern service by the great Police Acts of the nineteenth century. In our last chapter we shall use this vantage point both to consider some of the features which lay beneath the apparently moderate evolution of the last hundred years and, in this light, to speculate on the future.

*Conclusions*

1. The main emphasis of shift working was on the Early Shift (28·6 per cent in the provinces, 31·9 per cent in the Metropolitan divisions).

2. Split shifts were common in county forces but rare in boroughs and the Metropolitan divisions.

3. Office hours were worked by an average of 15·7 per cent in the provincial forces and 22·4 per cent in the Metropolitan divisions.

4. Working on a '24 hours responsibility' basis was fairly common in the county forces, but quite rare in boroughs.

5. Officers with 24 hours responsibility worked significantly longer hours than others, and this was particularly true in terms of active duty.

6. The main features of comparisons between the work of officers in Urban and Rural areas was that those in the country spent about ten hours a fortnight more on active duty than their urban counterparts.

7. Patterns of work were broadly similar, but most of the extra time was spent on patrolling. In the provincial forces rural officers did rather more crime investigation and foreign enquiry work, but in the Metropolitan divisions they did less of both.

8. In both the Metropolitan and provincial forces an average of just over 40 per cent of working time was spent in the station.

9. Traffic wardens spent least time in the station (average 10 per cent) and beat patrols averaged 26 per cent in the provincial forces and 31 per cent in the Metropolitan. Traffic departments had figures slightly higher than beat patrols,

10. Generally speaking borough forces had lower figures than county forces for the proportion of time spent in the station.

11. Report writing occupied, on average, 8·7 per cent of working time in the provincial forces and 10·6 per cent in the Metropolitan divisions. In the provincial forces this would mean that an average of 40 minutes a day were spent on report writing.

12. The incidence of report writing was heaviest on criminal investigation departments. For them it averaged 17·4 per cent, or nearly a sixth of working time.

13. As far as mobility was concerned, an average of 60 per cent of outdoor shifts were worked on foot or pedal cycle.

14. As would be expected mechanical transport was least used in boroughs, and most in counties.

15. It seems to have been a matter of policy whether mechanical transport was predominantly two- or four-wheel.

# XI

# General Conclusions

WE do not propose at this point to repeat the summaries already given in the preceding chapters, but shall proceed directly to consider the major issues underlying all the topics we have discussed. Two are of prime importance. The first is the broad question of the relationship between the resources the country is prepared to devote to its police service and the amount and nature of the policing it can get in return. The second concerns the place of specialization in the police and, related to it, the influence of technical change. We shall treat these matters historically and speculatively, not only considering the facts but also attempting to envisage how the service may develop in the future.

The discussion of both issues turns on the use of manpower. As we showed in Chapters III and IV pay and allowances have constituted over 70 per cent of current expenditure throughout the last fifty years, and probably ever since the modern police service came into being in the nineteenth century. As the cost of the service is dominated by the cost of manpower the return which the country gets for its investment has to be expressed in terms of the manpower available to deal with the tasks confronting the police. We have, therefore, examined both the total strength, and the classes of activity on which time has been spent.

It was not possible to relate expenditure on the police to the national income during the inter-war years, but over that period the service increased its share of total government expenditure (excluding defence), so that it cannot be said to have suffered unduly severely. During the fifteen years from 1950 to 1965 the police share of gross national expenditure, although subject to fluctuations, increased substantially. Gross national expenditure rose by 163 per cent, public spending (excluding defence) by 202 per cent and the cost of the police service by 256 per cent.

Over the same fifteen years the actual strength of the police service (excluding civilians) rose from 62,910 to 84,430. This

248

meant that the overall ratio to population fell from one police officer per 693 to one per 566.[1] Although the 1950 ratio was more adverse than any during the inter-war period, being partly a product of the immediate post-war situation, the 1965 figure was the most favourable achieved in the entire history of the service up to that date.

Ever since the second world war, however, there has been concern about what has been regarded as a shortage of manpower. How can this be explained in the face of an increased share of national expenditure and an improvement in strength related to population? Our next task must be to examine this paradox.

We must mention at once that local variations are an important part of the problem. The Select Committee on Estimates summarized the position for November 1965 in the following terms: 'Roughly it may be said that, although no forces are fully manned, and only a third of establishments are within tolerable distance of it, serious undermanning is restricted to the Metropolitan Police (25,000 to 18,204, i.e. 26 per cent short), and the conurbations, Birmingham, Liverpool and Leeds (though not Manchester). Thus out of a total deficiency of 15,000 men these four show 8,720.'[2]

The complaints of manpower shortage, however, have not been merely local, and we must consider the national position. In making the historical comparison implied by our question two factors are crucial: working hours and the nature of the work done. Precise comparisons are impossible because although we have detailed information about the present we lack it for the past. Nevertheless we have made the best estimates we can, and they are sufficient to show what the main influences have been.

Our detailed estimates were given in Chapter IV.[3] In them we calculated, as far as possible on a decennial basis, the total number of hours worked by police officers and, in later years, by the *service*, i.e. including civilians and cadets. Furthermore, just as the Police (Weekly Rest Day) Act of 1910 was not implemented for more than a decade in some forces, neither has it been possible

[1] These figures are higher than those given in Appendix I to H.M. Chief Inspector of Constabularys' Reports, because we have used actual numbers of police officers rather than establishments.

[2] *Estimates*, Sel. Cttee. 1st Report, p. xvii; 1966–67 (145).

[3] See Table IV.5, p. 78 and Appendix B.1.

to achieve the 42-hour week of the 1965 Police Regulations for more than a third of the officers in the service. To allow for this, we computed two sets of estimates for 1965: one based on regulation hours, the other based on the overtime position described by the Working Party on Police Manpower as it applied in April 1966 (the month in which our Metropolitan surveys were conducted). Each set of figures was related to the size of the population.[1]

The calculations based on the regulation hours show that in the 1960's the total time worked by police officers was substantially higher than at any earlier period. Even when the increase in population was taken into account, the total for 1961 was higher than for any year back to 1921. Calculated on the basis of the police *service*, that is including civilians, the 1961 and 1965 figures per thousand of the population were substantially higher than in any previous year in the entire history of the service.

If, moreover, we work on the more realistic basis of including the contribution of civilians and cadets *and* allowing for regular overtime, the 1965 position was even better in terms of hours of police cover per thousand of the population.

These improvements were not achieved without considerable cost. From 1921 to 1965 the number of police officers increased by 23,716 (40 per cent), and the number of civilians from virtually nil to just over 19,000. The employment of these extra 42,000 members of the service allowed the total number of hours worked (including overtime) to increase by about 66,000,000. In short, an increase in strength of over 70 per cent was needed to achieve an increase of 47 per cent in hours.

At first sight this might seem unreasonable, but it should be borne in mind that it was only possible to raise the total number of hours to this level by working regular overtime. We estimate that such overtime accounted for nearly ten million hours, and without it the increase in police service hours between 1921 and 1965 would have been 41 per cent rather than 47 per cent.

Important though the overtime was, the employment of civilians was even more crucial. This is shown by comparing the hours worked (including overtime) by police officers and by the police *service* in 1965, each calculated per thousand of the population. The figure for police officers' work was 3,426 (excluding

[1] The basis of our calculations is described in Appendix B.1.

overtime), and that for the service was 4,133. The civilians therefore added 707 hours (approximately 17 per cent) to the basic
total worked by police officers. This compared with 204 hours
due to police overtime.

The reason for the failure of police man hours to keep pace
with the increase in the numbers of police officers was the improvement of working conditions in the service. The importance
of this point can be illustrated by an example. Table XI.1 below
shows the theoretical number of hours worked by a constable at
three different dates. They assume he enjoyed perfect health, and
that he received the minimum official periods of leave. The first
column refers to the period at the beginning of this century, when
conditions were by no means uniform throughout the service. As
some forces worked a nine-hour day and some an eight we have
estimated on the basis of an average of eight and a half. Boroughs,
generally speaking, gave more leave than counties, so we have
given separate figures for each.

The second column is based on the position under the first set
of Police Regulations of August 1920. These remained in force
virtually unchanged in this respect until 1945 when six days extra
annual leave were allowed. The final column is based on the
Police Regulations of 1965, i.e. those obtaining at the time of our
surveys.

It must be re-emphasized that these are the regulation figures
and they do not allow for any overtime which was not compensated by time off in lieu. Neither, on the other hand, do they
subtract anything for the statutory refreshment break in each
shift.[1]

The essence of Table XI.1 can be expressed by saying that
since the first police regulations were introduced in 1920 the
official number of hours worked a year has been reduced by 16
per cent, and that, compared with the beginning of the century
the modern policeman should work between 29 and 31 per cent
fewer hours a year.

The amount of police cover available, however, is not merely
a matter of the total number of hours worked. In the past a great
deal of time went on patrolling intended to prevent crime and

---

[1] The duration of refreshment breaks varied from force to force, but from
1920 the minimum was usually half an hour. The 1965 Regulations prescribed
a standard three-quarters of an hour in an 8-hour shift.

maintain public order. A proportion of this time has now been eroded by other activities, quite legitimate in themselves, but nevertheless reducing the time available for this side of the work. The most obvious are training and traffic work.

TABLE XI.1

**Regulation hours of work for constables 1900, 1921 and 1965**

| | circa 1900 | | Police | Police |
| | Boroughs | Counties | Regs. 1920 | Regs. 1965 |
|---|---|---|---|---|
| Days of leave: | 2 per | 1 per | 1 per | 1 per week      = 52 |
| | month* = 26 | month = 13 | week   = 52 | 1 per fortnight = 26 |
| | | | | 1 per month    = 13 |
| | | | | Public holidays = 6 |
| | Annual = 7 | Annual = 7 | Annual = 12 | Annual          = 16 |
| Total | 33 | 20 | 64 | 113 |
| Working days per year | 332 | 345 | 301 | 252 |
| Length of working day | 8½ hrs† | 8½ hrs† | 8 hrs | 8 hrs |
| Official hours per year | 2,822 | 2932·5 | 2,408 | 2,016 |

\* Under the Police Regulations a month is taken to equal 4 weeks.
† Average: 8- or 9-hour days were fairly common.

It is fairly easy to make an allowance for training, as it was only introduced systematically on a large scale after the second world war. For practical purposes it can be assumed that the policeman of 1921 spent no time on training as such. Our survey results, however, showed that training in the provincial forces in 1965 accounted for 8·7 per cent (or roughly a twelfth) of working time. This proportion can be applied to the figures given earlier with the following results.

The constable working his official 2,016 hours a year would lose a further 175 hours; the hours worked by police officers in the country as a whole would be reduced by 14,774,000, and the aggregate hours per thousand population would fall by 312 a year. The police service total would, of course, be reduced correspondingly.[1]

It is more difficult to decide on the appropriate allowance to be made for traffic work. Although it accounted for 22·8 per cent

[1] Civilians spend a negligible amount of time on training.

of active duty time in the provincial forces and 19·3 per cent in the Metropolitan divisions we cannot assume that no traffic work was done in 1921. Indeed in some respects the absence of traffic lights and other measures of traffic engineering intended to facilitate the flow of vehicles may have meant that almost as much time was spent on traffic supervision. Traffic accidents, on the other hand, may have involved less time—they were certainly fewer but we do not know how much time went on each incident. Road Traffic Patrols, however, were only in an experimental stage even in the late 1930's, and it seems fair to treat the whole of the patrolling time of traffic departments as a post-1921 development.

On a conservative basis, therefore, the following adjustments to the 1965 figures seem reasonable: to exclude all time spent on patrolling by traffic departments, to halve the time spent on accidents and incidents and, correspondingly, to halve the amount of traffic court work. We recognize that traffic cases were very much fewer, but it seems unlikely that procedure was as streamlined as it is now. To halve the figure would not result in an excessively low estimate.

The results obtained by this procedure reduce the proportion of working time spent on traffic work in 1965 in the provincial forces from 22.8 per cent[1] to 13·2 per cent, and in the Metropolitan divisions from 19·3 per cent to 11·1 per cent. If we combine the two to get a single national figure[2] the proportion of working time spent on traffic work would drop from an average of 22·0 per cent to 12·7 per cent, i.e. a difference of 9·3 per cent. This can then be applied in the same way as the figure for training, with the following results.

The constable working his 2,016 hours would include in that number 187 hours which might be regarded as transfers to traffic from other work. Applied to the national figures this 'extra' traffic work would amount to the equivalent of 322 hours per 1,000 population for the police service as a whole.

If we now combine the time spent on training and on 'extra' traffic work we can see that together these activities would account

---

[1] This is the average derived from the survey forces without further weighting See p. 155.
[2] These are weighted averages which take into account the differences in strength between the Metropolitan and the provincial forces.

for 362 out of a total of 2,016 hours (18·0 per cent). Lastly we can relate these two figures to the reductions in working hours that have taken place since 1921. The main influences may be shown as follows:

Official hours worked per constable under
   Police Regulations 1920                 = 2,408
Reduction due to improved conditions    = 392 = 52%
Reduction in effective hours due to increased
   training                                = 175 = 23%
Transfer of time due to 'extra' traffic work  = 187 = 25%

                                              754  100%

Our conclusion on the overall question of working hours, therefore, is that, compared with 1921—which might be regarded in terms of strength as the heyday of the modern police force—what we might term 'working capacity' per constable has been reduced by about 31 per cent, i.e. from 2,408 to 1,654 hours per year. Half of this reduction has been due to a necessary improvement in working conditions, a quarter to an equally necessary increase in training, and a quarter to the substantial claims of extra traffic work.

If we apply the combined reduction of 18·0 per cent in respect of training and extra traffic work to the totals of Table IV.5 we find that, on the basis of the 1965 Police Regulations the 'working capacity' of the police *service* in hours per thousand of the population is reduced from 4,133 to 3,389. This is slightly below the 1921 level, but higher than any subsequent decennial year until 1961.

On the other hand we must recognize the effects of regular overtime working. We have reproduced the official figures which showed that in fact only one-third of the police officers of the country were working the 42-hour week in March 1966, although rather more than another third were working a 44-hour week. Most of the remainder were working a 48-hour week, with some doing 46 hours. When overtime is taken into account even the reduction of 18·0 per cent leaves the total 'working capacity' at 3,556 hours per thousand of the population, and this was higher than for any pre-war year back to 1921.

In more personal terms the effects of working 48-, 46- and 44-hour weeks are the loss of 34, 24 and 11 additional rest days respectively.[1] There is no need to work out the implications in detail, but it will be realized that regular overtime can make a substantial difference. For example the 48-hour man would work 2,268 hours a year instead of 2,016, thus nullifying nearly two-thirds of the improvements gained since 1921.

Although such overtime is to be regretted it must not be forgotten that, in effect, it amounts to a sizeable regular pay increase. For example the constable in the Metropolitan police with 3 or more years' service was, in 1966, paid overtime totalling £168 12s. 2d. on a basic pay of £880. This overtime was, therefore, the equivalent of increasing the basic rate by 19 per cent. Payments in other forces, and for less overtime, were correspondingly smaller, but still reached totals which, over the year, added up to significant amounts.

The practical importance of this situation is twofold. First its cost is quite considerable, and second there are likely to be psychological difficulties in reducing overtime if this will result in officers taking home less pay than that to which they have become accustomed. Possibly the solution to this question may have to be linked with the introduction of Unit Beat Policing.

In general it seems that the service has been partly deprived of many of the benefits which should have followed from the improvement in the statutory conditions of service. About two-thirds of the service enjoy all or most of these benefits, but at the same time the work load has undoubtedly increased, particularly in the forms of crime and traffic. We have already tried to estimate the impact of increased traffic work, but it is more difficult to make such estimates concerning criminal investigation work.

Undoubtedly the number of crimes reported has greatly increased. In 1921 the number stood at 103,258. By 1939 it had increased to 459,869 and by 1965 it had reached 1,133,882. Exactly how much extra work this entailed cannot be estimated, as we lack information about the numbers of detectives and how fully these crimes were investigated. We have shown that in 1965 in most forces the number of crimes reported averaged less than the Dixon Committee's norm of 150 per detective a year, but research may be needed to test the validity of this standard. Certainly the general impression given by our figures is that, whatever the force, the hours worked by the C.I.D. were

[1] Taverne Report, p. 61.

significantly longer than those of other departments. For the time being all that we can say is that C.I.Ds. are relatively hard pressed, but how this pressure can best be dealt with remains to be seen.

This brings us to our second main theme, the place of specialization in the police service. We could not help gaining the impression that one of the influences underlying the expressed difficulties of the service is the unsolved problem of specialization.

Specialization is a paradoxical phenomenon. It tends to be both a medium of change and an inhibitor of further development. A brief summary of the events outlined in our earlier chapters will help to elucidate the point.

The primary emphasis of the service when formed in the nineteenth century was the maintenance of public order and the prevention of crime. The means by which this was to be achieved was the visible presence of officers out and about patrolling their beats. The 'Peeler' initiated a new era in terms of physique and discipline. The problem of drunkenness showed that discipline was not achieved at once though, when established, it was remarkably strict. The new policeman formed part of an essentially simple organization. His strength and the code of his service meant that he was expected to cope with all situations on his own. In short, his function was a general purpose one.

In this public role the police were conspicuously successful. With this success and, above all, with the economic lift given to the service by the Desborough Committee, the security and status of the uniformed police were well and truly established. The limitations of the uniformed branch also became apparent. Not all crime was prevented by the patrolling officer, and special criminal investigation departments were developed in attempts to solve the crimes actually committed. Gradually members of these departments acquired more specialized skills, in which training began to be introduced, and in some forces the C.I.D. had its own line of promotion. All this could be justified on grounds of operational efficiency.

Between the two world wars traffic emerged as the second big problem. Experiments in introducing special mobile units for traffic patrolling were tried in a number of forces although the onset of the war in 1939 prevented systematic development. Nevertheless from these beginnings have grown the well-equipped traffic departments of today which, in some forces, have something of the air of a *corps d'élite*.

The most conspicuous specialism has been introduced in the form of the traffic warden. He, or she, represents almost the opposite extreme to the general purpose P.C. Physical standards are lower, training is minimal, function is highly restricted. The result, however, is that one warden appears to spend as much time on traffic supervision as about seven constables on beat patrol, and where wardens have been employed the amount of traffic supervision undertaken has sharply increased. Clearly this specialization has worked.

Less obvious, but important, special classes have also proliferated—not only general purpose administrators, but specialists in prosecution, traffic cases, the compiling of statistics, road safety officers, crime prevention officers, training officers, juvenile liaison officers, coroners' officers, finger-print specialists, photographers, scenes of crime specialists, river police, frogmen, dog-handlers, and so on. Many are civilians.

All these developments can be welcomed, both for what they achieve and for what they represent. The most obvious result is increased skill. More work is done better by fewer people. Enthusiasm is generated; people are more willing to work long hours, 'wastage' and sickness are less. Even more such developments represent adaptation to changes in the problems the service has to face. They show an awareness of need and a capacity to adopt new methods.

Such forms of growth are not all gain. They have two great disadvantages. They are apt to absorb the more experienced, intelligent, versatile and far-seeing members of the service. This inevitably reduces the relative standard of the remainder and is likely to have an adverse effect on their morale. Secondly, once isolated in this way the resources of manpower and equipment tend to be 'frozen' in the sense that they cannot be used for anything else.

After the second world war one of the most successful British Commanders, Field Marshal Lord Slim, wrote a memorable discussion of this point as it applied to the formation of special units in the Army. It is too long to quote in full, but the implications for morale of creating favoured units have rarely been better stated:

To begin with, they were usually formed by attracting the best men from normal units by better conditions, promises of excitement, and not a little propaganda. . . . Men thought to be below the standards set . . . were weeded out to less favoured corps. The result of these methods was undoubtedly to lower the quality of the rest of the Army, especially of the infantry, not only by skimming the cream off it, but by encouraging the idea that certain of the normal operations of war were so difficult that only specially equipped *corps d'élite* could be expected to undertake them. Armies do not win wars by means of a few bodies of super-soldiers but by the average quality of their standard units.[1]

Obviously the 'war against crime' is not exactly analogous, but there are enough parallels in the police to justify making the comparison. Traffic departments do very little non-traffic work, C.I.D.s are concerned only with crime, mounted police have limited scope, and so on. The really serious question must concern 'the quality of the rest of the Army'. Where the police are concerned this seems to be not so much a matter of the quality of the individuals concerned, as of the nature of the jobs left for them to do. The Working Party on Operational Efficiency and Management criticized the traditional beat system for 'the discouraging effect it undoubtedly has on many policemen' and had serious doubts 'about its efficiency as a method of policing many areas in modern conditions'.[2] We ourselves could not help gaining the impression that, although many police officers sincerely believed in the value of the traditional beat system, the structure of the service and its method of operation tended to minimize its effectiveness.

In the first place specialist departments tend to be filled at the expense of the others, so that any manpower shortage is located in the beat departments. Secondly we were not always convinced either that the principles of the beat system had been re-examined since it began to break down in the face of manpower shortages, or that these principles had been imparted to and accepted by patrol officers.

It seemed to us on the basis of our data and of our first-hand impressions, that the aims and methods of patrolling needed to

[1] Field Marshal Sir William Slim: *Defeat Into Victory*, London, Cassell & Co. Ltd., 1956, Chapter XXIII.
[2] Taverne Report, pp. 115–21.

be re-examined. This was all the more necessary in view of the rise in crime, the high rate of national investment in the service, and the recurring problem of 'wastage', particularly in the early period of service. If more time was to be spent explicitly on such vital matters as crime, and if this was to be obtained with the existing manpower, the obvious source was the time occupied with patrolling. Not only was this activity by far the largest single consumer of police time, but its results were essentially intangible.

The implication seemed inescapable that, rather than continue to lament a manpower situation described in traditional terms as a shortage, the police service should question the appropriateness of its criteria. This process in fact started while we were conducting our research, and the work of the Police Research and Development Branch and the Reports of the Working Parties, which we have quoted so frequently, represent the reappraisal and its first fruits.

Our contribution to this reappraisal, apart from providing background information is, once again, to make a historical observation. This is partly to question the adequacy of the traditional beat coverage, on account of the inefficiency of the communications involved. All policing entails either patrolling of a somewhat general nature or being available quickly to act in a fire-brigade type of role, i.e. getting rapidly to a situation where a policeman was needed. It seems highly likely that the old system placed great emphasis on patrolling because this in fact was all that it was capable of doing. If men were needed to deal with specific incidents it was necessary to have a reserve in the station as the communication system was almost entirely dependant on the patrolling officer following a strict routine or contacting his station on his own initiative: to call upon him for action was difficult. In this sense it was inflexible and not very efficient.

The traditional system therefore probably needed far more men than one relying on communication by personal radio. Once all officers can be reached in a matter of seconds the principles on which they should be deployed can be worked out afresh. Attention can be paid to the expectation of crimes being committed so that officers stand a better chance of being in the right place at the right time. Perhaps even more important it becomes possible for the officer to be given a more positive briefing because he can be more flexible in the use of his time.

Possibly the greatest contribution of Unit Beat Policing is, as we have said, its emphasis on the collection, and even more the use, of information. This is a process of redefining the parts of the patrol officer's time which previously were not occupied with specific activities. From being 'quiet' periods of patrolling they are re-defined as *opportunities* for collecting information and following up any contacts with the police. In itself such a change of attitude would be of limited value if it were not for the crucial step of appointing a collator whose job it is to listen to what the patrol officer has to say about his area and to assemble all such information so that it can be used. This is clear from the last of the instructions for area constables in Unit Beat Policing 'His effectiveness will be judged by the amount of information he feeds into the collator'.[1]

The implications of the development of Unit Beat Policing are likely to be widespread and numerous. Time alone will show them in their entirety. In the terms of this discussion, however, the most important are likely to be economy in manpower, the creation of a more crime conscious attitude among beat officers and, above all, better co-operation between specialists and non-specialists. In the long run the greatest benefit may be an improvement in the morale of the service.

It is not our function to make detailed suggestions for research into the methods of police work, but two general comments are appropriate at this stage. They concern administrative efficiency, and productivity.

No one who has seen much of the police service can fail to be impressed with the thoroughness of its administration. There is a commendable emphasis on meticulous accuracy. This is not only imparted in training but handed down as a very real and living tradition. Every virtue, however, has its corresponding defects and in this case there seem at times to be two possible dangers. The first is by no means confined to the police but occurs wherever public accountability is important. It is that the recording of actions and incidents is given so much importance that attention may be distracted from the action itself. In short, that paper work may become dominant. Here, again, there are encouraging signs: for example, the Monmouthshire Constabulary recently conducted a comprehensive survey of clerical duties with the aim of eliminating unnecessary operations and simplifying others. More

---

[1] Taverne Report, p. 142.

important, the Metropolitan police itself has recently employed a firm of management consultants to review the working of its administration. Operations of this kind are bound to be detailed and to take time, but we should imagine that the effort would be well rewarded.

The second danger is that things will go on being done in certain ways because they have always been done in those ways, and it is difficult for an organization which sets such store by efficiency not to conceive it in a rather narrow sense. In other words an emphasis on the efficient performance of known duties makes it more difficult to question their nature and purpose. This may not matter so much at the lower levels of the service, but it has its limitations as a training for the top.

Finally we must say a few words about productivity as, in its turn, it underlies both the main themes discussed in this chapter. Although, as we have shown, the service has managed to increase the amount of cover provided in terms of man hours to the highest figure ever recorded, this has been achieved in a context of local shortages and the systematic working of overtime. In a sense the service has attempted to swim against the modern tide of productivity by reducing hours of work for individuals, but increasing the size of the organization. This perhaps partly explains the continued expression of the belief that there has been a manpower shortage.

Whatever the reasons for the belief, constant reiteration has led to the realization that what has long been recognized in other fields might even be applicable in policing;[1] namely that increased capital expenditure could lead to economies in manpower, and therefore in running costs.

It is difficult to get a precise picture from the published statistics, but expenditure on vehicles and communications only developed at a substantial rate from about 1960 onwards and, as we have shown, investment in personal radios did not become large until after 1965. The importance of the personal radio, not only as a means of communication but even more for the flexibility of organization that it allows, can hardly be over-estimated.

[1] We say 'even' because we frequently encountered the view that police work and the police service were unique, almost impossible for outsiders to understand, and not susceptible to the application of economic criteria.

A.S.I.M.—18

An emphasis on the better equipped and more mobile police officer must also require new thinking about operational organization and training. Unit Beat Policing is clearly the first stage of reappraising operational methods and further studies will have to be undertaken to evolve the most effective ways of concentrating sufficient men in the right place at the right time. The men, furthermore, will have to be sufficient not only in number but in training. If full use is to be made of the capital that is being invested in the service all ranks will have to be trained to understand the implications of mobility and communications. It may well be that the police officer will need to know less about law, for advice will be easier to come by, but more about the tactics of operations. If the rapid investment in research is to be used to the full, ways will have to be found of bringing its results, and even more its attitude of trying to measure efficiency, to all members of the service.

If the 'war against crime' can no longer be fought successfully by the old methods of overworking the individual officers, then the only effective alternative must be the better use of the manpower already in the service. This, above all, will depend on capital investment, and on training to realize the full potentialities of the equipment and of the men and women who are to use it.

# APPENDIX A

## INSTRUCTION BOOKLET
### SURVEY OF POLICE DUTIES
(Including Civilians and Cadets)
Institute of Criminology, Cambridge

**Introduction**

This survey is part of a large study of the 'Cost of Crime'. It is designed to discover how much time is spent by police forces on different types of work. The only reliable way of finding this out is to make a survey of this kind. The survey includes enough forces of various types to provide an overall picture for the country as a whole.

We hope that the information gained will be of value in planning future developments in the service and also in giving the public a realistic picture of the nature of police work. You will appreciate that a survey of this kind is a major undertaking and the quality of its results will depend upon the accuracy with which each officer's work is recorded. Although the survey is bound to mean some extra work, we have tried to minimise the amount, and we feel sure that in view of the potential value of the results everyone taking part will try to make it a success.

The recording booklet has been designed to make both your and our task as easy as possible. Although it might at first appear rather involved, the daily recording should prove quite straightforward provided the instructions below are followed and the summary sheet will only require some simple addition for its completion.

Although the Institute of Criminology is responsible for organizing and conducting this survey, it is being carried out with the agreement and support of the Home Office and Her Majesty's Inspectors of Constabulary.

### FRONT COVER

Please begin by completing the details under the various headings. *Starting Date* will be the day on which the survey commences in your area.

**Force**    State full name.

**Division and Station**    Indicate appropriate details. Designation by letter and/or number where applicable.

**Rank and Number**    Policewomen should indicate by prefix before number. Civilians and senior officers state name.

**Age and Number of Years of Service**    As appropriate. If less than one year's service state number of months.

**Department**    Indicate, using the following grouping:

| | |
|---|---|
| Traffic Wardens | Administration |
| Traffic Dept. (incl. Patrols) | Station Staff |
| Beat patrols—all types | Training Course |
| C.I.D. | (only if full-time) |
| W.PCs | Training Instructors |
| Others—specify | |

OFFICERS with 24 hour RESPONSIBILITY should insert tick in the square provided.

**Time Spent Making Reports and in Station**    Keep a note each day of the time spent on writing, dictation, and typing of reports. At the end of each day convert to the nearest whole number of quarter hours and enter this in the appropriate daily square in Section C on the front cover. Cross through squares when no time is spent in this way. In this survey, a report is a written communication to a superior officer or to a court concerning action taken by an officer, results of enquiries, answers to queries, etc. Do not include letters, statements, or making entries in pocket book.

Time spent in station includes **all** time spent in any police station during tour of duty (including refreshment breaks). It has to be totalled at the end of each tour in the same way as Report time.


## DAILY RECORDS

The white sheets are designed to cover two whole weeks starting on a Monday and ending on the Sunday, 14 days later. Starting with the top sheet first make a cross in the appropriate day's square and then enter full particulars of tour, area, and method of transport when out of station by placing ticks in the squares provided, *except for days off duty, leave, sickness, etc.* On days off draw a line along the appropriate row and write the reason over the top, e.g. in C 20—'rest day'. If night duty, cross day in which duty commences.

**Tour of Duty**   Indicate by tick whether, early, late, night, split shift, or office hours. Offset tours should be treated as the regular shift to which they most correspond. Make **one entry only** for each day, in most appropriate column.

**Area**   Tick the square most descriptive of the area in which you are working. If working period is spent mainly indoors then tick square representing the type of area in which your station is situated. Make one entry only for each day. Use the following definitions.

1. **Urban**   Predominantly built up areas in towns or cities.

2. **Rural**   Areas sparsely populated but including villages and/or the outskirts of towns not completely built up.

3. **Mixed**   Areas which include parts of 1 and 2 above, also large villages or small towns of rural character.

**Method**   If working out of Station for the whole or part of the shift indicate by a tick the principal method of transport employed, whether on foot, cycle, motor-cycle or scooter, or car. If 'Out', but mainly in Court mark 'C' in square marked 'foot'. Make *one entry only* for each day in most appropriate column unless in Station, when no entry under 'Method' is required.

## SECTION D

### DUTY CLASSIFICATIONS

All duties have been classified under 20 different categories, and time spent on each category is to be recorded in quarter hour units by a diagonal dash / in one square across for each quarter hour period. It is not intended that you should make entries at quarter hour intervals, but it is suggested that entries should as far as possible be made at hourly intervals. (If more than one duty took place during any given quarter hour classify according to the activity which took the largest part of the time.)

**Extra Time**   If more than 8 hours are worked enter extra time in appropriate square of the extra time column. Write the number of quarter hour units, e.g. $1\frac{1}{2}$ hours extra time spent on crime investigation would be written as 6 in row 1. *Include all time actually worked* in excess of 8 hours, but disregard short periods of time spent parading before shifts officially begin.

**Half Days**   Make up remainder of basic day as leave and enter under C 20.

**Totals**    At the completion of each tour of duty add the number of dashes in each line across plus any quarter hours extra time entered in that line, and enter the total figure in the 'totals' column on the right. If less than 8 hours per day is normally worked the actual time worked should be entered, e.g. for a 7 hour day the daily total will be 28 quarter hours and this number should also apply for leave, etc.

## NOTES ON CLASSIFICATIONS

**Standby Duty**    Time spent in this way should be entered as for the duty to which one may be called, unless unspecified, then under C 17.

**Report Writing**    Time spent writing reports should be recorded under the heading referring to the subject of the report, *except that if the report is for use in Court it should be recorded in the section on Court work.*

**Combined Traffic and Criminal Offences**    All cases concerning vehicles should be classified as traffic offences unless involving larceny, T.D.A., unfit to drive or causing death by dangerous driving.

Classifications (C)

| | |
|---|---|
| C 1 | Investigations—Should include all work associated with criminal acts, including petty crime, but not traffic offences. |
| C 2 | Foreign Enquiries—Should include all work undertaken at the request of another police force or outside body. To include animal movement orders, issuing licences, aliens registration, etc. |
| C 3, 4 & 5 | Traffic—If it is not possible to assess whether a traffic accident or incident will result in 'Process', the distinction between C 4 & 5 should be based on the officer's opinion at the time as to whether process is likely. Some cases will be quite clear cut, others less so. Entries should be made under C 5 if there is any doubt. If this opinion turns out to be wrong there is no need to alter earlier entries. Enquiries following an incident should be recorded under the same classification as the actual incident, e.g. Enquiries following an accident likely to result in process should be recorded under C 5. |
| C 6 & 7 | Civil incidents and Public Order. These might occasionally overlap, or a civil incident develop into a case of public order. If in doubt enter under C 7 which should also include rowdyism. |

IMPORTANT. All duty & /or leave time must be recorded under one of the following headings in quarter hour units on the white sheets.

## Section D
## DUTY CLASSIFICATION

| 1 | INVESTIGATIONS. Enquiries, Crime Reports, Arrests, etc. (excluding traffic cases) |
|---|---|
| 2 | FOREIGN ENQUIRIES. For other Forces or Public Bodies |
| 3 | TRAFFIC — Traffic Supervision, Point Duty, Road Safety, etc. |
| 4 | Accidents not involving 'Process' |
| 5 | Incidents and Accidents which might result in 'Process' |
| 6 | CIVIL INCIDENTS. Domestic, Lost Children, Individual Problems |
| 7 | PUBLIC ORDER. Public ceremonies, Crowd Control (not involving arrests) |
| 8 | PRIVATE DUTIES. Paid for by Private Organisations |
| 9 | COURT. Include preparation of reports, travelling time and all time spent in court, whatsoever — CRIMINAL OFFENCES — Magistrates Court |
| 10 | Higher Courts |
| 11 | WORK — TRAFFIC OFFENCES, All Courts |
| 12 | CIVIL AND CORONER'S COURTS |
| 13 | JUVENILE COURTS, All cases. |
| 14 | FOLLOWING — All duties, including travelling spent with convicted persons. — ADULTS |
| 15 | CONVICTION — JUVENILES |
| 16 | PATROLLING. Routine duties excluding 1-15 above |
| 17 | GENERAL DUTIES, Supervision, routine standby, car maintenance, etc. |
| 18 | INTERNAL ORGANISATION |
| 19 | TRAINING and SPORTS (state which) |
| 20 | LEAVE and time off due to SICKNESS (state which). Also CANTEEN periods |

| Cross Day | Mon. | | TOUR | Early | Late | Night | Split | | | Extra Time | Totals |
|---|---|---|---|---|---|---|---|---|---|---|---|
| Tue. | Wed. | Thu. | AREA | Urban | Mixed | Rural | Office | | | | |
| Fri. | Sat. | Sun. | METHOD | Foot | Cycle | M/C | Car | | | | |
| | | | | 1st hour | 2nd hour | 3rd hour | 4th hour | 5th hour | 6th hour | 7th hour | 8th hour |
| 1 | | | | | | | | | | | |
| 2 | | | | | | | | | | | |
| 3 | | | | | | | | | | | |
| 4 | | | | | | | | | | | |
| 5 | | | | | | | | | | | |
| 6 | | | | | | | | | | | |
| 7 | | | | | | | | | | | |
| 8 | | | | | | | | | | | |
| 9 | | | | | | | | | | | |
| 10 | | | | | | | | | | | |
| 11 | | | | | | | | | | | |
| 12 | | | | | | | | | | | |
| 13 | | | | | | | | | | | |
| 14 | | | | | | | | | | | |
| 15 | | | | | | | | | | | |
| 16 | | | | | | | | | | | |
| 17 | | | | | | | | | | | |
| 18 | | | | | | | | | | | |
| 19 | | | | | | | | | | | |
| 20 | | | | | | | | | | | |

C 8            Private Duties—Arranged by special agreement.

C 9, 10, 11,   Court Work—Should include any work relating to the
12, 13         administration of justice whether as usher, prosecutor,
               witness, etc. Time spent in court should be entered
               according to the type of court and/or offence which cause
               the officer to be present. Include the preparation of
               antecedents but not of evidence (which should be
               included under investigation).

C 14 & 15      Following Conviction—Should include any work done
               with or for convicted persons and to include the time
               spent at Attendance Centres (even if classed as free
               time).

C 16           Patrolling—Should include only routine beat duties
               which cannot be classified under any of the above head-
               ings. This item includes patrolling in motor vehicles.

C 17           General Duties—To include General Supervision, rou-
               tine standby, enquiry desk (only when not classifiable
               under subjects of enquiries), switchboard, information
               room, car maintenance, etc. It is most important that
               only duties which cannot be accommodated in other
               classifications should be included here.

C 18           Internal organization—*Should only include internal police
               matters* e.g. the preparation of duty rotas, etc. Clerical
               work directly related to any of the above classifications
               should be entered accordingly.

C 19           Training and Sports—Indicate over the line the type of
               training or sport. Also include attendance at meetings
               and committees indicating whether relating to training
               or sports.

C 20           Leave and Sickness—Enter total quarter hours as for
               normal shift—indicate across line whether leave or sick-
               ness. Enter periods spent in Canteen on this line. Lunch
               breaks to be excluded altogether by civilians and those
               working split shifts.

   Read the following instructions with the booklet open so that the
sequence may be followed.

   **Procedure**   There are 14 separate daily sheets. After each has been
completed it should be folded back and inserted in the flap provided

at the back of the booklet. At the end of the fortnight all the daily sheets should be inserted in this way when it becomes possible to open out the inside cover to reveal the summary sheet Sections E and F. With Section F visible above, the various classification totals on each white sheet should be duly entered on the summary sheet in their correct sequence:—

1. Transfer daily ticks for Tour, Area and Method to the appropriate daily columns on Section F.

2. Transfer the various classification totals on each white sheet to the corresponding numbered daily columns in Section E.

3. Once all daily totals have been transferred from the white sheets the columns in Section F denoting Tour, Area and Method, should be totalled. Exclude days off, leave and sickness.

4. The classification totals in Section E should then be totalled down and across, making certain here that leave and days off sick are included in C 20. Then check that the sum of the horizontal totals equals the sum of the vertical totals.

When this has been done all the details from the front cover should be copied in the space on the summary sheet provided. Ignore Section marked 'Office use only'.

It is important that all details are transferred accurately on to the summary sheet.

When duly completed the booklet should be folded as first received and handed in to the collecting officer as soon as possible.

A member of the Institute of Criminology will be available during the period of the survey should any problems or queries arise. Should you be in doubt on any point please let the appropriate officer know your difficulty or query without delay.

**Please carry the booklet with you on duty. We do not mind if it gets a little grubby so long as it is kept up to date.**

# APPENDIX B

## 1.—Method of Calculation of Police Service Man Hours 1861–1965

This Appendix describes the methods used for calculating the figures shown in Table IV.5 on p. 78.

Column (1)  All years were Census years except for 1938, 1949 and 1965. As no Census was held in 1941, we took the last full peace time year, i.e. for year ended 29/9/38. 1949 was included to show the position towards the end of the immediate post-war period, while 1965 was the last year covered by our study.

Column (2)  Census figures were used where appropriate. The figure for 1938 was taken from 1961 Census Preliminary Report Table 1, 'Mid-Year Estimate'. Figures for 1949 and 1965 were taken from Table A.1, 'Mid-Year Estimates' from Registrar General's Statistical Review of England and Wales 1965, Part 2.

Column (3)  Totals were those of strength for ordinary duty taken from the *Annual Reports of H.M. Inspectors of Constabulary*.

Column (4)  The totals of Col. (3) were adjusted to allow for sickness by reducing the strength by the percentage rate of sickness. For police officers we applied the sickness rates of the Metropolitan police to the country as a whole.

Column (5)  Hours worked by police officers were calculated on the basis of days worked per officer per year multiplied by the number of officers (corrected for sickness). For the years up to and including 1891 police officers were assumed to work a 9-hour day. For all later years an 8-hour day was used. Civilians were counted as working an 8-hour day till 1961, but the 1965 figure was based on an average of 7·6 hours, in order to allow for a 38-hour week.

The number of working days in the year was estimated on the basis of the police regulations for dates from 1921 onwards, while for earlier years we made estimates from such records as were available.

From 1921 onwards we subtracted one day per officer per year from the regulation average to allow for the extra leave granted to senior ranks and, in later years, constables with longer service. Although this might seem a rather small adjustment we convinced ourselves by attempting to produce weighted averages that this simpler method gave reasonably accurate results as the number of officers entitled to extra leave is relatively small. In any case we preferred to err on the conservative side in making the allowance so that, if anything, our figures for hours worked by police officers do not show the full effect of extra leave.

Our special estimate for 1965 allowing for regular over-time was based on the numbers working 42-, 44-, 46- and 48-hour weeks as shown in Appendix A of the Report of the Working Party on Manpower (Home Office: *Police Manpower, Equipment and Efficiency*, London H.M.S.O., 1967, p. 60). The weighted average number of days worked per year is shown below.

The number of days worked by civilians were based on enquiries made of local authorities concerning local government practice.

The number of days worked per year by each police officer estimated in this way and used in our calculations were:

| Year | Avge days worked | Year | Avge days worked |
|------|------------------|------|------------------|
| 1861 | 352 | 1931 | 300 |
| 1871 | 352 | 1938 | 300 |
| 1881 | 347 | 1949 | 288 |
| 1891 | 341 | 1951 | 288 |
| 1901 | 339 | 1961 | 288 |
| 1911 | 338 | 1965 | 251 |
| 1921 | 300 | 1965* | 266 |

* Weighted average allowing for overtime.

Column (6)   Col. (5) + Col. (2) expressed per thousand population.

Column (7)   Figures taken from *Reports of H.M. Inspectors of Constabulary*. They include members of the first police reserve working full time, civilians in clerical, domestic and technical full time employment, cadets (youths and girls), traffic wardens (men and women). The staff of

the Receiver of the Metropolitan Police have been
excluded.

Column (8)    The adjustment was made in the same way as for police
officers, but the only available basis for estimation was
the figure of 2·7 per cent derived from our manpower
surveys of 1965–66. It has been assumed that this rate
applied in all the years for which figures of civilian
strength have been shown.

Column (9)    This is simply the total of Col. (5) with the figure for
civilians added. All civilians were treated as working an
8-hour day, 265 days a year from 1949–61, and a 7·6-
hour day 239 days a year in 1965.

Column (10)   This is the total of Col. (9) expressed per thousand of
the population.

# 2.—Test of Significance of Correlation Coefficient

THE statistical significance of the product moment correlations was tested by means of Student's distribution. In small samples the approximate distribution of $r$ is such that we may consider

$$t = \sqrt{\frac{(n-2)r^2}{(1-r^2)}}$$

where $t$ has $n-2$ degrees of freedom.

This test is robust even for small values of $n$, see M. G. Kendall and A. Stuart, *The Advanced Theory of Statistics*, Vol. II, p. 470. London, Griffin, 1961.

# 3.—Method of Calculating Overtime for Manpower Surveys

As has been explained in the text it was not always possible to tell from the recording booklet exactly how many of the hours worked by an officer were overtime. We had an exact figure for hours worked in excess of the normal 8-hour tour of duty, but such time might be compensated by time off in lieu. We worked, therefore, on the basis that where the total of hours worked plus leave exceeded 112 in a fortnight any time in excess of that number was treated as overtime. (This is the total derived from a 42-hour working week, i.e. 84 working hours per fortnight and 28 hours leave.)

While this method counts any hours due to long tours of duty it does not distinguish between hours spent on duty and on leave. In particular it does not account for extra shifts. This had to be done in two further stages.

First, all shifts worked in excess of eleven in a fortnight were regarded as overtime (at 8 hours per shift). This total was then added to the figure for long tours of duty (which had been recorded in the manner already described). For forces not working systematic overtime these two figures were combined to form the total overtime for the force.

Second, where forces did work systematic overtime there was also the possibility that an officer working eleven or fewer shifts had included an overtime one in his total. For example, he might have taken one or two extra days of leave due to him. To allow for this possibility we made the assumption that one in twelve of the shifts worked by those totalling eleven or fewer working shifts were overtime shifts. This was done on the basis that approximately one shift in twelve was compulsory overtime. The forces treated in this way were the Metropolitan, Essex and Bedfordshire. A similar procedure was applied, but treating 1/24 as overtime, with the two forces (Birkenhead, Leicestershire and Rutland) working a 44-hour week.

In this process we also made the assumption that none of this overtime was worked by traffic wardens or civilians. This was possibly unfair to some civilians, but the recorded overtime figures for civilians were small, and returns by forces where police officers worked regular overtime showed that, generally speaking, their civilians did not do so.

# 4.—Test for Representativeness of Number of Crimes Committed During Survey Period

COMPARISONS were made between the number of crimes reported to the police during the survey period ($x$) and the annual number of crimes reported to the police (and recorded in *Supplementary Criminal Statistics*, 1965, Table 4, total a, i) divided by 26 thus producing an average rate per fortnight ($y$). There were twelve observations of each variable.

This gave $\bar{x} = 272 \cdot 58$

$\bar{y} = 230 \cdot 14$

The difference between means is in the direction that would be expected from the practice of writing off some crimes initially reported as crimes but later reclassified on grounds that no crime had been committed. In any case using a $t$ test the means were definitely not significantly different.

Since we had no knowledge of the underlying distribution of the variables and the number of observations was small we also applied a non-parametric test due to Wilcoxon. This is described in Kendall and Stuart, *op. cit.*, Vol. II. Ch. 31, Sections 53–62. Using this test we obtained a value of $z = 0 \cdot 404$ where $z$ is approximately a standard normal variate. This value is clearly not significant.

On the basis of these tests it was safe to assume that the figures for the survey period were not unrepresentative.

# APPENDIX C

# Selection and Characteristics of Sample Forces

THE sample was intended to include approximately 10 per cent of the provincial forces in terms of average strength and total expenditure. The figures used when drawing the sample were those for 1962–63, which at that time were the latest available.

The 123 police forces of England and Wales were divided into eleven strata in order to cover the following main characteristics: size, type of force (county or borough), crime rate and, as a separate category seaside borough resorts. As we had agreed not to include forces already participating in the Home Office sponsored survey of drunkenness, we had first to exclude all such forces. Fortunately they comprised a random sample, selected by the Government Social Survey which was conducting the drunkenness survey.

Stratification by size used different groupings according to whether forces were those of boroughs or counties—counties on average being considerably larger than boroughs. Crime rates were divided into High and Low according to whether the number of indictable offences per 1,000 population was above or below the median value for boroughs or counties as the case might be. Bedfordshire, which was a medium-sized county, was added to bring the total sample size nearer to the desired total sample size.

The results of this process are summarized in the table below:

| | Method of stratification | Total of forces in stratum | Excl. on account of drunkenness Survey | Force selected in each stratum | Average strength | Civilians | Total expenditure £000 | Expenditure per police officer £ |
|---|---|---|---|---|---|---|---|---|
| (i) | Borough seaside resorts | 8 | 3 | Hastings | 129 | 23 | 226 | 1,750 |
| (ii) | Boroughs average strength over 800 | 6 | 3 | Bristol | 885 | 235 | 1,434 | 1,620 |
| (iii) | Counties average strength over 1,000 | 9 | 5 | Essex | 1,338 | 365 | 2,477 | 1,851 |
| (iv) | Boroughs average strength up to 200 L.C.* | 22 | 12 | Bath | 131 | 14 | 211 | 1,607 |
| (v) | Boroughs average strength up to 200 H.C.* | 10 | 6 | Barrow-in-Furness | 133 | 11 | 199 | 1,496 |
| (vi) | Boroughs average strength 201 to 800 L.C. | 11 | 5 | Birkenhead | 307 | 105 | 457 | 1,517 |
| (vii) | Boroughs average strength 201 to 800 H.C. | 15 | 7 | Plymouth | 400 | 32 | 594 | 1,486 |
| (viii) | Counties average strength up to 500 L.C. | 14 | 6 | Pembroke | 173 | 23 | 283 | 1,638 |
| (ix) | Counties average strength up to 500 H.C. | 9 | 5 | Dorset | 476 | 94 | 785 | 1,680 |
| (x) | Counties average strength 501 to 1,000 L.C. | 9 | 4 | Leicestershire | 621 | 150 | 1,019 | 1,641 |
| (xi) | Counties average strength 501 to 1,000 H.C. | 10 | 5 | Northumberland | 657 | 110 | 1,084 | 1,649 |
| | | | | Bedfordshire | 580 | 145 | 1,030 | 1,776 |
| Total | | 123 | 61 | | 5,830 | 1,307 | 9,799 | — |
| | Total as % all forces | 10·0 | | | 10·0 | 11·1 | 10·0 | |
| | Average of all forces | | | | | | | 1,673 |
| | Average for sample | | | | | | | 1,643 |

* L.C. and H.C. represent Low and High Crime respectively.

# APPENDIX D

## TABLE D.1

### Tables relating to hours of work, overtime and abstractions

| | Total hours potential duty time (1) | Total hours abstractions (2) | Abstractions as % of potential duty time (3) | Total hours working time* (4) | Total strength of force (5) | Average hours worked by force (6) | Total overtime worked by police officers and cadets (7) | No. of police officers and cadets (8) |
|---|---|---|---|---|---|---|---|---|
| *Provincial forces* | | | | | | | | |
| *First surveys* | | | | | | | | |
| Plymouth | 49,442 | 21,504 | 43·5 | 31,845 | 434 | 73·4 | 1,573 | 412 |
| Hastings | 17,575 | 8,166 | 46·5 | 11,056 | 157 | 74·2 | 413 | 140 |
| Pembroke | 23,174 | 9,593 | 41·4 | 15,852 | 201 | 78·9 | 1,128 | 183 |
| Dorset | 60,406 | 25,651 | 42·5 | 41,028 | 531 | 77·3 | 2,298 | 476 |
| Bristol | 130,701 | 59,395 | 45·4 | 85,560 | 1,152 | 74·3 | 2,632 | 1,022 |
| Bath | 17,408 | 8,113 | 46·6 | 11,654 | 152 | 76·7 | 2,273 | 139 |
| Barrow-in-Furness | 16,344 | 7,046 | 43·1 | 10,480 | 146 | 71·8 | 263 | 138 |
| Birkenhead | 45,773 | 18,864 | 41·2 | 29,947 | 401 | 74·7 | 2,361 | 382 |
| Leic. and Rutland | 88,681 | 39,014 | 44·0 | 57,878 | 772 | 75·0 | 6,058 | 696 |
| Northumberland | 90,395 | 39,187 | 43·3 | 60,356 | 771 | 78·3 | 6,084 | 705 |
| Bedford | 60,667 | 21,821 | 36·0 | 46,033 | 529 | 87·0 | 5,576 | 469 |
| Essex | 182,371 | 71,867 | 39·4 | 128,615 | 1,603 | 80·2 | 16,072 | 1,406 |
| Total | 782,937 | 330,221 | 42·2 | 530,904 | 6,849 | 77·5 | 46,731 | 6,168 |
| *Metropolitan* | | | | | | | | |
| 'B' Division | 74,850 | 24,951 | 33·3 | 58,841 | 626 | 94·0 | 10,338 | 598 |
| 'S' Division | 82,518 | 28,175 | 34·1 | 63,050 | 711 | 88·7 | 8,993 | 669 |
| Total | 157,368 | 53,126 | 33·8 | 121,891 | 1,337 | 91·2 | 19,331 | 1,267 |
| C.T.D. Special Squads | 46,137 | 16,956 | 36·8 | 34,730 | 400 | 86·8 | 4,806 | 395 |
| | 25,416 | 4,456 | 17·5 | 21,285 | 178 | 119·6 | | |
| *Provincial forces* | | | | | | | | |
| *Second surveys* | | | | | | | | |
| Hastings | 17,876 | 8,097 | 45·3 | 11,650 | 157 | 74·2 | 639 | 142 |
| Pembroke | 23,496 | 10,388 | 44·2 | 15,147 | 202 | 75·0 | 1,188 | 186 |
| Dorset | 63,315 | 26,504 | 41·9 | 41,391 | 552 | 75·0 | 2,330 | 494 |
| Total | 104,687 | 44,989 | 43·0 | 68,188 | 911 | 74·8 | 4,157 | 822 |

* Working time was defined as potential duty time minus time spent on leave and sickness. Sport in duty hours was included, but the time involved

TABLE D.2

Allocation of active duty by function (total force)

| | Law enforcement | | Administration of justice | | Treatment of offenders | | Civil duties | | Total |
|---|---|---|---|---|---|---|---|---|---|
| | Hours | % | Hours | % | Hours | % | Hours | % | =100% |
| *Provincial forces* | | | | | | | | | |
| *First surveys* | | | | | | | | | |
| Plymouth | 16,106 | 76·6 | 2,003 | 9·5 | 191 | 0·9 | 2,738 | 13·0 | 21,038 |
| Hastings | 5,177 | 73·2 | 487 | 6·9 | 85 | 1·2 | 1,326 | 18·7 | 7,075 |
| Pembroke | 7,212 | 77·7 | 759 | 8·2 | 31 | 0·3 | 1,279 | 13·8 | 9,281 |
| Dorset | 16,634 | 77·6 | 2,385 | 11·1 | 210 | 1·0 | 2,200 | 10·3 | 21,429 |
| Bristol | 34,943 | 72·2 | 3,936 | 8·1 | 221 | 0·5 | 9,307 | 19·2 | 48,407 |
| Bath | 4,916 | 73·3 | 908 | 13·5 | 86 | 1·3 | 797 | 11·9 | 6,707 |
| Barrow-in-Furness | 5,518 | 80·8 | 549 | 8·0 | 89 | 1·3 | 677 | 9·9 | 6,833 |
| Birkenhead | 13,794 | 73·9 | 1,659 | 8·9 | 85 | 0·5 | 3,115 | 16·7 | 18,653 |
| Leic. and Rutland | 24,280 | 73·8 | 4,213 | 12·8 | 233 | 0·7 | 4,158 | 12·7 | 32,084 |
| Northumberland | 25,597 | 72·7 | 4,324 | 12·3 | 253 | 0·7 | 5,020 | 14·3 | 35,194 |
| Bedford | 18,416 | 71·6 | 3,778 | 14·7 | 318 | 1·2 | 3,221 | 12·5 | 25,733 |
| Essex | 55,480 | 74·0 | 8,426 | 11·2 | 795 | 1·1 | 10,307 | 13·7 | 75,008 |
| Total | 228,073 | | 33,427 | | 2,597 | | 44,145 | | 308,242 |
| Average (per cent) | 74·0 | | 10·8 | | 0·8 | | 14·4 | | 100·0 |
| *Metropolitan* | | | | | | | | | |
| 'B' Division | 32,786 | 82·9 | 3,604 | 9·1 | 153 | 0·4 | 2,984 | 7·6 | 39,527 |
| 'S' Division | 31,001 | 80·0 | 4,739 | 12·2 | 129 | 0·3 | 2,888 | 7·5 | 38,757 |
| Total | 63,787 | | 8,343 | | 282 | | 5,872 | | 78,284 |
| Average (per cent) | 81·5 | | 10·7 | | 0·4 | | 7·4 | | 100·0 |
| C.T.D. | 16,676 | 78·1 | 1,997 | 9·4 | 46 | 0·2 | 2,635 | 12·3 | 21,402 |
| *Provincial forces* | | | | | | | | | |
| *Second surveys* | | | | | | | | | |
| Hastings | 5,431 | 70·1 | 547 | 7·1 | 109 | 1·4 | 1,660 | 21·4 | 7,747 |
| Pembroke | 6,716 | 71·6 | 687 | 7·3 | 94 | 1·0 | 1,885 | 20·1 | 9,382 |
| Dorset | 17,273 | 71·1 | 3,074 | 12·8 | 432 | 1·8 | 3,177 | 13·3 | 23,956 |
| Total | 29,420 | | 4,308 | | 635 | | 6,722 | | 41,085 |
| Average (per cent) | 71·6 | | 10·5 | | 1·5 | | 16·4 | | 100·0 |

## TABLE D.3

### Allocation of active duty by area of operation (total force)

| | Traffic Hours | % | Crime Hours | % | Civil order Hours | % | Internal organization Hours | % | Total = 100% |
|---|---|---|---|---|---|---|---|---|---|
| *Provincial forces* | | | | | | | | | |
| *First surveys* | | | | | | | | | |
| Plymouth | 4,514 | 20·7 | 7,211 | 33·0 | 9,313 | 42·6 | 817 | 3·7 | 21,855 |
| Hastings | 2,015 | 25·2 | 1,964 | 24·5 | 3,096 | 38·6 | 938 | 11·7 | 8,013 |
| Pembroke | 2,322 | 21·5 | 2,876 | 26·7 | 4,083 | 37·8 | 1,505 | 14·0 | 10,786 |
| Dorset | 5,189 | 20·6 | 8,104 | 31·8 | 8,226 | 32·7 | 3,741 | 14·9 | 25,170 |
| Bristol | 12,270 | 23·5 | 13,995 | 26·8 | 22,142 | 42·5 | 3,740 | 7·2 | 52,147 |
| Bath | 1,540 | 19·9 | 2,338 | 30·2 | 2,829 | 36·5 | 1,042 | 13·4 | 7,749 |
| Barrow-in-Furness | 1,521 | 20·8 | 1,610 | 22·0 | 3,702 | 50·6 | 481 | 6·6 | 7,314 |
| Birkenhead | 4,887 | 25·0 | 4,356 | 22·3 | 9,410 | 48·2 | 880 | 4·5 | 19,533 |
| Leic. and Rutland | 10,324 | 28·9 | 9,853 | 27·6 | 12,707 | 35·6 | 2,839 | 7·9 | 35,723 |
| Northumberland | 7,062 | 17·6 | 10,174 | 25·3 | 17,958 | 44·7 | 4,965 | 12·4 | 40,159 |
| Bedford | 7,830 | 26·9 | 8,587 | 29·5 | 9,316 | 32·0 | 3,396 | 11·6 | 29,129 |
| Essex | 18,335 | 22·1 | 26,189 | 31·5 | 30,484 | 36·7 | 8,052 | 9·7 | 83,060 |
| Total | 77,809 | | 97,167 | | 133,266 | | 32,396 | | 340,638 |
| Average (per cent) | | 22·8 | | 28·6 | | 39·1 | | 9·5 | 100·0 |
| *Metropolitan* | | | | | | | | | |
| 'B' Division | 6,557 | 15·5 | 16,942 | 40·1 | 16,028 | 37·9 | 2,572 | 6·5 | 42,099 |
| 'S' Division | 8,489 | 19·9 | 9,630 | 22·6 | 20,638 | 48·3 | 3,926 | 9·2 | 42,683 |
| Total | 15,046 | | 26,572 | | 36,666 | | 6,498 | | 84,782 |
| Average (per cent) | | 17·7 | | 31·4 | | 43·2 | | 7·7 | 100·0 |
| Total and percentage adjusted to allow for C.T.D. contribution | 16,743 | 19·3 | 26,634 | 30·6 | 36,686 | 42·3 | 6,711 | 7·8 | 86,744 |
| C.T.D. | 20,369 | 85·2 | 747 | 3·1 | 238 | 1·0 | 2,559 | 10·7 | 23,913 |
| *Provincial forces* | | | | | | | | | |
| *Second surveys* | | | | | | | | | |
| Hastings | 2,308 | 25·8 | 2,130 | 23·9 | 3,309 | 37·1 | 1,182 | 13·2 | 8,929 |
| Pembroke | 3,044 | 28·2 | 2,940 | 27·2 | 3,398 | 31·4 | 1,425 | 13·2 | 10,807 |
| Dorset | 6,710 | 24·5 | 8,916 | 32·5 | 8,329 | 30·4 | 3,463 | 12·6 | 27,418 |
| Total | 12,062 | | 13,986 | | 15,036 | | 6,070 | | 47,154 |

TABLE D.4

Tables relating to crime investigation

| | Population* of area (1) | No. of crimes† reported in survey period (2) | Arrests made in survey period (3) | Strength of C.I.D. (4) | Police officers‡ in C.I.D. (5) | Civilians in C.I.D. (6) | Police officers in force (7) |
|---|---|---|---|---|---|---|---|
| **Provincial forces** | | | | | | | |
| *First surveys* | | | | | | | |
| Plymouth | 210,090 | 222 | 82 | 50 (16)§ | 47 | 3 | 412 |
| Hastings | 66,346 | 73 (60)§ | 16 | 17 (16) | 15 (14)§ | 2 (2)§ | 140 (141)§ |
| Pembroke | 94,800 | 43 (45) | 14 | 15 (16) | 15 (16) | — (1) | 183 (185) |
| Dorset | 312,487 | 363 (382) | 57 | 46 (51) | 39 (43) | 7 (8) | 476 (485) |
| Bristol | 434,260 | 260 | 234 | 115 | 102 | 13 | 1,069 |
| Bath | 80,856 | 137 | 47 | 21 | 19 | 2 | 139 |
| Barrow-in-Furness | 65,310 | 137 | 24 | 15 | 13 | 2 | 138 |
| Birkenhead | 143,680 | 103 | 53 | 39 | 35 | 4 | 382 |
| Leic. and Rutland | 452,920 | 278 | 47 | 71 | 57 | 14 | 696 |
| Northumberland | 491,200 | 355 | 82 | 75 | 63 | 12 | 705 |
| Bedford | 257,913 | 178 | 85 | 61 | 53 | 8 | 477 |
| Essex | 1,179,060 | 1,122 | 216 | 218 | 171 | 47 | 1,426 |
| Total | 3,788,922 | 3,271 | 957 | 743 (748) | 629 (633) | 144 (116) | 6,243 (6,255) |
| *Metropolitan* | | | | | | | |
| 'B' Division | 216,810 | 965 | 107 | 102 | 90 | 12 | 598 |
| 'S' Division | 385,230 | 460 | 121 | 73 | 63 | 10 | 669 |
| Total | 602,040 | 1,425 | 228 | 175 | 153 | 22 | 1,267 |
| **Provincial forces** | | | | | | | |
| *Second surveys* | | | | | | | |
| Hastings | 66,346 | 47 | 13 | 14 | 12 | 2 | 40 |
| Pembroke | 94,800 | 47 | 25 | 17 | 15 | 1 | 179 |
| Dorset | 312,487 | 401 | 80 | 55 | 42 | 9 | 468 |
| Total | 473,635 | 495 | 118 | 86 | 69 | 12 | 687 |

* Source: *Police Almanac 1965.*
† Source: Return made by each force.
‡ This number excludes cadets.
§ Numbers in parentheses = average of both survey periods.

## TABLE D.5

### Distribution of crime investigation work—by departments

| | Traffic dept. | Beat patrols | C.I.D. | W.P.Cs. dept. | Admin. | Station staff | Other duties | Crime investigation | |
|---|---|---|---|---|---|---|---|---|---|
| | | | | | | | | Total hours =100% | As percentage of active duty time |
| **Provincial forces** | | | | | | | | | |
| *First surveys* | | | | | | | | | |
| Plymouth | 5·7 | 30·5 | 55·4 | 1·0 | 2·0 | 3·1 | 2·0 | 5,786 | 20·7 |
| Hastings | 9·1 | 19·5 | 59·7 | 6·2 | 2·2 | 2·5 | 0·5 | 1,705 | 18·1 |
| Pembroke | 1·3 | 44·3 | 31·2 | 4·8 | 11·4 | 6·2 | 0·5 | 2,516 | 18·5 |
| Dorset | 6·0 | 39·9 | 41·5 | 2·6 | 0·8 | 4·5 | 4·4 | 6,713 | 19·3 |
| Bristol | 1·6 | 10·2 | 55·0 | 2·0 | — | 7·0 | 24·0 | 11,462 | 16·0 |
| Bath | 2·2 | 25·5 | 64·2 | 5·9 | — | 1·6 | 0·3 | 1,868 | 20·0 |
| Barrow-in-Furness | 0·9 | 14·2 | 79·4 | 2·0 | 1·3 | 1·8 | — | 1,217 | 13·0 |
| Birkenhead | 4·6 | 6·5 | 72·5 | 2·7 | 0·1 | 1·9 | 11·4 | 3,465 | 12·8 |
| Leic. and Rutland | 4·0 | 25·4 | 55·2 | 1·5 | 2·6 | 8·7 | 2·3 | 7,574 | 15·2 |
| Northumberland | 1·2 | 25·8 | 60·2 | 1·9 | 3·5 | 6·2 | 1·0 | 7,669 | 14·9 |
| Bedford | 2·2 | 23·1 | 51·4 | 3·4 | 1·0 | 9·6 | 8·8 | 6,640 | 17·0 |
| Essex | 0·9 | 26·6 | 61·2 | 3·7 | 0·5 | 2·0 | 4·6 | 21,757 | 19·6 |
| Total | 2,083 | 19,192 | 44,342 | 2,233 | 1,180 | 3,856 | 5,461 | 78,372* | 452,716* |
| Percentage | 2·7 | 24·5 | 56·5 | 2·8 | 1·5 | 4·9 | 6·9 | 100·0 | 17·3 |
| *Metropolitan* | | | | | | | | | |
| 'B' Division | 0·4 | 23·9 | 58·6 | 1·3 | 0·3 | 0·9 | 14·2 | 14,818 | 29·6 |
| 'S' Division | 1·9 | 32·4 | 60·2 | 0·5 | 0·4 | 2·7 | 1·5 | 7,712 | 14·1 |
| Total | 221 | 6,059 | 13,341 | 244 | 79 | 347 | 2,239 | 22,530 | 104,242 |
| Percentage | 1·0 | 26·9 | 59·2 | 1·1 | 0·4 | 1·5 | 9·9 | 100·0 | 21·6 |
| **Provincial forces** | | | | | | | | | |
| *Second surveys* | | | | | | | | | |
| Hastings | 1·0 | 21·9 | 53·4 | 3·9 | 5·1 | 2·3 | 2·4 | 1,852 | 18·9 |
| Pembroke | 1·8 | 45·6 | 36·5 | 5·1 | 4·9 | 5·7 | 0·15 | 2,556 | 19·4 |
| Dorset | 4·4 | 39·2 | 45·6 | 1·1 | 1·4 | 2·7 | 5·3 | 7,009 | 19·0 |
| Total | 558 | 4,321 | 5,122 | 287 | 322 | 385 | 422 | 11,417 | 59,698 |
| Percentage | 4·8 | 37·8 | 44·8 | 2·5 | 2·8 | 3·3 | 3·6 | 100·0 | 19·1 |

* This total includes 25 hours worked by those on training courses but not shown under departments.

## TABLE D.6

### Time spent on different types of court work

| | Criminal courts Magistrates' Hours | % | Higher Hours | % | Traffic courts (all types) Hours | % | Civil and Coroners' Hours | % | Juvenile Hours | % | Total hours =100% |
|---|---|---|---|---|---|---|---|---|---|---|---|
| *Provincial forces* | | | | | | | | | | | |
| *First surveys* | | | | | | | | | | | |
| Plymouth | 1,089 | 55·6 | 68 | 3·5 | 681 | 34·7 | 45 | 2·3 | 77 | 3·9 | 1,960 |
| Hastings | 110 | 22·6 | 33 | 6·8 | 247 | 50·7 | 66 | 13·6 | 31 | 6·4 | 487 |
| Pembroke | 226 | 29·8 | 81 | 10·7 | 315 | 41·6 | 114 | 15·0 | 22 | 2·9 | 758 |
| Dorset | 832 | 34·9 | 156 | 6·5 | 1,107 | 46·4 | 187 | 7·8 | 103 | 4·3 | 2,385 |
| Bristol | 1,340 | 34·0 | 581 | 14·8 | 1,326 | 33·7 | 298 | 7·7 | 392 | 9·6 | 3,937 |
| Bath | 208 | 22·9 | 124 | 13·7 | 380 | 41·9 | 144 | 15·9 | 52 | 5·7 | 908 |
| Barrow-in-Furness | 141 | 25·7 | 26 | 4·7 | 158 | 28·8 | 87 | 15·8 | 137 | 25·6 | 549 |
| Birkenhead | 381 | 23·0 | 331 | 20·0 | 732 | 44·1 | 121 | 7·3 | 94 | 5·7 | 1,659 |
| Leic. and Rutland | 1,149 | 27·8 | 708 | 16·8 | 1,954 | 46·4 | 213 | 5·1 | 189 | 4·5 | 4,213 |
| Northumberland | 1,629 | 37·7 | 344 | 8·0 | 1,699 | 39·3 | 373 | 8·6 | 279 | 6·5 | 4,324 |
| Bedford | 989 | 26·2 | 438 | 11·6 | 1,888 | 50·0 | 261 | 6·9 | 202 | 5·3 | 3,778 |
| Essex | 2,400 | 28·5 | 803 | 9·5 | 4,281 | 50·8 | 508 | 6·0 | 434 | 5·2 | 8,426 |
| Total | 10,494 | 31·4 | 3,693 | 11·1 | 14,768 | 44·2 | 2,417 | 7·2 | 2,012 | 6·0 | 33,384 |
| *Metropolitan* | | | | | | | | | | | |
| 'B' Division | 1,379 | 36·0 | 442 | 11·8 | 1,580 | 42·3 | 186 | 5·0 | 150 | 4·0 | 3,737 |
| 'S' Division | 1,225 | 25·8 | 450 | 9·5 | 2,668 | 56·3 | 282 | 6·0 | 114 | 2·4 | 4,739 |
| Total | 2,604 | 30·7 | 892 | 10·5 | 4,248 | 50·1 | 468 | 5·5 | 264 | 3·1 | 8,476 |
| C.T.D. | 135 | 6·8 | 119 | 6·0 | 1,599 | 80·1 | 74 | 3·7 | 70 | 3·5 | 1,997 |
| C.I.D. | 635 | 60·2 | 420 | 39·8 | | | | | | | 1,055 |
| *Provincial forces* | | | | | | | | | | | |
| *Second surveys* | | | | | | | | | | | |
| Hastings | 109 | 19·9 | 29 | 5·3 | 307 | 56·1 | 71 | 13·0 | 31 | 5·7 | 547 |
| Pembroke | 140 | 20·4 | 116 | 16·9 | 339 | 49·3 | 58 | 8·4 | 34 | 4·9 | 687 |
| Dorset | 811 | 26·4 | 526 | 17·1 | 1,410 | 45·9 | 189 | 6·1 | 138 | 4·5 | 3,074 |
| Total | 1,060 | 24·6 | 671 | 15·6 | 2,056 | 47·7 | 318 | 7·4 | 203 | 4·7 | 4,308 |

## TABLE D.7

### Time spent report writing and in police stations

| Provincial forces (first surveys only) | Total report time | Total R.T. as % of Total W.T. | Total station time | Total S.T. as % of Total W.T. |
|---|---|---|---|---|
| Plymouth | 3,144 | 9·9 | 12,131 | 38·2 |
| Hastings (1) | 885 | 7·5 | 5,661 | 48·2 |
| Pembroke (1) | 1,584 | 10·0 | 6,681 | 42·2 |
| Dorset (1) | 2,756 | 6·7 | 17,724 | 43·2 |
| Bristol | 5,749 | 6·9 | 32,329 | 38·6 |
| Bath | 935 | 8·1 | 4,439 | 38·4 |
| Barrow-in-Furness | 401 | 3·8 | 3,363 | 32·1 |
| Birkenhead | 2,302 | 7·7 | 10,995 | 36·9 |
| Leics. & Rutland | 3,748 | 5·8 | 23,068 | 35·6 |
| Northumberland | 4,700 | 7·8 | 21,918 | 36·4 |
| Bedford | 5,191 | 11·4 | 22,046 | 48·3 |
| Essex | 14,991 | 11·7 | 56,678 | 44·1 |
| Total | 46,386 | 8·7 | 217,033 | 40·6 |

| Metropolitan | | | | |
|---|---|---|---|---|
| 'B' Division | 6,148 | 10·4 | 24,253 | 41·1 |
| 'S' Division | 6,799 | 10·8 | 26,562 | 42·1 |
| Total | 12,949 | 10·6 | 50,815 | 41·6 |

## TABLE D.8

### Sickness rates related to rank

| | *No. in rank* | *Total hours* | | *Sick leave as %* |
|---|---|---|---|---|
| | | *Sick leave* | *Potential duty time* | *of potential duty time* |
| *Provincial forces** | | | | |
| Constables—urban areas | 2,884 | 8,661 | 327,337 | 2·6 |
| —mixed areas | 811 | 653 | 93,317 | 0·7 |
| —rural areas | 453 | 991 | 52,550 | 1·9 |
| Detective constables | 322 | 263 | 40,082 | 0·6 |
| Sergeants | 136 | 129 | 17,303 | 0·7 |
| Women officers | 187 | 401 | 20,969 | 2·0 |
| Civilians | 606 | 1,103 | 63,032 | 1·7 |
| | | | | |
| *Metropolitan* 'B' & 'S' Divisions | | | | |
| Constables—urban areas | 745 | 2,101 | 85,729 | 2·5 |
| —mixed areas | 126 | 287 | 14,538 | 2·0 |
| —rural areas | 12 | 16 | 1,363 | 1·2 |
| Detective constables | 98 | 183 | 13,561 | 1·3 |
| Sergeants | 39 | 104 | 5,462 | 1·9 |
| Women officers | 31 | 171 | 3,502 | 4·9 |
| Civilians | 70 | 83 | 7,809 | 3·1 |

* Where forces were surveyed twice only the first round survey results were used in compiling this table.

# APPENDIX E

# The Employment of Traffic Wardens in Some Survey Areas

THE table below gives the detailed figures for traffic supervision in each division of those forces which employed traffic wardens at the time of our surveys. It will be seen that even in these forces wardens were employed in only one or two divisions, so that comparisons with traffic supervision in other parts of the force area are also possible. We have standardized the figures by showing the time spent on traffic supervision by those officers doing any supervision, and also indicating the proportion such officers (and civilians) form of the divisional strength.

The most significant fact is that traffic supervision by police officers (and civilians in an administrative capacity) was maintained at levels comparable with those prevailing in divisions where wardens were not employed.

It will also be seen that in most divisions having wardens the proportion of police officers and civilians was not much lower than in other divisions of the same force. The divisions having relatively low figures were Bristol 'A' and Bedfordshire 'B', but the two Essex divisions with wardens also had high involvement of non-wardens in traffic supervision. The Bedfordshire and Bristol figures may indicate a genuine reduction of the load on the police as their wardens seem to have taken a greater share of the total than in the two Essex divisions.

## Contribution of traffic wardens to traffic supervision (1965–66)

| Force and division (1) | Total hrs on traffic supervision by police officers and civilians (exclud. wardens) (2) | No. of police and civilians doing traffic supervision (3) | Total police and civilians (4) | % doing supervision (3)÷(4) (5) | Avge hrs on supervision per police officer/civilian doing any supervision (6) | Avge hrs on patrolling by police officer (7) | Wardens total hrs on traffic supervision (8) | Avge hrs per warden (9) | Proportion of all supervision done by wardens (10) % |
|---|---|---|---|---|---|---|---|---|---|
| *Essex* | | | | | | | | | |
| Braintree | 350 | 65 | 119 | 55·0 | 5·3 | 36·2 | — | — | — |
| Brentwood | 561 | 64 | 110 | 58·0 | 8·7 | 30·1 | — | — | — |
| Chelmsford | 849 | 103 | 159 | 65·0 | 8·2 | 31·0 | 760 | 76·0 | 47 |
| Clacton | 394 | 84 | 142 | 59·0 | 4·6 | 37·1 | — | — | — |
| Harlow | 534 | 92 | 155 | 59·0 | 5·8 | 27·4 | — | — | — |
| Colchester | 760 | 95 | 147 | 65·0 | 8·0 | 32·4 | 673 | 67·3 | 47 |
| Grays | 721 | 104 | 170 | 61·0 | 6·9 | 31·0 | — | — | — |
| Basildon | 1,225 | 165 | 251 | 66·0 | 7·4 | 30·4 | — | — | — |
| Saffron Walden | 205 | 44 | 63 | 70·0 | 4·6 | 33·0 | — | — | — |
| *Bedfordshire* | | | | | | | | | |
| B—Bedford | 551 | 111 | 182 | 61·0 | 5·0 | 34·2 | 606* | 75·8 | 52 |
| C—Biggleswade | 315 | 69 | 99 | 69·7 | 4·6 | 31·6 | — | — | — |
| D—Dunstable | 502 | 72 | 106 | 67·9 | 7·0 | 32·8 | — | — | — |
| *Bristol* | | | | | | | | | |
| A—Central | 1,136 | 139 | 244 | 56·9 | 8·2 | 38·4 | 3,288 | 70·0 | 74 |
| B—Bedminster | 742 | 114 | 184 | 61·9 | 6·5 | 37·9 | — | — | — |
| C—Redland | 852 | 118 | 192 | 61·4 | 7·6 | 28·9 | — | — | — |
| D—St George's | 687 | 90 | 168 | 53·5 | 7·1 | 36·2 | — | — | — |

* This number has been adjusted to exclude time entered under this heading by the supervising sergeant or civilian clerk.

# Index

absenteeism, 11
abstractions, 131, 162–3, 278
  as percentage of duty time, 141
  civilians, 143, 144, 163, 220
  C.I.D., 177–8, 194
  differences between urban and rural
    areas, 234, 235
  negative correlation between hours of
    work and, 142–3
  policewomen, 215
  seasonal differences, 204–5, 209
  survey results, 140–5, 204–5, 215
  24 hour responsibility and, 232
  see also leave; meal breaks; sickness;
    training
accidents, 253
  high correlation with traffic offences,
    183–4
  recording of, 94
  seasonal differences, 202
  traffic work and, 161
administration, 260–1; see also internal
    organization
administration departments:
  juvenile court work, 199
  station and report time, 238, 239
  traffic work and, 189, 191, 192–3, 195
  working time, 147
administration of justice:
  C.I.D. time spent on, 178
  survey definition, 128–9
  work load, 154–5, 163, 196, 279
  see also court work
advertising:
  for recruits, 86
  of senior posts, 98
aliens, registration of, 37, 120
allowances, 17, 41, 43, 74, 75–6
  detective duty, 74, 76
  rent, 16, 17, 45, 74, 75–6
  see also housing
amalgamations, 5, 10, 32, 118
  advantages of, 32–3, 116
  effect on promotion, 29–30

antecedents, preparation of, 128, 179 n.,
    196
areas of operation:
  survey classification of, 129–30
  work load and, 155–7, 280
  see also civil order; criminal work;
    internal organization; traffic work
arrests:
  not significantly correlated with crime
    rates, 167
  numbers in survey period, 167–8
  numbers related to criminal work time,
    175–6, 177, 194
assaults on police, 23
Association of Chief Police Officers of
    England and Wales, 123 n.
Association of Municipal Corporations,
    221
Atcherley, L. W., 25
attendance centres, 129

Banton, M., 233
beat patrol officers, 91
  criminal work and, 174
  mechanization of, 4, 55, 68, 109–10,
    244, 245–6
  mobility of, 4, 68, 109–10, 238–9, 244–5
  personal radios, 68, 180, 245, 259
  station and report time, 238–9, 241, 246
  traffic work and, 3, 183, 189, 190, 191,
    192, 195, 206–7, 209
  working time, 147
  see also unit beat policing
beat patrol system, 6, 7, 258–9; see also
    beat patrol officers
bicycles, use of, 25, 68, 107, 238, 241–2,
    244, 245, 247
Booth, C., 17, 22 n.
borough forces:
  growth of, 8–12
  ratio of police to population, 48–9
  wages, 15, 16, 18
Bowley, A. L., 14 n., 15 n., 19 n., 20,
    23 n., 31 n., 38 n., 41 n., 44 n.

Bow street runners, 21
Bradley, J., 125 n., 128 n.
buildings, 2, 6, 11, 52–3, 69, 71, 72, 104–7
burglar alarms, 93–4
Burn, W. L., 26 n.

cadets, 53 n., 54, 79, 81, 86–7, 250
Callaghan, L. J., 164–5
capital expenditure, 41, 42, 52–3, 69,
    71–2, 104–5, 183, 261–2; see also
    buildings; communications;
    housing; transport
cars, see motor vehicles; private motoring
central government, police and see ex-
    chequer grants; Home Office
Chartists, 8, 9
Chief Constables, 9, 30, 33, 121, 122
civil duties:
    C.I.D. time spent, 178
    survey definition, 128
    work load, 154, 155, 163, 279
civilians, 4, 90 n., 91–6, 219–26, 240,
    250–1
    abstractions and, 143, 144, 163, 220
    career structure, 95–6, 114
    future policy for, 225–6, 227
    hours of work, 4, 78, 95, 220–1, 227
    in C.I.D.s, 93, 170, 171–3, 193
    increased use of, 54, 78, 80, 81, 91–2,
        117, 210, 250
    Metropolitan Police, 81, 211, 212–13,
        226
    numbers employed, 210–13, 226
    occupations of, 54, 80, 81, 93–4, 95–6,
        221, 227, 257
    overtime working, 220, 227
    proportion in large forces, 92
    recruitment problems, 95
    see also traffic wardens
civil incidents:
    civilians and, 222
    definition, 129–30
    policewomen and, 215, 216, 227
    seasonal differences, 207, 209
    time spent on, 161–2, 163
civil order:
    survey definition, 129–30
    work load, 155, 157, 163, 280
Civil Service Commission, 95, 98
Clark, C., 38 n.
clerical work, 25, 52, 64; see also crime,
    records; report writing; statistical
    information

clothing, see uniform
command:
    structure of, 29–30, 35, 49–52, 96–7
    training in techniques of, 89–90
communications, 66, 68, 91, 111–13, 158,
    164
    between forces, 17–18, 21, 33, 35
    between Home Office and police; see
        Police Council; Police Federation
    civilian role in, 81, 93–4, 117
    within forces, 39–40, 52, 53–4
    see also radio; telegraph system; tele-
        phone; teleprinters; telex
conditions of work, 21–4, 35, 40, 41,
    79–80, 89, 228, 251, 254
co-operation between forces, 38, 55–61,
    66–7, 115–16, 118; see also com-
    munications; training
correlation coefficient, significance test,
    142, 273
cost of living, 14–15, 71
    bonuses, 36, 42–3, 44
county forces:
    as proportion of total strength, 82–3
    growth of, 9–12
    ratio of police to population, 48–9
    wages, 15, 16, 17, 18
County Police Acts 1839 and 1840, 9
'Courtesy Cops' scheme, 56, 57
court work, 3, 120, 128–9, 196–200
    civil and coroners, 197, 198–9, 200,
        208, 222, 223
    civilians and, 222, 223
    criminal, 3, 128, 160, 197, 198, 199–
        200, 208–9, 222, 223, 283
    juvenile, 197, 198–9, 208, 215, 222,
        223
    policewomen and, 215, 216, 227
    related to criminal investigation, 178–9,
        186–7, 193
    seasonal differences, 202, 209
    survey categories, 131
    time spent on, 196, 197, 199–200,
        208–9, 242, 283
    traffic offences, 3, 161, 186–7, 192–3,
        195, 197–200, 208, 209, 222–3,
        227, 253, 283
    types of, 197–9
crime:
    investigation of, 7, 11, 68–9, 119, 128,
        158–60, 281–2; see also criminal
        work; detectives; forensic science
        laboratories

crime—*contd.*
  prevention of, 7, 11, 69, 99, 100, 119,
    128, 174, 181, 257
  rates:
    C.I.D. strength and, 173, 193–4
    C.I.D. working hours and, 175–6
    in survey areas, 167–9, 193, 202, 275
    not significantly correlated with
      arrests, 167
    rise in, 61, 63–4, 66, 68–9, 82, 109,
      116, 255
    seasonal differences, 202
  records, 52, 53 n., 55, 60–1, 69, 113, 171
criminal court work, 3, 128, 160, 197,
    198, 199–200, 208–9, 222, 223, 283,
  seasonal differences, 202
Criminal Investigation Departments, 91
  abstractions, 177–8, 194
  allocation of duty time by function,
    178–9
  case load, 3, 169–173, 176, 181, 193,
    194, 255
  civilians in, 93, 170, 171–3, 193
  expansion of, 68–9, 173–4
  first formed, 24, 256
  report writing, 179, 194, 239, 241, 247
  sickness rate, 177–8, 194
  station time, 179–80, 238, 239
  strength, 169–71, 173–4
    related to crime rates, 173, 193–4
  transport used, 244
  working time, 147, 148, 163, 255–6
Criminal Justice Act 1967, 193, 196 n.,
    198, 200
criminals, mobility of, 60, 68, 115, 118
criminal work, 166–82, 247
  civilians and, 221, 222, 224
  crime rates and, 167–9
  distribution between departments,
    174–5, 194, 282
  policewomen and, 215, 216, 227
  related to criminal court work, 178–9,
    186–7, 194
  related to juvenile court work, 199
  seasonal differences, 202
  survey definition, 129
  time spent related to arrests, 175–6,
    177, 194
  time spent related to crime rate, 175–6
  unit beat policing and, 180–2
  work load, 155, 156, 160, 163, 280
  *see also* Criminal Investigation Depart-
    ments

Critchley, T. A., 7 n., 10 n., 23 n., 24 n.,
    31 n., 34 n.

demonstrations, political, cost of, 139 n.
Desborough Committee, 1, 10, 30, 36–8,
    40–1, 43, 44, 46, 49–50, 63, 65–6,
    256
  (1923), 45
detectives, 24–5
  case load, 3, 169–173, 176, 181, 193,
    194, 255
  hours of work, 147, 148, 255–6
  training of, 25, 57, 99, 100, 117
  'unit of work', 169
  *see also* Criminal Investigation Depart-
    ments
*Detective Work and Procedure*, Cttee., 57, 58,
    169
discipline, 8–9, 11, 23–4, 89
dismissals, 14, 23, 28, 87
District Recruitment Boards, 65
Districts, 11, 19
District Training Centres, 74, 98–9
  cost of, 100–2, 104
District Training Scheme, 65
Dixon, Sir Arthur L., 36 n., 59, 121 n.,
    170, 171, 173–4, 255
dogs, 59, 110, 147, 231, 257
driving schools, 57, 99, 117
drunkenness, 1, 6, 11, 23
Dunning, Sir Leonard, 10, 26, 37
Durham survey, 121 n.
duties:
  classification for survey, 127–33
  *see also* escort duties; extra duties;
    general duties; private duties

earnings:
  off-duty work, 21
  *see also* wages and salaries
economic situation, effect on police
    between wars, 41–6
efficiency, measurement of, 11, 40, 41 n.,
    262
*Employment and Distribution of Strength in
    the Metropolitan Police*, Cttee.
    (Dixon), 170, 171, 173–4, 255
enquiries, foreign, *see* foreign enquiries
equipment, 25, 53–4; *see also* communica-
    tions; transport
escort duties, 128–9, 131
establishment, 249
  definition of, 90 n.

realistic, 84, 90
reappraisal needed, 164–5
size of, 32, 34, 35, 90–1
*see also* vacancies
*Estimates*, Sel. Cttee. (1966–67), 3, 87, 88,
  115, 135, 160, 219, 221, 249
examinations, 29, 97–8
exchequer grants, 69 n., 100
  eligibility for, 11–12, 34
  witholding of, 40, 59
expenditure, 116
  capital, 41, 42, 52–3, 69, 71–2, 104–5,
    183, 261–2
  local authority, 43, 55, 71–4, 104–7
  on forensic science laboratories, 114
  on training, 100–3
  on transport, 107–8
  related to national expenditure, 2, 4,
    42, 69–71, 248
  *see also* finance
expenses, 41
extra duties, 25–6, 37, 120

facsimile transmitting equipment, 68, 113
Factories Act 1847 (Ten Hour Day Act),
  22
finance:
  co-operative schemes, 55–61, 66–7
  forensic science laboratories, 58–60,
    68
  traffic patrols, 55–6
  training, 100–3
  *see also* exchequer grants; expenditure;
    Special Services Fund
fingerprint system, 25, 35, 68, 113, 171,
  257
fire service, manned by police, 25–6
Flying Squad, working time, 147, 148
  151, 152, 153
forces:
  co-operation between, 38, 55–61, 66–7,
    115–16, 118; *see also* communica-
    tions; training
  numbers of, 6, 12, 19, 32–3, 83
  selection for survey, 134–6, 276–7
  size of, 47–9, 83, 84, 117
  small, 12, 32, 33, 47, 83, 84
  *see also* borough forces; county forces
foreign enquiries:
  civilians and, 222, 224
  seasonal variations in, 207
  time spent on, 161, 163, 246
  types of, 131–2

forensic science laboratories, 2, 54, 55,
  58–60, 66, 68, 74, 94, 100, 114–15,
  117
  expenditure on, 114
Fraud Squad:
  report writing time, 179
  working time, 147, 151, 152
  functions:
    survey classification, 128–9
    work load by, 153–5, 279
    *see also* administration of justice; civil
      duties; law enforcement; treat-
      ment of offenders
Functions of Traffic Wardens Order
  1960, 218 n.
Functions of Traffic Wardens Order
  1965, 94, 218 n.

Geddes Committee, 44, 45, 52–3
general duties:
  civilians and, 221, 222
  definition of, 131
  policewomen and, 215, 216, 227
  work load of, 158
General Strike, 63
grants, *see* exchequer grants

Hammond, J. L. and B., 8 n.
handwriting, scientific study of, 58
Hart, J. M., 10 n., 33 n., 34 n.
Hendon:
  Police College, 53 n., 56–7
  Police Driving School, 57
  Wireless School, 57
holiday areas 3–4
  policing of, 200–8, 209
holidays, *see* leave, annual
Home Office:
  advertising campaign, 86
  Adviser on Scientific Aids, 58–9
  borough forces and, 10
  communications with police, *see* Police
    Council; Police Federation
  county forces and, 9, 10–11
  increased powers of, 40–1
  pension funds and, 28
  Police Research and Planning Branch,
    74, 75, 115, 118, 164, 170–1,
    180, 259
  radio system and, 93, 94, 111–12
  *see also* exchequer grants; expenditure;
    finance; Police Regulations;
    wages, scales of

homicide, 121, 141
hours of work, 21–2, 77–80, 116, 145, 163, 249–52, 278
  abstractions as percentage of, 141
  calculation of, 270–2
  civilians, 4, 78, 95, 220–1, 227
  differences:
    counties and boroughs, 150
    provinces and Metropolis, 147, 148, 150
    urban and rural areas, 234–5, 246
  negative correlation between abstractions and, 142–3
  policewomen, 147, 214, 227
  seasonal changes, 204, 205
  survey results, 145–9, 203–5
  24 hour responsibility and, 231–3, 246
housing, 2, 16, 45, 53, 69, 72, 75–6, 104–6

inspections, 11, 34, 35
Inspectors of Constabulary, 10–11, 74, 90–1
internal organization:
  civilians and, 221, 222, 223, 227
  policewomen and, 215, 216
  survey definition, 130
  work load, 157, 280

Johnson, G. B., 121 n.
justice, administration of, see administration of justice
justices of the peace, 9, 27
juvenile courts, see court work: juvenile
juvenile liaison work, 129, 257

Kendall, M. G., and Stuart, A., 273, 275

laboratories, see forensic science laboratories
Lancashire survey, 121 n., 137
law enforcement:
  C.I.D. time spent on, 178
  survey definition, 128
  work load, 154, 163, 279
  see also crime, investigation of; crime, prevention of; public order
leave, 1, 2, 23, 37, 79, 145, 170 n., 234, 252
  annual, 17, 23, 35, 77, 79, 116, 153 n., 252
  effect on work load, 203–6, 209
  as percentage of total abstractions, 143, 144, 163

Lee Committee, 45
licensing activities, 26
Licensing Acts, enforcement of, 26
local authorities:
  expenditure, 43, 55, 71–4, 104–7
  work done for police, 81
Local Government Act, 1888, 12, 32
London Government Act, 1963, 7 n.

management, training in, 89–90, 99, 100
manpower equivalents, definition of, 137
manpower survey, see survey
Martin, J. P., 128 n.
Mather, F. C., 8 n.
May Committee, 46
meal breaks, 2, 4, 22–3, 144 n., 146 n., 234, 235, 251
  as percentage of total abstractions, 143, 144
Metropolitan and City Police Company Fraud Branch, see Fraud Squad
Metropolitan Police:
  civilian strength, 81, 211, 212–13, 226
  command structure, 50
  Criminal Record Office, 113
  founding of, 6, 7
  manning up allowance, 80
  ratio of police to population, 48
  Receiver's Department, 81, 212
  sample chosen, 135–6
  Solicitor's Department, 54, 95
  special squads, see Flying Squad; Fraud Squad; Stolen Vehicles Branch
  strike, 37
  see also Hendon: Police College; Police Driving School
Metropolitan Police Act 1829, 7
Metropolitan Police Act 1839, 7
mobility, 238, 241–6, 247
  beat patrol officers, 4, 55, 68, 109–10, 238–9, 244–5
  between forces, 33–4
  of criminals, 60, 68, 115, 118
  see also transport
modus operandi classification, 25, 35, 94
motor cycles, 55, 68, 107, 109–10, 117, 242, 243–4, 245
motoring offences, see traffic offences
motor traffic, increase in, 61–2, 66, 68, 82, 116–17
motor vehicles, 54–5, 68, 117, 238, 241–5, 247
  expenditure on, 104, 105, 107–8

maintenance of, 81, 94, 111
radio equipped, 109, 110–11, 112, 117
Road Fund Grant for, 55
specialized use of, 109–11
Mowat, C. L., 44 n., 63
Municipal Corporations Act 1835, 8
Municipal Corporations (New Charters)
     Act 1877, 32
murder, 121, 141
mutual aid agreements, 33, 41

national expenditure, police expenditure
     and, 2, 4, 42, 69–71, 248
National Expenditure, Cttee. (Geddes), 44,
     45, 52–3
National Expenditure, Cttee. (May), 46
nightwatchmen, 7, 8–9, 28

Oaksey Committee, 66, 75, 89, 91, 97
off-duty work, 21, 24
overtime, 2, 79, 82, 143, 145, 146, 250–1,
     254–5, 278
  calculation of, 274
  civilians compared with police, 220,
     227
  seasonal changes in, 204, 205
  survey results, 149–53, 162, 163, 204,
     205

parades, 22
parish constables, 7, 9, 21
Parris, H., 10 n., 11 n.
patrolling, 222, 239, 251–2, 258–9
  differences between urban and rural
     areas, 234, 235, 246
  effect of traffic wardens on, 218
  policewomen and, 215–16, 227
  seasonal differences, 208, 209
  survey definition of, 131
  survey sub-division, 129 n.
  work load of, 157, 158, 159, 163, 164
  see also beat patrol officers; traffic
     patrols; unit beat policing
pay, see wages and salaries
Peacock, A. T., and Wiseman, J., 43, 61
Pearson's product-moment correlation
     coefficient, 142
pensions, 12, 17, 26–9, 31, 33–4, 35, 42,
     46, 72–4, 88–9
  funds, 9, 26, 28–9, 45
photography, 53, 66, 171, 257
pilot survey, 122 n., 128

Plug Plot riots, 7
point duty, 7, 22, 62, 94
Police, R. Com., 75, 84
Police Act 1856, 10, 11, 35
Police Act 1890, 28, 31
Police Act 1919, 36, 38, 40, 41
Police Act 1964, 74
Police Advisory Board, 149
Police and Prison Officers' Union, 37,
     38, 63
Police College, Hendon, 53 n., 56–7
Police College (national), 2, 58, 65, 66,
     74, 90, 99, 100, 117
  cost of, 101–2, 104
Police Conditions of Service, Cttee. (Oaksey),
     66, 75, 89, 91, 97
Police Council, 39–40, 44, 45, 65
Police Federation, 39–40, 44, 45, 65, 66,
     86, 228
Police Manpower, Equipment and Efficiency,
     Working Parties (Taverne Re-
     port), 149–50, 164, 180, 225, 228,
     236, 250, 258, 259, 271
Police Pay (New Entrants), Cttee., 46
Police Promotion Examinations Board,
     98
Police Regulations 1920, 41, 66, 251, 252,
     254
Police Regulations 1965, 145 n., 214, 250,
     251, 251 n., 252, 254
Police Service of England , Wales and Scotland,
     Cttee. (Desborough), 1, 10, 30,
     36–8, 40–1, 43, 44, 46, 49–50, 63,
     65–6, 256
Police (Superannuation) Act 1906, 28
Police (Weekly Rest Day) Act 1910, 37,
     79, 249
Police Weekly Rest Day, Sel. Cttee., 39–40
policewomen, 4, 81, 106, 117, 199, 214–16
  abstractions, 215
  hours of work, 147, 214, 227
  numbers employed, 211, 212, 226
  resignations of, 88 n.
  station and report time, 238, 239
  traffic work by, 207, 216
  training time, 215
  transport used, 244–5
  types of work done by, 215–16, 227
  wastage rate, 211 n.
policy, local variations in, 121–2
Popkess, A., 58
population, ratio of police to, 11, 46–9,
     249

Pratt, H. R., 57 n.
prisoners, escorting of, 120, 128–9
private duties, 130, 222
private motoring, increase in, 61–2, 66,
    68, 82, 116–17
probationers, resignations of, 85, 87, 88
productivity, 261–2
promotion, 29–32, 35, 37, 56, 97–8
    favouritism in, 30, 31
    transfers and, 33–4, 98
prosecutions, local variations in, 121
provincial forces, development of, 8–12
public order:
    civilians and, 222
    preservation of, 7–8, 9, 119, 128, 130,
        162, 163
    seasonal differences, 207
public relations, 69

radio, 2, 55, 57, 59-60, 66, 68, 71, 93–4,
    109–113, 117
    personal, 4, 60, 68, 103, 112–13, 117,
        180, 181, 245, 259, 261
ranks:
    changing proportions in, 29–30, 50–2,
        96–7
    standardization of, 30, 49–50
recreational facilities, 52, 53 n.
recruitment, 1, 12–14, 16, 64–5, 66, 83–7
    advertising and, 86
    civilians, 95
    educational standard of, 8, 12, 86, 87
    pay of, 46
    qualifications of, 9, 12, 85–6, 87
refreshment breaks, see meal breaks
Regional Crime Squads, 115–16, 118
regional services, 41, 58–61, 66–7
Regulations, see Police Regulations
rent allowances, 16, 17, 45, 74, 75–6
report writing, 22, 93, 120, 124, 239, 241,
    247, 284
    beat patrol officers, 239, 241
    C.I.D., 179, 194, 239, 241, 247
resignations:
    compulsory, 14
    reasons for, 89
    voluntary, 14, 77, 83–5, 87–90
retirement, 27, 28, 31–2, 64, 88–9
Richardson, H. W., 41 n.
road accidents, see accidents
Road Fund, 55
Road Traffic Act 1930, 55, 62
Road Traffic Act 1934, 62

Road Traffic and Roads Improvement
    Act 1960, 218 n.
Royal Institute of Public Administration,
    90
rural and urban areas, differences in
    police work, 233–6, 246

St Johnston, Sir T. Eric, 121 n., 137
salaries, see wages and salaries
sample:
    characteristics of, 138, 276–7
    exclusions from, 134
    selection for survey, 132, 134–6, 276–7
scenes of crime specialists, 114–15, 171,
    257
seasonal differences, see holiday areas
separation:
    causes of, 14
    rates of, 13–14, 24, 88
    see also dismissals; resignations, wastage
shift working, 22, 79, 94, 149, 203–4,
    205,
    228–31, 233, 246; see also overtime
shoplifting, 121, 216
sickness, 2, 35, 77, 79
    as percentage of total abstractions, 143
        144, 163
    differences between urban and rural
        areas, 234, 235
    rates by rank, 285
    rates in C.I.D., 177–8, 194
    seasonal differences, 204–5
Simpson, Sir Joseph, 57
Slim, William J., Field Marshal 1st
    Viscount, 257–8
social change, impact on police work,
    61–4
Special Branch, 24
specialization, 3, 4, 24–5, 35, 54, 68, 117,
    123, 256–8
Special Services Fund, 58–60, 61, 74
speed limits, enforcement of, 62
sports, time spent on, 143, 144, 146 n.
standard of living, 1, 14, 36–7, 42–3
stations:
    C.I.D. time spent in, 179–80, 238, 239
    expenditure on, 69, 71, 72, 106–7
    need for new, 52–3, 106
    staff working time, 147, 238, 239
        on traffic work, 189, 191, 192
    time spent in, 238–40, 246–7, 284
statistical information, collection of, 52,
    69, 94, 257

statistical significance, tests for, 142–3, 273
status, 1, 2, 6, 12, 17, 25, 34–5, 36, 37–8, 66, 75, 256
Stolen Motor Vehicle Investigation Branch, see Stolen Vehicles Branch
Stolen Vehicles Branch, 100
    working time, 147, 151, 152, 153
strength, 46–9, 52, 66, 77–82, 116, 117, 248–50
calculation of numbers needed, 11, 90–1
C.I.D., 169–71, 173–4
definition of, 90 n.
effective, 2, 139–45, 162
    annual leave and, 203
    high correlation with traffic offences, 184–5
    reduction in, 44
strikes, 35, 37, 40, 65; see also General Strike
Student's *t* distribution, 142, 273
superannuation, see pensions
supervision, time spent on, 158
survey:
    briefing procedure, 124–5, 126–7
    classification of activities, 127–33
    data processing, 136–7
    dates conducted, 125
    design of, 119–37
    exclusions from, 134
    pilot study, 122 n., 128
    purpose of, 122
    recording booklet, 125, 127–8, 263–9
    recording procedure for, 123–7
    selection of forces for, 134–6, 276–7
    selection of sample, 132, 134–6, 276–277

Taverne Report, see Police Manpower, Equipment and Efficiency
telegraph system, 25
telephones:
    increased use of, 52, 53–4, 93
    private systems, 54, 113
teleprinters, 54, 93, 113
telex, 113
Temporary Deductions from Police Pay, Cttee. (Lee), 45
Ten Hour Day Act 1847 (Factories Act), 22
tipping, 21
trade union, see union

traffic departments, 183
    contribution to criminal work, 174
    court work and, 192–3
    methods of transport used, 242, 243–4
    seasonal differences in work of, 206–7, 208, 209
    station and report time, 238, 239, 246
    strength related to traffic offences, 184–5, 190–1
    traffic incident work, 190–1
    traffic supervision by, 189–90, 195; see also traffic wardens
    work load, 183–5
    see also traffic patrols
traffic lights introduced, 62, 253
traffic offences:
    civilians' work on, 54
    seasonal differences, 202
traffic patrols, 2, 68, 91, 117, 253, 256–7
    Courtesy Cops, 56, 57
    finance of, 55–6
    inter-force co-ordination of, 68, 118
    South West experiment, 122 n., 183
    working time, 147
    work load, 186, 187, 188
    see also patrolling; traffic departments
traffic wardens, 3, 4, 79, 94, 95, 117, 160, 217–19, 257, 286–7
    finance of, 219
    impact on traffic work, 183, 187, 188, 218
    powers of, 217, 218 n.
    numbers employed, 211, 213, 219 n.
    station and report time, 239, 241, 246
    traffic supervision by, 188–90, 195, 217–19, 227, 257, 286–7
    working time, 147, 149, 217–18
traffic work, 3, 119, 182–93, 194–5, 252
    by beat patrol officers, 3, 183, 189, 190, 191, 192, 195, 206–7, 209
    civilians and, 222–3
    differences between urban and rural areas, 234, 235
    distribution between departments, 188–93
    seasonal differences, 206–7
    increase in, 61–2, 82, 252–4
    main types of, 185–6
    Metropolitan Police, 187–8, 192, 234, 235
    policewomen and, 207, 216
    seasonal differences, 202, 206–7, 208, 209

traffic work—*contd.*
    survey divisions of, 130–1
    work load, 155–6, 160–1, 280
        Metropolitan Police, 161, 163
    *see also* court work, traffic offences
training, 2, 24–5, 56–8, 64–5, 66, 98–100,
    117, 252, 253–4
    advanced courses, 56–7; *see also* Police
        College
    cost of, 100–3
    detectives, 25, 57, 99, 100, 117
    in management techniques, 89–90, 99,
        100
    scenes of crime specialists, 114–15
    time spent, 102–3, 143, 144, 163
        as proportion of working time, 236–7
        policewomen, 215
        seasonal differences, 204–5, 209
    *see also* Police College
training instructors, working time, 147,
    148, 239
transfers between forces, 33–4, 98
transport, 4, 25, 54–5, 66, 68, 91, 107–11,
    238, 241–6, 247
    expenditure on, 107–8
    *see also* bicycles; motor cycles; motor
        vehicles
Transport, Ministry of, 69
treatment of offenders:
    C.I.D. time spent, 178
    survey definition, 128, 129
    work load, 154, 155, 163, 279
Trenchard, H. M., 1st Viscount, 53
Truck Acts, 16 n.

unemployed, unrest among and police
    work, 63, 66
uniform, 12, 25, 40, 41
union, 21, 37, 38, 40, 63
Unit Beat Policing, 3, 5, 6, 117, 157 n., 162,
    164, 180–2, 238, 255, 259–60, 262
universities:
    co-operation with police, 58
    recruitment of graduates from, 87

urban and rural areas, differences in
    police work, 233–6, 246

vacancies, 13, 45, 47, 50, 81, 84, 87, 90,
    96, 249
vehicles, *see* motor vehicles
Vincent, Sir Howard, 24
wages and salaries, 1, 14–21, 35, 37–8,
    40, 41, 66–7, 72–7, 116, 255
    between the wars, 42–6, 66
    comparability with other occupations,
        15–16, 17, 38, 66, 75–7, 116
    cuts in, 44–5, 46, 66
    Desborough scales, 37–8, 44, 46, 65–6
    differentials, 18, 19–21, 80
    new recruits, 46
    regional differences, 14, 17–21
    scales of, 9, 10, 15, 16, 43–4
wardens, *see* traffic wardens
war-time duties, 37
wastage, 1, 16, 83–5, 87–90
    cost of, 88
watch committees, 8, 9, 10, 15, 27–8,
    34
weights and measures, inspection of, 26
Wilcoxon test, 167 n., 275
Williams, A., 3 n.
wireless, *see* radio
Wireless Depots, 60, 74
Wireless School, Hendon, 57
women employed as civilians, 54
women police, *see* policewomen
working time, 220, 251, 252
    percentage spent in station, 239
    percentage spent report writing, 239,
        241
    *see also* hours of work; work load
work load, 2–3, 64
    by area of operation, 155–7, 280
    by function, 153–5, 279
    C.I.D., 3, 147, 148, 163
    effect of annual leave on, 203–6, 209
    seasonal differences, 201–2, 208, 209
    survey results, 145–9, 153–62, 201–2